African Pentecostals in Catholic Europe

AFRICAN PENTECOSTALS IN CATHOLIC EUROPE

The Politics of Presence in the Twenty-First Century

ANNALISA BUTTICCI

Harvard University Press

Cambridge, Massachusetts

London, England

2016

Second printing

Library of Congress Cataloging-in-Publication Data

Butticci, Annalisa, author.
  African pentecostals in Catholic Europe : the politics of
presence in the twenty-first century / Annalisa Butticci.
    pages cm
  Includes bibliographical references and index.
  ISBN 978-0-674-73709-9
  1. Catholic Church—Relations—Pentecostal churches.
  2. Pentecostal churches—Relations—Catholic Church.
  3. Pentecostalism—Italy.   4. Nigerians—Italy—Religion.
  5. Ghanaians—Italy—Religion.   6. Immigrants—Italy.
  7. Religion and sociology—Italy.   8. Italy—Religious life
and customs.   I. Title.
  BX8764.2.B88 2016
  289.9'408996045—dc23
                                                    2015030829

Contents

African Pentecostals in Catholic Europe

Introduction

Surely the Lᴏʀᴅ is in this place; and I knew it not.
—Genesis 28:16, NIV

Iᴛ ᴡᴀs ᴏɴ a cold Sunday morning toward the end of winter that I walked through Corso del Popolo in Padua, past the railway station to the majestic Tempio della Pace (Temple of Peace). Named to memorialize the soldiers who died during World War II, the church contains the remains of nine hundred victims of the war. This Catholic parish in the northeastern Italian city of Padua is located at a busy five-way intersection in the midst of the financial district, law courts, trade fair, and several university departments, hardly an ideal location for nurturing the life of a parish that consists of around 450 families, most of whose members are elderly.

Once, that picture was very different. Once upon a time, young people in Padua used to go to the parish buildings alongside the Tempio della Pace to play basketball. In the 1970s and 1980s, several basketball teams gravitated to the area around the church, and several of the more talented players even became known on the national circuit. Up until a few years ago, a sport like basketball could foster cohesion. Sadly, sports associations' merger of several teams combined with demographic changes and town planning decisions have slowly emptied the Tempio della Pace of its young people. Over the years, urban and generational changes in the district have drastically reduced the number of parishioners and the activities organized by the parish. Nonetheless, the parish is well known for its volunteers who provide food and clothing for the poor, and who work with other local charitable associations.

That Sunday morning when I crossed the threshold to the Tempio della Pace, I saw that the church was deserted. But through the sound system came the clear voice of the priest, Don Elia Ferro, celebrating Mass. His voice echoed around the vast and empty church. The electric lighting had been turned off and the only light was the daylight filtering through the windows. In such a huge, empty place, the steps I took in my elegant high-heeled shoes echoed. I tried to tiptoe, then found myself wondering why. After all, whom was I disturbing? The priest was not at the altar and the pews were deserted. I went past the rows of empty benches to the middle of the main nave. From there I could see the huge Christ on the cross above the main altar and the statue of the Madonna to the left-hand side of the altar.

The disembodied voice continued to recite the liturgy, amplified by the microphone and the powerful sound system; he seemed to be celebrating in a void:

> *"Lord, we have sinned against you: Lord, have mercy."*
> Silence.
> *"Lord, show us your mercy and love."*
> Silence.
> *"May almighty God have mercy on us, forgive us our sins, and bring us to ever-*
>   *lasting life."*

I began to think the Mass or prayer might be a recording and that I had been mistaken about what time Holy Mass was scheduled. In front of the statue of the Madonna I sat down to see whether people would eventually come. The Madonna had a long white and blue dress cinched at the waist, and a long veil covered her hair. She had naked feet with which she was crushing the head of an open-mouthed serpent who seemed to be admitting defeat. The Madonna's arms were open, as if she were preparing to embrace someone, and her eyes had that sweet look that I see on all statues of Mary. I gazed at her face for a while, and it seemed that she was also gazing at me. This is what the priest and my grandmother used to tell me: "She sees you all the time, so beware of what you do, and don't cause her to cry because of your misdeeds!" I never lost that habit of looking at the face of the statues, straight at the eyes of saints and the Madonna, and I have always been amazed by how real they seem to the beholder. This statue had fresh flowers and lighted candles around her. That empty church, despite a scheduled Mass going on, seemed to me to be a sign of the inexorable unchurching of society so much debated by scholars.[1] But then I caught sight of a sign on a pillar beside the statue of the Madonna that said that today Mass was being held in one of the church's little outer chapels. I quietly stood up and followed the signs to the rear of the altar, and I came to a small door through which I could hear the priest speaking, and now also the voices of his congregation.

I glanced through the gap in the half-open door and saw Don Elia celebrating Mass in a tiny room that served as a chapel. He was standing before about twenty people between fifty and seventy years of age. The priest seemed to have chosen the little chapel because it was easier to keep it warm during the cold winter months, but his microphone was connected to the main sound system and consequently resounded throughout the building.

I slid into the little chapel, hoping that my late arrival would pass unnoticed. Don Elia talked about the fasting and abstinence required of the faithful during Lent. At the end of his brief homily, he gently invited those attending to pray in silence, and to meditate and listen to the voice of God in the privacy of their own hearts. The people bent their heads. Some wrapped themselves in their coats and others adjusted their posture before becoming immobile, absorbed in prayer. Don Elia also bowed his head, and stood with his eyes closed and his hands clasped.[2]

After the silent moment of prayer, the liturgy continued, led by Don Elia's gentle voice. The people participated in the liturgy, carefully following the order of service in the pamphlet. It was during the silence of the consecration of the host that a muffled sound of voices crying out the name of Jesus, of garbled words, and occasional thumps caught my attention. Yes, I thought to myself, they are audible even from here. The sounds were coming from the building next door, the parish hall, where nine different Pentecostal churches were celebrating their own services, singing, praying, speaking in tongues, shaking, trembling, falling down, and rolling on the floor under the power of the Holy Spirit.

Those were the churches I had been studying for the last months. I could recognize some of the pastors by their voices: Pastor Sunday, Pastor Augustine, Pastor Stella, Pastor Clement. I knew their own unique way of saying amen and particular phrases of which they were fond, such as "Put your hands together for Jesus!" or "Praise God!" I could tell which church was singing because I knew their favorite songs and the way they sang and clapped. I knew, for instance, that Pastor Augustine loves to sing the songs of the popular band The Voice of the Cross. He usually starts the service with the song "Good Morning Jesus" and

continues to sing half of the repertoire of the band during the first worship session of the service. Next door to Pastor Augustine's church, Pastor Clement instead likes to worship with songs in West African pidgin
English like the song "Satan Fall Down" that goes as follows:

> *Satan fall down for ground oh*
> (response) *Mash him, mash him*
> *I be you fall down for gutter*
> (response) *Mash him, mash him*
> *You go fall down for ditch oh*
> (response) *Mash him, mash him*
> *I be you fall down for ground oh*
> (response) *Mash him, mash him*
> *I be you fall down for ditch oh*
> (response) *Mash him, mash him*

Which means:

> *Satan will fall down in the ditch*
> *Mash him, mash him*
> *I will make you fall down in the gutter*
> *Mash him, mash him*
> *I will make you fall down*

When people sing "Mash him, mash him," they aggressively stomp
the floor, miming the gesture of really mashing Satan and making the
floor of the room and also Don Elia's nerves shake like guitar strings. In
other rooms, at the same time, other African Pentecostal churches were
celebrating their Sunday service, and people were passionately praying, vigorously speaking in tongues, fearlessly falling down and rolling
on the floor under the power of the Holy Spirit that according to them
was there, visible, audible, tangible, and even smellable in the scent of
sweating, praying bodies, the fragrance of soap and starch, and in the
scent of the rivers of olive oil flowing from the pastors' hands to people's
hands and heads.

In speaking with Pentecostals about their sensations, they describe
the perception of a presence that touches them, presses them down to
the floor, talks to them, and speaks through them. It is the Holy Spirit
and the whole body feels it because, as Brent Plate would contend, it
gets under one's skin.[3]

These intense moments of perceived *real presence* are, as Nimi Wariboko argued in his book *Nigerian Pentecostalism*, "the engine of pentecostal

spirituality as well its Achilles' heel; its strength and its weakness at the same time."[4] This real presence is not only the engine of Pentecostalism but, as Robert Orsi argues, also of Roman Catholicism.[5] For Catholics, the flesh and blood of Christ are really, truly, and substantially present in the Eucharist, just as divine power is present in sacred images, sacramental substances, in relics, in the statues of Mary and the saints.

This book looks at real presence, or real presences, as focus and locus of both spiritual and political power, and examines the role these real presences play in the relationship between Roman Catholicism and African Pentecostalism. I will explore this relationship by focusing on what I call *aesthetics of presence* such as practices, objects, images, substances, and bodily sensations by means of which human beings generate and give material form to real presence.[6]

Clashes, Continuities, and Ambiguities

Christianity is redefining historical global configurations of power in contemporary societies of the Northern and Southern Hemispheres. Roman Catholicism and Pentecostalism, in their various cultural expressions, are at the forefront of this historical change. However, there are considerable tensions between Catholics and Pentecostals, and despite various attempts to establish a fruitful dialogue through ecumenical initiatives, historical doctrinal differences, suspicions, and ambiguities still remain.[7] Even Pope John Paul II has publicly defined Pentecostalism and its multiple expressions as "sects" that act like rapacious wolves, causing division and discord in Catholic communities. Equally controversial was Pope Benedict XVI's Declaration "Dominus Iesus," in which he stated that non-Catholic churches cannot be considered proper churches because they "suffer from defect," do not have divine origin or salvific efficacy, and "constitute an obstacle to salvation."[8]

For their part, Pentecostals condemn as heretical and idolatrous Catholic doctrine and devotional practices, and often denounce Catholic historical privileges and relationships with political institutions and powers. The Pentecostals' anti-Catholicism has sometimes taken remarkable, extreme forms—as in Brazil, where Pentecostalism has attracted hundreds of thousands of Catholics—and where tension between Catholics and Pentecostals has reached significant social and political dimensions.[9] A rather emblematic event happened in October

1995 when a bishop of the Pentecostal Universal Church of the Kingdom of God attacked a statue of the Virgin Mary on a live television show to demonstrate his disdain for the Catholics' "idol worship." Bishop Sergio Von Helder hit and kicked the statue twenty-two times on the Universal Church's television program, saying of the statue, "This doesn't work miracles."

Pope Francis has made several efforts to promote unity between Catholics and Pentecostals. Recently, he sent a video message to a Pentecostal gathering in Texas and had two meetings with Pentecostal pastors in Italy, one in July 2014 in Caserta and the other in May 2015 at the Vatican. In the first meeting, which he said was a personal visit to an old friend who happens to be a Pentecostal pastor, he apologized for the persecution of Italian Pentecostals that occurred during Mussolini's fascist regime. At that time, as I will discuss more in Chapter 1, Pentecostal gatherings were banned and Pentecostals were forced to meet secretly to escape the regime's repression and police harassment.

Interestingly enough, Pope Francis's efforts to promote ecumenism met some support but also harsh criticism from both Catholics and Pentecostals. Along with those who celebrated the pope's initiatives there were several who remained unconvinced about the possibility of a real change in the relationship between the two Christian faiths. Some Italian Pentecostal and Protestant churches released a joint statement reiterating the historical Pentecostal critique of Catholic heresy and imperialism, and declaring these Catholic-Pentecostal ecumenical initiatives as incompatible with the irreconcilable differences between Roman Catholicism and Pentecostalism.

While I was in Nigeria, Ghana, and Italy, I heard Pentecostal pastors voicing strong comments against Catholic idolatrous practices and veneration of images, use of material forms, objects, substances, embodied practices, and gestures. Their attitude toward Catholicism reflected the iconoclastic nature of the Reformation that Martin Luther described as follows:

> In order to grasp safely and fortunately a true and unbiased knowledge of this sacrament [the Mass], we must above all else be careful to put aside whatever has been added by the zeal and devotion of men to the original, simple institution of this sacrament—such things as vestments, ornaments, chants, prayers, organs, candles, and the whole pageantry of outward things.[10]

Echoing the spirit of these Reformation words, Pentecostal pastors continue to repeat, "These things are not necessary to salvation!"[11] As the national chair of a Nigerian Pentecostal church, Pastor Sola said, "They are all just religious practices that have come to acquire some value in the churches but they are not essential to salvation. We do not need all that. I cannot imagine Peter carrying incense around with him. I cannot see where he, or Christ, are doing such things. Incense burning and all that are the old, obsolete way."

Sometimes such opinions are not just spoken but written and published. In his famous prayer book *Prayer Rain*, Daniel Kolawole Olukoya, founder and general overseer of the Mountain of Fire and Miracles Ministries (one of the most popular Pentecostal churches in Nigeria), included a special set of prayers for achieving release or deliverance from the *spirit of religion* such as Roman Catholicism. Among the various evil spirits associated with Catholicism, there is a whole list of saints and madonnas, rosaries, candles, miraculous medals, ashes on Ash Wednesday, human bone relics on the altars, the crucifix, and genuflection before altars, to name just a few.[12] The list is long and includes as many as 120 evil spirits that allegedly coexist with Catholic material forms, practices, and aesthetics.

And yet as I also show in this book, Pentecostals themselves make abundant use of images and sacramental objects and substances. Olive oil, bells, holy water, holy robes, and sophisticated attire are nearly always central features of Pentecostal practices and events. Given this reality, why do Pentecostals condemn Catholic veneration of images and paraphernalia, and yet include in their religious aesthetics some of the sacramental substances also used by Catholics? Why, as I show in Chapter 3, does the New Life Pentecostal Ministries in Italy adorn the main altar of its church with a huge reproduction of the *Transfiguration of Christ* of Raphael, the great Renaissance masterpiece that is currently exhibited in the Vatican Museum and in Saint Peter's Basilica in the Vatican? Why do Pentecostals invest Catholic images and statues with evil powers and yet go to Catholic churches and basilicas to pray? And why do they run away from relics of saints disgusted and frightened? Aren't relics just superstitions according to Protestants?

In response to these and other questions, the book challenges several established assumptions and theoretical approaches of the study of religion and Pentecostalism. One of these assumptions is the definition of Pentecostalism as a segment of Protestantism.[13]

The link between Pentecostalism and Protestantism presumably lies in their doctrinal commonality, and in the history of some of the Pentecostal churches that were born out of schisms and divisions of mainstream Protestant churches. It lies also in some Pentecostal elements of Protestant ethics, and in their open and mutual hostility toward and critique of Catholic doctrine and practices. However, while I do acknowledge the Protestant elements of Pentecostalism, my focus is on one of the biggest paradoxes of Pentecostals' Protestant anti-Catholicism, a paradox that is also one of Pentecostalism's most vital theological and experiential dimensions: its catholicity manifested in the incarnational and sacramental principle that claims a divine presence in visible and tangible form in the here and now.

Catholicity and Aesthetics of Presence

In this book, rather than focus on the apparently irreconcilable differences and improbable dialogue between Pentecostalism and Roman Catholicism, I will look at what both pulls them together and separates them. This mysterious pulling force is a constitutive theological feature of Pentecostalism that, with the exception of some works by Pentecostal theologians, previous anthropological and sociological studies have overlooked, namely, the catholicity of Pentecostalism.[14] The word *catholicity* is not synonymous with Roman Catholicism, nor is it the property of one particular denomination. The word *catholicity* relates both to the classic concept of the universality and unity of the church, but also, as I want to emphasize in this book, to the wholeness and unity of the divine and human revealed in the physical worlds.[15] In other words, catholicity is the sacramentality manifest in the conflation of spirit and matter that generates perceived real presences of divine and supernatural powers pulsating in the material world, in nature, objects, and substances, as well as in the human body.

In this sense, catholicity undergirds the sacramental or incarnational principle or, as anthropologist Birgit Meyer puts it, a principle of mediation through which real presences, or the beyond, the invisible, the supernatural, and the transcendent to which religion refers is made tangible and becomes "really" present in this world.[16]

The question of real presence, or real presences, has always been charged with anxiety and tensions.[17] In this regard Matthew Engelke talked about the "problem of presence" and the core paradox of Christian thought: the simultaneous presence and absence of God—a question that, as we shall see in this work, has tantalized the mind and imagination of theologians, intellectuals, and artists.[18] In his research on the Masowe Church in Zimbabwe, Engelke particularly addressed the relationship between materiality and presence and highlighted the profound ambiguities of the impossible commitment to immateriality that paradoxically makes matter all the more important.[19]

In this book, I intend to show how Pentecostalism's impossible commitment to immateriality paradoxically illuminates its gritty materiality and its deep and visceral longing for real presence that it shares with Catholicism and also African traditional religions.

Historian Orsi has written extensively on the question of real presences, exploring the material and embodied world of presence in Catholicism and the everyday practices of corporealization of the sacred, such as "the practice of rendering the invisible visible by containing it as an experience in a body—in one's own body or in someone else's body—so that the experiencing body itself becomes the bearer of the presence for oneself and for others."[20] In this process, or corporalization, Catholic embodied practices and material culture, such as images, rosaries, and statues, play a major role in making the beyond visible and tangible. But as Orsi rhetorically asks in his work, how does this happen? In this book, I will look at aesthetics that generate perceived real presences. These presences are not mere representations or signification of the divine and the supernatural but are perceived as real, tangible, visible, and audible manifestations or evidences of the divine and the supernatural. In this book, *aesthetics of presence* refers to the perceived visual, kinesthetic, audible, and somatic properties of the sacred and supernatural. These aesthetics involve the human sensorium, the artful combination of gestures, words, images, and objects that turn the transcendent and the indefinite into an accessible real presence that human beings can feel, perceive, smell, touch, and hear.[21]

Presence, immediacy, mediation, remediation, and hypermediation are terms I will engage in this book to underline the analogy between the body, religious images, and objects that Pentecostals engage to mediate real presences. These terms migrated from modern media studies to religious studies and gave birth to the flourishing aesthetic and "media turn" in the study of religion.[22] The mediality, materiality, and sensuality of religious aesthetics are indeed intriguing lenses through which to observe religious aesthetic formations, changes, and interactions that involve not only meanings and ideas but also the very material and sensual elements of religion that have been long neglected by belief and meaning-centered approaches. These lenses illuminate more than belief, to paraphrase Manuel Vazquez, and put at the center of this study the embodied and sensuous place-shaping religious practices by means of which Pentecostals and Catholics invoke and give material form and presence to divine and supernatural presences.[23]

Certainly, the global scenario of the contemporary relationship between Roman Catholicism and Pentecostalism is very diverse and follows the nuances of the incredible heterogeneity and fluidity of these two expressions of Christianity.

As Harvey Cox wrote in *Fire from Heaven*, "Pentecostalism is diverse, volatile, and mercurial. It will not sit still long enough for someone to paint its portrait, or stop changing long enough for anyone to chart its trajectory."[24] This volatility triggers uncertainties that stem from the concomitant presence of conflicting tensions, including the tensions between continuity and change, institutionalization and charisma, emotion and discipline.[25]

But there is more.

During my fieldwork in Italy, Nigeria, and Ghana I was able to see just how complex this scenario can be. Visiting the various Pentecostal churches in Lagos, Accra, and Northern and Central Italy, I met with such a diversity of practices and material worlds that every effort I made to classify them proved futile. This was exactly what I had been led to expect by Matthews Ojo, author of the book *The End Time Army*, when we completed a short period of fieldwork together in Lagos.[26] He said, "When you speak about Pentecostalism in Nigeria your greatest difficulty will lie in honoring its homogeneity and heterogeneity. You must not be tempted to generalize!" These words of caution guided my first forays into the world of African Pentecostalism.

There is indeed a great deal of diversity in the various expressions of Pentecostalism. Views on deliverance from evil—an aspect that seems very important in Nigerian and Ghanaian Pentecostalism and that, as we shall see in Chapter 2, is one of the main issues on which Pentecostalism and Catholicism disagree—are very diversified. During my research in Lagos, I was rather surprised to see such different approaches to the concept of deliverance, or liberation from the evil forces afflicting individuals' spiritual and social life. Some churches, like the Mountain of Fire and Miracles Ministries, had made deliverance their mission and strength, while others, like the Redeem Evangelical Mission (TREM), were rather distrustful of the various deliverance practices and programs that form part of the city's religious events. Peace Okonkwo, wife of Mike Okonkwo (general overseer of TREM in Lagos), represents this latter view. She told me, "I do believe in Satan, but I don't believe in deliverance. If you are a good Christian, you pray and the Holy Spirit is with you, so how can a demon enter your body?"

So while hundreds of thousands of people attend deliverance programs in Onike, Yaba (headquarters of the Mountain of Fire and Miracles Ministries), and at its Prayer City, where they writhe on the ground and grapple with the forces of evil while pastors shout furious prayers and order the evil forces to abandon their bodies, there are many others who look on, express doubts, and sometimes even make derisive comments about what they see happening.[27]

There are just as many differences in how Pentecostals of different stripes view any number of other aspects of Pentecostal worship. For instance, although it is true that music and dance accompany prayers and songs of praise in Pentecostalism, perhaps more than in other churches, it is also true that not all the churches support what they perceive as a lack of restraint in one's worship expression. Several pastors of the Deeper Christian Life Bible Church and of the Mountain of Fire and Miracles Ministries, both in Italy and in Nigeria, have told me: "If people want to dance, they should go to a club, not to church."

These few examples illustrate the heterogeneity and complexity of Pentecostalism. This heterogeneity characterizes not only Pentecostalism in the city of Lagos, which has been defined as the most Pentecostal city in the world, but also Pentecostalism globally.[28]

This same heterogeneity also exists in Catholicism, even though—unlike global Pentecostalism—it has a strongly global hierarchical and centralized structure. It has only one headquarters that is assumed to be the sole source of theological reflection, from where rules and recommendations on liturgy, belief, and religious practices emanate. Despite its centripetal forces and strongly hierarchical and centralized structure, even Roman Catholicism has increasingly come to terms with different, often conflicting theological currents and internal debates, just as

inescapable cultural differences have historically and contextually characterized the various expressions of Catholicism around the world. Such
differences are the effect of cultural strategies that the Catholic Church
itself has sometimes adopted, for example through Vatican II and the
inculturation strategies that recognized and promoted the nuanced local
expressions of contemporary world Catholicism.

To give an example: In Italy, the home of the papacy, Catholicism
is deeply entangled with cultural geographies and with local cosmologies and imaginaries. Italian Catholicism itself incorporates elements of
pre-Christian cults that have survived the passage of time, and traces
of them can still be seen in the churches and cathedrals today, where
pagan symbols and signs of the Roman Empire sometimes can be found
not far away from the tabernacles and high altars of the basilicas.[29] For
instance, an attentive observer walking within the huge basilica of Saint
Anthony in Padua, which is featured several times in this book, would
notice the paintings of two charming pagan *sibillas* (sibyls) at the beginning of the visual narrative of the books of the Bible adorning the naves
of the basilica. Here one can also see a marble statue of Aesculapius,
the Roman god of medicine, and his clock; and a marble phoenix, the
mythological bird symbol of death and resurrection.

The composite and multiple voices of Catholicism have generated a
mosaic of different spiritual expressions, movements, and renewals. The
Catholic Charismatic Renewal is a vivid example. With its bottom-up administration of the sacred, its embodied and enthusiastic prayer, and its
emphasis on the power and gifts of the Holy Spirit, the "movement" has
garnered both encouragement and suspicion among Church hierarchies.[30]

Among these various expressions of Catholicism, popular (or folk)
Catholicism has for centuries been the most resilient, visceral, and "immediate product of crude sensations," as Gramsci puts it, collecting and
keeping alive a heritage of pre-Christian pagan religions dominated by
the profound relationship between man and nature.[31] This is the Catholicism of devotion to the saints and madonnas, of pilgrimages, of miraculous places and objects that sometimes even appear to usurp the
sovereignty of God.[32] For centuries, this has been the religion of Italy's
"second-class" citizens, who had their own Catholicism with its "second-
class" religious practices magisterially narrated by Ignazio Silone in his
book *Fontamara*, by Carlo Levi in *Christ Stopped at Eboli*, and by Pier Paolo
Pasolini in his novels and films.

If there are already such different aspects to Italian Catholicism, then the facets of world Catholicism and the different forms of expression it takes around the globe are bound to be numerous indeed. Faced with such a complex picture, dare we even consider embarking on any analysis of African Pentecostalism and Roman Catholicism aesthetics of presence in the twenty-first century? In this volume, I attempt to take on this challenge with a narrow focus on a particular contact zone to shed light on what is the greatest paradox of Pentecostal anti-Catholicism and Catholic anti-Pentecostalism: their shared sacramentality.

The Politics of Aesthetics in the Contact Zones

This book analyzes Pentecostal aesthetics of presence that take place in an intriguing contact zone: Italy. As I will discuss extensively in Chapter 1, this zone is characterized by a marked imbalance of power between Roman Catholicism, the former Italian state religion, and African Pentecostalism, a minority religion professed largely by first-generation African immigrants.[33]

Italy, home of Catholicism and seat of the papacy, has over the last thirty years become the destination of a significant migratory flow from Western Africa, specifically from Nigeria and Ghana. Along with their suitcases and dreams of a brighter future, these migrants have also brought with them their own form of Pentecostalism, shaped by their different cultures and religious worlds. This contact zone illuminates the encounter between two expressions of Christianity that, as I will discuss, are the fruit of a long and articulated historiography of multiple transcultural encounters that happened in different times and spaces.

In the contact zones I present in this book, tensions between Catholics and Pentecostals occur about many things: about the styles of the aesthetics of presence; about the role and place of images, material forms, substances, the body, and the senses.

The material and sensuous world of the Pentecostalism of Nigerian and Ghanaian migrants in Italy is particularly interesting. In Italy, Pentecostals find themselves immersed in the majestic architecture, stunning sacred art, sacramental objects, pompous public ceremonies, and processions of relics and of statues of Mary and the saints. Catholics walk with these statues and relics along with representatives of the church's hierarchy, public authorities, musical bands, and religious brotherhoods.

They perfume the route with incense, strew the streets with flower petals, light candles, and sprinkle holy water.

Pentecostals observe the spectacle of Catholic aesthetic and power in Italy and often shake their heads and react with disgust before the remains of human bodies that Catholics venerate as relics. Intriguingly, they recognize in some of these Catholic practices the rituals of the traditional religion of those they define as their idolatrous forefathers. When I interviewed Pastor Sola, of the Deeper Christian Life Bible Church in Italy, he told me:

> We know what Catholicism is all about because we saw it in Africa. In African traditional religions, there are a lot of rituals. For example, we have African initiated churches where they light candles, so what is the difference between that candle lighting and the one that is done in the Catholic Church? None! They use incense. What is the difference with that of the Catholic Church? None! They sprinkle water and oil too. What is the difference between a person going to the Catholic Church dipping their hand into something and touching their head and making the sign of the cross? They are very similar rituals. It is very easy for somebody who is into African religion to adapt to the Roman Catholic Church because they are just the same!

Pastor Sola's words highlight that the Italian contact zone reveals complicated and entangled relationships among Roman Catholicism, African Pentecostalism, African traditional religions, and also the enduring presence of the pagan idols of the Roman Empire. In this contact zone, these aesthetic communities meet and clash while part of their material worlds made of objects and images migrates across their porous cultural, religious, and temporal barriers, generating contradictions and ambiguities.

Meyer argues that all religious aesthetics are common, shared, and produced in regimes of emotions and sensations.[34] They shape the process of religious mediation as do ideas, passions, emotions, moods, values, and practices; and they sustain collective identities and subjectivities within a particular religious space, city, or even a nation. In her work, Meyer talks about aesthetic formations in order to highlight the dynamic nature of aesthetics. Certainly, aesthetics are not fixed and they change over time. The word *formation* perfectly captures the fluidity of aesthetics. Although in this book I do also focus on formation, fluidity, and especially the transcultural dynamics through which objects and images cross religious community boundaries to generate real presences, I still prefer to keep the word *community*, and in a very Durkhemian sense to examine what marks a community and what separates it from other communities or groups.

Here, I look at the relationship between Catholicism and Pentecostalism not as a problem of presences, to paraphrase Engelke, but as a problem of the politics of presence. To do so, I draw on Jacques Rancière's intellectual project of the politics of aesthetics and on the ideas behind the aesthetic turn in political thought that, as Nikolas Kompridis writes, deals with

> the problem of voice and voicelessness, the problem of the new, the problem of integrating (rather than dichotomizing) the ordinary and the extraordinary, the problem of judgment, the problem of responsiveness and receptivity, the problem of appearance, and of what is given to sense to make sense of, and more generally, the problem of the meaning and scope of aesthetic dimension of politics.[35]

In this sense, politics is the capacity to feel, perceive, speak, and talk when one is not supposed to.[36] In other words, as Rancière argues, politics is the disruptive staging of dissensus, such as the interruption or suspension of an aesthetic order that defines "delimitation of spaces and times, of the visible and the invisible, of speech and noise that determine the relationship between forms of action, production, perception and thought."[37] Rancière calls this delimitation *distribution of the sensible* where people, objects, things, emotions, and feelings have a determined place and role in what is common to the community. Understanding what is connected between aesthetic communities and what is not, and also what is at stake in these gaps and commonalities, is what the "politics of aesthetics" means. In this book, by using an aesthetic lens, I will try to disclose what connects Catholics and Pentecostals, and also what separates and differentiates them.

In their edited volume *Materializing Religion*, Elisabeth Kennan and William Arweck write:

> Materiality marks out religion and cultural "differences" as assuredly as the horizon divides earth, sea and sky. . . . Our materiality, notably our religious materiality, unites and separates us, making us recognizably "us" and "them". . . . Material expressions of religion bring out, as perhaps nothing else can, where we stand, what we are prepared to say and do, and who we are (not).[38]

So, what will Catholics' and Pentecostals' aesthetics of presence and their sensuous and material world tell us about their connections and disconnections? How do these embodied and deeply felt aesthetics of presence separate them and pit them one against the other?

As I will discuss extensively in Chapter 1, Pentecostal churches are one of the great novelties in the history of the last thirty years of African migration, and they are the most resilient non-Catholic, non-Italian, and nonwhite subjects of the last century in the history of religious pluralism in Italy. Their presence is the result of a dynamic movement of people and a creative spirit that has given rise to a cultural and religious expression unprecedented in the history of religious pluralism in Italy. The African Pentecostal churches of Italy are populated mainly by men and women who have arrived in Italy since the nineties. The majority of them have experienced the most difficult period of African immigration; they have been socially marginalized; they experience blatant racism and criminalization. Many members of the Pentecostal churches do not have a residence permit. Many (although certainly not all) have been exploited by the Nigerian or Italian mafia, or criminal organizations trafficking in men and women destined for the sex and drug markets, or have been employed in conditions of quasi slavery on farms in Southern Italy. Some of these African people have suffered badly from the economic recession, from the failure of multicultural policies for migrants in Mediterranean Europe, and from the building of barricades by the fortress of Europe.[39] No longer useful to a deflated economy, these men and women have seen powerful signs of a particular Italian form of racism nourished by the Western invention of Africa's otherness and by the specificity of Mussolini's colonial ideas of Africans as savage and underdeveloped.[40]

How do Pentecostal aesthetics of presence respond to the imposed peripheral existence that African Pentecostals espouse as black, African, non-Catholic, working-class migrants? And what do their aesthetics of presence tell us about the relationship between Roman Catholicism and African Pentecostalism?

Structure of the Book

The first chapter profiles African Pentecostalism in Italy and discloses the multilayered relations of power that African Pentecostals experience both within and outside their communities. African Pentecostalism in Italy is a new reality in the Italian context. It is the fruit of a relatively recent history of African migrations from West Africa to the Mediterranean countries. Predominantly attracted by the once flourishing Italian economy, immigrants are now facing the challenges of a massive economic crisis and increasing social tensions and conflicts both within and outside the various communities. In this chapter, I highlight the contemporary shape of power of Roman Catholicism in Italy, and I place African Pentecostalism in the long sweep of the history of Roman Catholics' struggle in Italy over the power to administer the sacred.

Chapter 2 analyzes what happens in the Italian contact zones. These contact zones are not a neutral ground in which Pentecostals and Catholics have equal standing. They are Catholic parish halls rented or borrowed from the local Catholic priest where the African Pentecostal churches hold their Sunday services. What happens when Catholics and Pentecostals physically meet and share the same space to pray, worship, anoint, or deliver people from evil powers?

Chapter 3 looks at the place of relics in Catholic and Pentecostal aesthetics. In the Catholic order, relics create and consolidate the spiritual and social power. This shows that the relics are not only intrinsic to Catholic aesthetics of presence; to Catholics a relic is an object of veneration and passion, something charged with charisma and power. It arouses devotion, excitement, loyalty, a sense of identity, memory, and national pride. Relics were—and probably still are—constitutive of Catholic social and political power, of a religious, aesthetic, and social order. To Pentecostals, relics are disgusting, polluting, evil forces that unchain social and spiritual chaos by blurring the barriers between the world of the living and the dead. What is their disgust telling us about their place, role, and power within a Catholic aesthetic order?

Chapter 4 focuses on the remediation of Raphael's *Transfiguration of Christ* by the New Life Pentecostal Church in Italy. In this church, underneath an industrial shed amid the desolation of an industrial zone in Northern Italy, an enormous reproduction of the upper portion of Raphael's *Transfiguration of Christ*—one of the great works of art of the Italian Renaissance, defined by Vasari (Raphael's biographer) as the most famous, the most beautiful, and most divine—decorates the altar. Why has the church chosen to reproduce this particular painting? Aren't Pentecostals against worshipping images?

The conclusion responds to the ultimate question about the aesthetics of presence: What is at stake with the aesthetics of real presence? Why do human beings want to make the divine and the supernatural visible, tangible, and real?

1

African Pentecostalism in the Storm

*Cursed be he that perverteth the judgment of the stranger, fatherless, and widow.
And all the people shall say, Amen.*

—Deuteronomy 27:19, NIV

IN ITALY, AFRICAN Pentecostalism dwells at the bottom and the periphery of Italian society. Yet the space it occupies is not just physical; it also represents geopolitical religious areas, or contact zones, with their own power structures, social struggles, and religious aesthetics and practices. These aesthetics are the sensory fabric of a population in motion, often swept aside by petrodollar economies and politics of exploitation and control of the movement of the labor force from the global South.

To illuminate and frame the aesthetics of African Pentecostals in Italian society and within the Catholic aesthetic regime, it is important to set their presence in the broad socioreligious framework defined by migration, the international division of labor, and Italian ethnoreligious politics. In this chapter, I highlight the complexity of the Italian religious field, as Bourdieu would describe it—and I profile the role and place of African Pentecostalism in light of the wider Italian socioreligious history.[1]

Although in this book I focus on the relationship between Italian Roman Catholicism and Pentecostalism as practiced by Nigerian and Ghanaian migrants in Italy, the Italian religious arena is an intricate web of connection and disconnection. African Pentecostals traverse this arena alongside the ramifications of relationships of solidarity and exploitation, and alliances and divisions with various subjects both within and outside their communities.

Against the background of a Catholic-dominated European and pre-dominantly white society, the African Pentecostal community is defined by being non-Catholic, non-Italian, and black economic migrants. Yet they also have connections and disconnections with other religious community (both Christians and non-Christians) that are shaping the contemporary Italian religious field.

Within their own communities, African Pentecostals navigate diverse positions defined by their ethnic affiliations, gender, status as document-ed or undocumented migrants, and of course, by the various roles they hold as members or leaders in their churches and associations. On the stage on which they operate, Pentecostal churches experience the same turbulence that stirs the lives of an incredibly diverse population in motion. They are part of a crowded arena of religious institutions (including other African religious groups that are not only Pentecostal but also Methodist, Anglican, and Catholic) and associations distributed across various parts of the country.

With these scenarios in mind, I will try to describe this turbulence, starting with a brief introduction to the history of African Pentecostalism in Italy.

Between Motions and States of Exception

Pentecostal churches are one of the great novelties in the history of the last three decades of African migration in Italy. The presence of these churches in Italy is the result of a massive movement of people from West Africa. African Pentecostals in Italy are primarily men and women who emigrated in the last fifteen to twenty years. In Italy, the increase of migrants is 16.8 percent per year. Five out of every ten immigrants are Europeans, and of these half are EU citizens, four are Africans and Asians, and one is Central/South American. African countries represent 26 percent of the resident foreign population. The largest communities come mostly from North, West, and East Africa. With regards to West Africa, the most significant national groups come from Senegal (90,863 units), Nigeria (66,833 units), and Ghana (51,602 units).[2]

In 2013, after the United Kingdom and Germany, Italy was the third country of destination for Nigerians and Ghanaians coming to Europe, followed by Spain and the Netherlands. Recent African immigration to Europe has been more difficult than ever. No longer useful to a deflated economy, these people have been exploited, criminalized, and marginalized. As Ferruccio Gambino showed in his book *Migranti nella tempesta* (*Migrants in the Storm*), they have been experiencing the perverse relationship between racism, international migratory movements, and international division of labor.[3] In the name of a neoliberal job market, migrants in Italy are deliberately deprived of fundamental rights and ghettoized by ethnicity, place of origin, and religion; and by means of carefully designed social and legislative devices, they are inexorably drawn into an illegal underworld and exploited by criminal networks.

The world in which African Pentecostals are immersed in Italy is steeped in tensions that reveal how racism has always been embedded in Italian society. This racism, crowned by the racial laws of Mussolini's fascist regime—whose pictures on the colonial postcards that arrived from Ethiopia portrayed black men and women as little more than animals—and recently revitalized by the Italian right-wing political parties and the xenophobic Lega Nord (Northern League), has always been what Alessandro Mezzadra called an *internal supplement* of the national and international division of labor.[4] This "supplement" was amply applied in the years after World War II to the Southern Italians who migrated en masse to Northern Italy, which was gradually becoming more industrialized. Italian racism became the driving force behind a social hierarchization and national division of labor that runs through the formal and informal economies, the latter still an unshakeable pillar of the Italian economic system. Before the arrival of migrants from abroad, it was the Italians from the south and the islands who bore the brunt of the discrimination and labor exploitation that helped to make the fortunes of industrialists and entrepreneurs who populated the scene of Italy's economic miracle. With the arrival of the first significant wave of foreign migrants in the 1970s and 1980s, the burden of this racial prejudice was deliberately transferred onto the backs of the migrants attracted by the strong demand for labor in the factories of northeastern Italy and in the agricultural sector of the south. There were also job opportunities for home cleaners and caregivers of the elderly, and in the informal economy as a whole.[5] With time, the jobs and accommodations offered to these migrants left them more and more marginalized, and exposed to an increasing process of discrimination, criminalization, and incarceration. However, contrary to appearances, this is not simply a result of the relationship between immigration and crime. Recent studies show how prison sentences are influenced by the low social and cultural status of the accused and their (lack of) knowledge of the law and the judicial system, the social alarm raised by the crimes committed, and by selective police controls.[6]

Moreover, racial prejudice against migrants in general and Africans in particular slowly became institutionalized and informally consolidated by migration and citizenship laws that have turned them into second-class citizens. This racism has become the mainstay of a society at the mercy of savage job market rules, a shadow economy, a battle to accumulate wealth, and an unruly property market, in which the people most severely affected are the most vulnerable and the most easily blackmailed. Since the 1980s, African migrants have been experiencing steadily worsening living and working conditions, making them a significant and growing proportion of the marginalized people in Italian society. They are frequently depicted and perceived as unwanted, dangerous, and criminal.[7]

The entire migrant population suffers from these negative mechanisms, but the racial prejudice against Africans has particular features. Their socially constructed and imposed stereotypic "Africanness" has emerged as the dominant markers that define their social relations and their racial, cultural, geographical, religious otherness, and inferiority.

Such inferiority has been deviously shaped by power dynamics through which the West has molded the imaginary of a continent constantly in need of being rescued, educated, civilized, and domesticated.[8] From the slave masters to the colonizers and the neocolonial African self-proclaimed rescuers, the constructed inferiority of Africans has always served economic and imperialistic interests. Today, as Nimi Wariboko argued in his reflections on Nigerian Pentecostalism and race, it is gross national product (GNP) that defines the worth of Africans:

> There is a wicked theory of GNP afoot in the world; and it is in the face of Africans. Low levels of economic development in Africa have come to be interpreted as black persons' greater vulnerability to death and shame, and have indeed marked them as surplus population, unworthy lives, those to be excluded from the global centers of power. The logic of this hermeneutics of GNP is part of the axiomatics of the current global formation, which before any engagement and dialogue, determines which race or people is to be taken seriously beyond the pale of politically correct tolerance in world economic-political affairs. Today, the connection

between GNP and racism is an important and particular site of the destructive weight of the world on Africans.[9]

In line with Wariboko's argument, one of my interviewees, a very successful Nigerian accountant in Italy, described the course that Italian racial prejudice has taken against Nigerians:

> When I arrived in Italy as a student more than twenty-five years ago, the tellers at the bank were opening the doors for me. At that time, I was a reflection of the wealth that my country was experiencing. Moreover, they knew that African students in Italy were coming from wealthy families. Now, if I go to the bank, they barely let me in.

In addition to this economic-imposed profile, selective police control, the overrepresentation of migrants in criminal activities, and the labeling of African migrants as criminals together have led Italians to consider Nigerians as what Asale-Angel Ajani called a "dangerous race." In her research in Italy, Ajani noted how easily Italians substitute the term *Nigerian* for "prostitute" or "drug trafficker/dealer." In Italy, *Nigerian* has thus become synonymous with "African criminal."[10]

This trend has been nurtured by the shameful wide-scale trafficking of human beings between Nigeria and Italy, the country known as the primary destination for young Nigerian women and men. By the early 2000s, poorly educated and unskilled young Nigerians had become highly vulnerable to dishonest agents, smugglers, and traffickers who promised passage to Italy and a job. Many of these migrants were destined for the sex and drug markets, and other highly exploitative informal economies organized by unscrupulous, criminal Italians and Nigerians.[11] The numbers of young Nigerians employed in drug dealing, set to work in appalling conditions in the fields of Southern Italy, or exploited by the urban shadow economy (selling counterfeit goods, for instance) are equally alarming. Living rough in sheds or makeshift lodgings in the country, or in overcrowded, unhealthy tenements in the city suburbs, these men and women are extremely vulnerable, exposed to all sorts of abuse and violence at the hands of the Italian and Nigerian mafia.

The situation of Africans in Italy today is hardly encouraging. Here, as in other European countries such as France, Spain, Belgium, Greece, and Portugal, the rising tension due to both the persistence of dynamics of social segregation and exploitation and episodes of brutality on the part of the police and other authorities has been triggering the protests of exasperated young Africans living in the ghettoes of Cova da Moura in Lisbon, San Denis in Paris, Roquetas de Mar in Spain, Thessalonica in Greece, and Milano and Castel Volturno in Italy. These are the consequences of a deeply ingrained racism and of the failure of the various migration policies in multicultural Europe.

Meanwhile, Italy is faced with an African presence that dates back many decades. There are now second- and third-generation Afro-Italians who claim to be Italian, a fact that causes those to tremble who continue to dream of a white, Catholic Italy in which African people remain the unwanted and inferior "other." This constructed otherness subtly justifies the discrimination of African people and their segregation in Italian-style ghettoes destined for the surplus population, and marginalizes their work as disposable labor that occupies what Maurizio Ambrosini and other Italian scholars have called the five *P* jobs: *precari, pesanti, pericolosi, poco pagati,* and *penalizzati* ("precarious," "tiring," "perilous," "poorly paid," and "socially stigmatizing").[12]

The first emblematic event of the story of African migrant labor in Italy that inaugurated a long season of racial violence happened in 1989. The story concerns the assassination of Jerry Masslo, a South African immigrant killed in fields outside Naples, where the young man was harvesting tomatoes for a pittance. Jerry had come to Italy to escape the racial persecution in his home country. He had run away from apartheid and saw Italy as a promised land. His previous life had been tainted with discrimination, terror, and bloodshed. His father and daughter had been killed in South Africa during a protest march for black people's rights. On March 21, 1988, Masslo arrived in Rome and applied for political asylum. The Italian authorities rejected his application because at that time, according to the law, asylum was available only to citizens escaping communist countries. Jerry was detained at the airport for two weeks and then released with no clearly defined legal status. He went looking for work. Already in those years, the living conditions of the seasonal farm laborers were appalling; the immigrant workers that Jerry joined had no accommodations. Some of them spent their nights in temporarily empty graves at the local cemetery. Two days before he was killed, Jerry was interviewed by one of the Italian national broadcasters, and he spoke out about the migrants' working conditions in the fields outside Naples:

In Italy I thought I would find a place to live in peace and be able to cultivate my dream of a future without barriers or prejudice. But I have been disappointed. Having a black skin in this country limits life in society. There is racism here too, in the form of acts of daily violence against people who ask nothing more than solidarity and respect. We of the Third World are contributing to the growth of your country, but this apparently means nothing. Sooner or later, one of us will be killed and then someone will notice that we exist.[13]

Jerry Masslo's brutal assassination two days later seemed, for a while, to shake the Italian people's conscience about racial prejudice and the inhuman conditions of migrant workers in Italy. Jerry Masslo was given a state funeral that was broadcast live on a national TV channel. The funeral was followed by the first national-scale "black" strike against racism. More than two hundred thousand people marched through the streets of Rome. Jerry's assassination prompted the birth and multiplication of the first antiracist associations, and the first law on immigration, passed in 1992.

Yet in 2014, the same conditions that Jerry Masslo experienced in 1989 continue to humiliate African laborers—and continue to fill the coffers of multinational companies that set the prices of a near-bankrupt Italian agricultural sector.[14] Jerry Masslo's story was only the first of a long series of violent episodes among the increasing numbers of tragic deaths of migrants attempting to cross the Mediterranean, which for the last century has served as Europe's largest cemetery of migrants' bodies. Meanwhile, the borders have become emblematic of Agamben's state of exception, as Hans Lucht argued in his breathtaking ethnography on the migratory journey across the Sahara Desert and Mediterranean Sea, of Ghanaian migrants living in Southern Italy.[15] Lucht gives a vivid account of their struggle for a life worth living in geopolitical spaces in which their lives are reduced to a state of bare life, a life that is constantly exposed to death and totally subject to the violence of national and international legislation implemented by policemen and border guards.

In recent times, tensions and conflicts between Italians and African migrants have triggered several race riots. A particularly serious episode occurred in Southern Italy in 2010 when a thousand African workers rebelled against their inhuman working and living conditions in the tomato fields. The assassination of seven Ghanaian migrants in Castel

Volturno (Naples) prompted another race riot. The Ghanaians owned a tailor's shop and had refused to come to terms with the local mafia. It was to those same migrants that the South African singer Miriam Makeba, the voice for freedom against the brutally racist South African apartheid system, gave her last concert and her last breath.

Makeba died in Castel Volturno on November 9, 2008, just after singing her song "Pata Pata" for the last time. She was participating in a concert against racism and the local mafia. A few weeks earlier, that mafia had killed seven Ghanaian immigrants who had refused to pay for their protection. Miriam Makeba performed in the square in Castel Volturno before an audience that, although it included representatives of the local authorities, associations, and activist groups, consisted mainly of ghettoized Africans who lived in industrial sheds and crumbling old houses at the mouth of the Volturno River, and who worked in miserable conditions of quasi slavery. These men and women heard and danced to Makeba's songs of freedom and hope, and gave her what was to be her final ovation. Soon after leaving the stage, Miriam Makeba fell to the floor and breathed her last.

During the nights and days of sorrow that followed, the African immigrants watched over her body and never left her until her body was returned home. At the morgue, a young African left her a bunch of flowers and a note with the words: "Bye Mama, you are our symbol." Fate, it seems, had decided that Miriam Makeba should die in another Africa, in the province of Caserta, where the mafia continues to kill Africans who dare to rebel. Miriam Makeba was an international symbol of the fight against apartheid, segregation, and racism, and she had come to Italy to sing in protest. She had dedicated her life to the struggle for civil rights and she died "in the field" in Castel Volturno, in what is known as this "province of Lagos," as a journalist ironically called this area of Campania to emphasize the strong link between it and Nigeria.

Certainly, not all Africans who make their way to Europe struggle against death and experience conditions of quasi slavery in Italy. As recent research shows, in the past the majority of undocumented migrants entered Italian territory with regular visas and passports, and became undocumented only when their documents expired. It is difficult to give an estimate of the actual number of undocumented African migrants in Italy, but certainly they are not the majority; and although many suffer under the grip of a bankrupt economy and have lost their jobs, other Africans have managed to secure a stable life with a job contract and property. The Africans who arrived in Italy over the last decade are a particularly diverse population, as Steven Vertovec's approach on superdiversity suggests.[16] They are a range of transnationally connected, socioeconomically differentiated, and legally stratified immigrants.

However, despite the superdiversity that gives this population a different kind of access to social resources and that places individuals in diverse positions of power in the Italian socio-religious field, the lives and experiences of the most vulnerable portion of this population also affects and stigmatizes the majority.

The whole web of relations of power is further complicated by the role played by criminal organizations, often other Africans who exploit their fellow countrymen with the same voracity with which the multinational lobbies are strangling the agricultural economies in which Africans are working in quasi-slavery conditions. Those countrymen exploit these vulnerable immigrant Africans into selling drugs, engaging in prostitution, or selling counterfeit goods, a practice called *shoroti*.

African Pentecostal churches usually respond nobly in such situations. As in other Pentecostal diasporic communities in Europe, they support their members' search for housing, jobs, and ways to attain permanent residence in Italy. The churches and their pastors are at the forefront of helping young men and women caught up in human trafficking; they provide all kinds of resources, hospitality, economic support, and networking activities to enable a social repositioning of those who wish to find legal work.[17] But sometimes pastors themselves engage in practices of dubious legality, such as taking money from young prostitutes in exchange for prayers to protect them against the violence of their customers and the police, a reality I do not intend to trivialize.

In the context of these multilayered relations of power between Pentecostals and Roman Catholics, Africans and Italians, I ventured into Pentecostal communities that rent rooms in empty Catholic parish halls or in industrial warehouses lost in the sprawling city suburbs, into spaces furnished only with plastic chairs, fake flowers, and paper decorations around the altars. It is in these churches that the various individual and collective experiences of black Pentecostal migrant men and women engulfed me. In these churches Pentacostals engage in quite different relations of power, this time with supernatural and divine forces. It is thanks to these forces that they can sing in dissent and joy, as Miriam Makeba did, recalling the past, retelling the present, and envisaging the future. As this book discloses, their stories are enmeshed in a web of contemporary politics of race, neoliberal global regimes, and neoreligious hegemonies, all of which we can see in the embodied and transubstantiated cosmologies of their religious aesthetics. For the last thirty years of this migration from Africa to Italy, we have been able to see in these small Pentecostal churches how stories of deception, humiliation, and shame that exude from African bodies are cleansed in rivers of olive oil and holy water, purified through deliverance, and refilled with new narratives of dignity.

African Pentecostalism in Italy

The history of today's Nigerian and Ghanaian Pentecostal churches in Italy dates back to the end of the 1980s and the early 1990s, when the first significant migratory movement from West Africa reached Italy. Those were the years when there was a strong demand for labor in the farming sector in Southern Italy and from the industries in the north of the country. Large numbers of people landed first in the southern and central regions of the country (particularly in Sicily, Campania, and Lazio) and then gradually moved north toward Veneto and Lombardy. During the years of these early migratory flows, very few churches worshipped in the English language. The exceptions were the American Pentecostal missions, such as the All Christian Fellowship, All Believers Fellowship, International Christian Fellowship, and the churches that provided a translation service, as in the case of some of the Assemblies of God. For many of the African Pentecostal churches currently operating in Italy, these options served as a launching pad for what has now become a movement with hundreds of churches. The account of Pastor James of Nigeria is an example of such:

> When I arrived in Italy someone took me to a church that was an Assembly of God. I had already gone to a Catholic Church but I didn't understand the language; it seemed strange. So I was looking for a church where they spoke English. A young lad took me to the Assembly of God and I could understand the message the pastor was preaching at last. There was a translation in English, so at least I could understand what was happening. There were no African churches at the time. In addition

to the language problems, there were also issues concerning the way the Catholic liturgy was conducted in Italy.

Pastor Austin of the International Redeemed Church likewise told me:

> When I came to Italy I went to the local parish where I was living, but mass was very different from how we celebrated in Nigeria. There was none of the ardor, that fire that I felt when I was praying in my parish in Enugu. So I began to organize a prayer group so that we could pray the way they do in Africa, with fire in our veins!

At the time, the Italian Catholic Church had yet to develop a pastoral multilingual and multicultural program for migrants. Today there are priests who come from the countries of the most numerous migrant populations and the liturgy is celebrated in different languages, but this is a relatively recent phenomenon.

As Pastor Austin told us, the Ghanaian and Nigerian Christian immigrants began to set up their little prayer groups in the early 1980s, and some asked the local Catholic churches and the Assemblies of God for permission to use their spaces.[18] An emblematic example of this process is the Church of Pentecost (COP) of Ghanaian origin, which is currently the most well-established and widespread of the African Pentecostal churches in Italy, followed by the Deeper Christian Life Church (Deeper Life) of Nigerian origin. The COP began its activities in Italy thanks to the initiative of a group of economic migrants who settled first in Castel Volturno and later moved to Udine. The first prayer group consisted of six people who began to meet in 1990. The promoters of these meetings were Daniel Wiafe (currently the representative of the COP in Italy) and his wife. Soon after, the group obtained the support of the Reverend Willis, an Italian American pastor of the Evangelical Church in Udine, who granted the group the use of his place of worship.

A year later, the church already had thirty-five members. It was then that Pastor Wiafe wrote to the headquarters of the COP in Accra, Ghana, and seven months later what they called a missionary was sent temporarily from Accra to Udine to consolidate the church and establish an executive committee for the COP mission in Italy. By 1991, the COP was operating in four places, and by 1993 there were a further eleven new sites. In the meantime, the head office in Accra had sent a coordinator to train pastors and administer the now well-established mission in Italy. The missionary appointed for Italy was unfortunately obliged to leave because his application to renew his residence permit was rejected by the authorities. He succeeded in returning only in 1995 when the number of churches had increased to twenty-one. In 2001, the COP had forty-seven churches in twelve districts. By this time, the organization could count on twelve ordained pastors (responsible for the districts), forty-nine deacons, and seventy-three deaconesses. The COP had 2,710 adult members and 699 children living in Italy. That same year (2001), the Italian mission purchased a head office in Brescia, followed by others in Milan, Vicenza, and Bologna. In 2011, the COP had approximately seventy-one churches organized into eighteen districts, directed by eighteen officially ordained pastors. The members of the Italian mission had increased to approximately 7,900 (with 233 new members in 2011 alone). The members' nationality was mainly Ghanaian, with only three Italians registered with the church, and 140 Africans of other nationalities.

The story of the COP in Italy, and of its rapidly expanding resources and membership, is unquestionably the result of a far-reaching missionary project that, once the first seeds had been sown by the economic migrants, has gradually become aligned with the view of the church as delineated in Accra.

Alongside the COP and Deeper Life, there are other churches too, such as the Redeem Christian Church of God, the Lord's Chosen, Christ Embassy, Action Chapel, Mountain of Fire and Miracles Ministries, Saint Joseph Chosen Church of God, Christian Pentecostal Mission International, and other Pentecostal churches with headquarters in Nigeria and Ghana. Other churches, such as the New Life Pentecostal Ministries, were first successfully established in Italy and then opened branches in Ghana and in England. But there are also churches founded in Italy by male and female pastors with weak leadership and extremely limited resources, and these suffer tremendously as a result of the economic crisis and a poorly consolidated membership exposed to the insecurity of the migrant's life. Such churches are short-lived and their experiences are only temporary features on the African Pentecostal and charismatic scene in Italy.

These churches have to cope with the many challenges that any new church has to face, specifically, economic difficulties including the cost of renting space and utilities due to the extreme mobility and inconsistency of their members, and the internal tensions that prompt separations and dissolutions. It is relatively simple to open a church but very difficult to keep it alive. Despite the efforts of religious leaders, in many cases it is hard to obtain a stable, solid "clientele" because the members are constantly moving from place to place and the churches have multiplied into myriad small groups. Mobility and vulnerability are the traits that make it difficult to accurately map these churches in Italy. In recent years, many small churches closed down because most of the members who were struggling with unemployment eventually left Italy to search for jobs in the United Kingdom or Germany. During my last months of fieldwork in Italy, I saw several congregations slowly shrink, move to smaller facilities, and finally close down.

In this context of severe economic challenges, the smaller and more isolated churches typically close down, whereas the strongest churches, with established national and transnational organizational backing, gain terrain by picking up the members left behind by the dying churches. Churches such as Deeper Christian Life Church, Church of Pentecost, Mountain of Fire and Miracles Ministries (and others) open new branches, and thanks to the work of trained and experienced pastors, consolidate their economic and social capacities.

As mentioned, the pervasive mobility of the members makes it difficult to provide an accurate number of African Pentecostal churches in Italy. However, I will attempt to provide a compass by which to navigate the phenomenon in two significant areas, namely, in the province of Padua (after Turin, this is the geographical area with the highest concentration of Nigerian immigrants in Italy), and the province of Vicenza (the geographical area with the highest concentration of Ghanaians in Italy). As of January 1, 2011, the Nigerian population in the province of Padua totaled 3,610. I have identified thirty-one Pentecostal and charismatic churches in the area, plus one Nigerian Anglican church and one Catholic parish that attracted most of the Nigerian Catholics in the province, where about 300 faithful attend the regular Sunday Mass and the most important liturgical celebrations attract as many as 500. (By comparison, the local Anglican Church draws approximately sixty people.) The charismatic Pentecostal churches typically have congregations of thirty to forty each, although in some cases there may be only a dozen people. In Vicenza, as of January 1, 2011, the Ghanaian population totaled approximately 5,579 people. In this area, there were thirty

Pentecostal and charismatic churches, plus a Catholic community (less well attended than the Nigerian one in Padua, with approximately 150 members) and an Italian Methodist church attended by about eighty Ghanaians. To these figures, and to the distribution of the Nigerian and Ghanaian faithful among the various expressions of Christianity, I have applied a variable of 10 percent to account for the people who are unaffiliated or irregular church goers. So we can estimate that there is one Pentecostal and charismatic church for every 100 Nigerians, and one for every 130 Ghanaians. Extrapolating these figures to a national scale, we could therefore expect to find nearly 500 Nigerian Pentecostal and charismatic churches, and 350 Ghanaian churches.[19]

A more recent study estimates the presence of 250,000 evangelical immigrants and a national scenario in which one evangelical out of three is an immigrant. The study highlights what the authors call an arena or an archipelago of diverse evangelical churches through which people move and dwell while surfing from one church to another according to linguistic affinity, ethnic affiliations, and liturgical styles. The archipelago of churches is indeed ample and made up of islands of various kinds, some connected to other islands and others totally isolated.

Attempts to create national bridges between churches through representative bodies have often failed. Some African pastors joined Italian Pentecostal networks to promote religious equality and rights in Italian society. But their presence in these representative bodies is scant. For instance, Reverend Adenitire, one of the first Nigerians to start his own church in Italy, told me that there are often tensions concerning the position and role of African Pentecostal pastors on the executive board of the Italian Pentecostal networks and federations. He stated, "I left the federation of Pentecostal churches in Italy because I was deeply disappointed by their attitudes towards the African pastors. They involve us when it is time to struggle and march in Rome in front of the parliament, but when it is time to appoint people to the decision-making board, they do not consider us!" In short, African Pentecostals seem to have little representation in the various Italian Pentecostal associations.

Difficult connections between African Pentecostal churches and Pentecostals of different theological persuasions; strained relations between ethnic groups like the southwestern Nigerian Yoruba and the southeastern Nigerian Igbo, Edo, and Bini, as well as between Nigerians and

Ghanaians; and infighting due to ongoing separations, trace a broad web of power and tensions.

Nonetheless, while facing the challenges of such fragmented contexts and the tensions that at times arise out of their inherent and profound internal conflicts, African Pentecostals continue to define and refine their role and place in Italian society alongside and against Roman Catholics. In trying to make sense of their imposed marginal role as a religious authority, these pastors often refer to the overwhelming power and prestige of the Catholic Church, its big cathedrals, pulpits, and columns, its sacred images and statues visible on every corner of Italian urban spaces, as well as the ubiquity of Catholic dogmas and doctrines in Italians' religiosity.

In fact, despite African pastors' dreams and aspirations, they have not succeeded in becoming missionaries to the Italians, and their churches have remained an exclusive space for Africans. After almost thirty years, they have not managed to attract and include members from outside of their own African immigrant communities and ethnic groups. Italians do not attend African Pentecostal churches, and as I will show in the following section, neither do they attend Catholic churches. Still, they define themselves as Catholic, and although they distance themselves from the Catholic institutions, the Catholic habitus seems to persist.

Between Ethnonational Catholicism and Catholic Aesthetic Hegemony

In his recent study on Catholicism in Europe, Ingo Schröder defined Catholic majority societies as those societies across Europe in which the Catholic Church has for centuries dominated the religious field without any strong competitors.[20] Italy is undoubtedly one of these societies, along with Ireland, Portugal, Spain, Poland, France, Lithuania, Slovenia, and Croatia. Italy occupies a peculiar position among these countries because with only a few brief interruptions, it has been the seat of the papacy and the land from which Catholicism has spread to become one of the world's mastodontic religious realities.

The power of the papacy in Rome, in Italy as a whole, and in the rest of the world clearly has been changing. The universal truth of Catholicism has often been challenged, and now, even in Italy, the relationship between the Catholic Church and the State is not what it once was.

Since 1984, Catholicism is no longer a state religion. However, by virtue of its long relationship with the country, the Catholic Church had always benefited from strong political support in Italy, which persisted throughout the thirty years of government by the Christian Democratic Party.[21] Before the constitution was adopted in 1947, the 1929 concordat governed Italy's relationship with the Catholic Church.[22] In 1984, a revised version of the concordat formally confirmed Italy as a secular state, but it maintained the principle of state support for religion that could also be extended to non-Catholic religions if requested and approved by Parliament.[23]

In this entangled history of religion and state in Italy, one can also trace the painful history of Italian Pentecostalism.[24] A ruling known as the Buffarini-Guidi circular, issued by Mussolini's government in 1935, ordered that prefectures all over Italy outlaw Pentecostal gatherings, which the circular defined as "religious practices contrary to the social order and harmful to the physical and psychological integrity of the race." This was the result of the clergy's pressure on the regime to have Pentecostals outlawed. During that time, stories of persecution (particularly in the south) tell of individuals beaten by police and priests alike, houses broken into and ransacked, people sent to jail for holding the Bible, and people being refused burial in cemeteries. According to the historical records, in 1929 there were at least 149 Pentecostal assemblies in Italy. After the fall of the Fascist regimes, those churches had publicly disappeared and met in open fields or in private homes behind closed doors.[25] The circular survived the end of the Fascists and was not revoked until April 16, 1955.

Today, after the Catholic Church and the Jehovah's Witnesses, the Evangelical Christian Churches of the Assemblies of God in Italy is the third largest organized religion in Italy; they have more than 1,000 churches and 140,000 members in Italy. Unlike the Assemblies of God and the other religions that have a special agreement with the state, African Pentecostal churches, along with all the other churches and religions including Islam, are not recognized as churches but are considered to be cultural associations.[26] Because of their legal status, these churches have limited access to the larger material resources of the state, including authorized places of worship. Pastors are not recognized as religious authorities, so they cannot make official visits to prisons and schools, nor can they perform marriages that are recognized by Italian law. They cannot rent premises for religious activities or benefit from the economic support granted to the Catholic Church, such as exemption from real estate taxes. Nor can pastors obtain visas or residence permits to stay in Italy for religious reasons because the state does not recognize their religion.

A practical example of the consequences of the legal status of African Pentecostalism in Italy comes from the story of a small Ghanaian Pentecostal church named Christ Peace and Love situated in Gorle, a small town in Northern Italy. Local authorities confiscated the church's property for violating the law on the legitimate use of spaces for religious purposes. The church reacted with a peaceful protest led by the pastor and his congregation. The African and Italian local newspapers followed the case of the little church for several weeks, and the online African newspaper *The International African Herald* reported on the event as follows:

> On the 28th of November, 2011 in Palazzolo, a province of Brescia, Italy, hundreds of Christian protesters took to the streets demanding without pretention a place to pray, a place of worship. These were members of the Pentecostal Evangelical Church of Palazzolo, a small town in Northern Italy. And after a year, a similar event was repeated. The Christ Peace and Love Evangelical Church in Bergamo, in collaboration with all evangelical churches in Bergamo, invites all believers to join in a peaceful demonstration against the Gorle municipality on Sunday 25th November. Pastor Emmanuel, who is in charge of the church in Bergamo, says there will be multitudes of believers praying, singing, and worshiping in front of the municipality, everyone, including the old and young, with billboards and placards.[27]

The local authority in Gorle (a municipality governed by the xenophobic Lega Nord Party) justified its decision to close down and confiscate the property of the church by saying that it had violated the regional authority's regulations on the use of industrial warehouses. They stressed that the warehouse was authorized only for manufacturing purposes, not as a place of worship. According to news reports, Gorle's mayor said that, in accordance with the Italian Constitution, the town adapts religious services to the needs of the people and that three churches (all of them Catholic) are enough for the town's citizens. He continued:

> The situation presented was not seen as an important issue to include in the urban plan, so, if these people think they are a necessary part and should be included in the community, then they are free to present their plan or else to worship at the Catholic churches already available in the area, if the priest in charge allows them to do so.[28]

Following its eviction, Pastor Emmanuel moved the church to another building, which was subsequently closed by the same local authorities for the same reason. In response, on the following Sunday,
church members worshipped in front of the municipal offices in the
rain. Pastor Emmanuel, who led the protest, said:

> We have decided to hold this peaceful demonstration to plead our
> cause, a cause which is affecting almost every Evangelical church in the
> Bergamo area. The voice of a child who stood with her father in the
> rain last Sunday asks to be heard because without a church for us there
> is no future.[29]

In April 2013, the regional authority's court responded to the small
Pentecostal church's appeal and annulled the local authority's confisca-
tion, obliging the latter to return the space to the little church, which is
now free to worship in the former warehouse it had purchased.

The struggle of African Pentecostals in Italy goes beyond the ob-
stacles created by the ethnoreligious politics of the Italian State, which
decides their legal position and access to material resources and social
authority. Their greatest battle is against the consolidated Catholic hegemonic cultural and religious power that has proved much more resistant
than the Italian people's support for the Catholic Church's institutional
objectives and their religious observance of the rulings of their mother
church. In this regard, Pastor Jeff, the national chair of a very successful
Nigerian Pentecostal church that has been operating in Italy since 1994,
said, "You have the big towers, the big pulpits, and you find nobody in
there. Only the old women when they are close to the grave, carrying
the walking stick, go to church. The youths are in parties and nightclubs.
So spiritually, they are bankrupt!"

Indeed, recent research has shown that the Italian lifestyle has
changed and with it, religious practice.[30] The number of people attending official Catholic rituals, like Sunday Mass, and taking holy sacraments (Communion, confession, confirmation, and last rites) is declin-
ing, whereas peripheral, extraliturgical practices, symbols, and signs of
popular piety remain very much alive alongside the official Catholic
system of beliefs and practices. In the public arena, the Catholic Church
retains a dominant social, political, and cultural presence, and it deploys
numerous forces and resources that form an integral part of Italy's civil
society. The Catholic Church's active involvement and influence in the
political sphere on issues such as immigration, religious diversity and

freedom, same-sex marriage, the welfare state, and bioethics, among others, still shows its influence in shaping the contours of contemporary Italian society. As Garelli argued, the Italian religious field seems to reflect the ambivalence of a religion of tradition that is experiencing the challenges of an increasing Euro-American "unchurching" process and the energy of a modern ethnonational Catholicism, whereas scholars like Vincenzo Pace and Marco Marzano stress the role of Catholicism as a custodian of Italian identity and memory.[31] I, however, look at Catholicism in Italy beyond nationalism and identity, and I see it as way of being and doing, of sensing the sacred though a disposition of the mind and body that shapes a certain religious and social world view. It is a habitus in the Bourdieuian sense with its own aesthetic formation.[32] In this regard, Pastor Sola made an astute and witty remark:

> It is far more difficult to spread the Gospel here than in a land that has never known any Gospel. It is easier to keep Italians out of the Catholic churches than to keep Catholicism out of the Italians. For Italians, Catholicism is something very profound. It is more than a religion. It is something that has to do with their memory, their fathers, their way of life.

Pastor Sola clearly sees that although Italians are not in church, Catholicism is very much in them. So, even though Italians have become emancipated from the life of their parishes and they are quite independent on matters of Catholic ethics and moral rules, they have a religiosity that responds to a mindset, a disposition, and a predisposition toward the sacred that permeates the very fabric of life. Such a habitus also assesses their relationship to any other religious habitus, which is typically perceived as being "other," far from the one universal truth proclaimed by the Catholic Church.

Today, the fact that Catholicism's weakening institutional affiliation challenges its social power does not mean that Catholicism is disappearing. As Schröder argued, in Catholic-majority societies that are undergoing a gradual unchurching, the Catholic habitus has proved much more resistant to change than the people's involvement in the Catholic churches. This situation casts some doubt on recent claims that the Catholic Church might be slowly dying in Italy, defeated by the country's increasing religious diversity.[33] As a matter of fact, the new religions that now occupy some Italian ground have not succeeded in substantially and radically altering the power relations in the religious field or, most important, the Italian Catholic habitus. Despite the expansion of the diverse religions of the migrants in Italy and the growing numbers of "do-it-yourself Catholics," or people disappointed with the Catholic institution (as discussed in Marzano's works), the number of Italians converting to other faiths or participating in the activities of these new religious communities is negligible.³⁴ Although other religions are offering alternative religious goods, the Italians remain essentially faithful to their Catholic habitus, which do not necessarily involve going to church on Sunday or receiving the sacraments, as studies on contemporary forms of secularization in Europe have shown.³⁵

In this regard, Pastor Sola made another good point. In his experience, it was extremely difficult to attract Italians to African Pentecostalism, and even when Italians did become involved in the Pentecostal churches, it was more difficult still to overcome the Italians' resilient Catholic devotional practices toward the saints:

> Roman Catholic dogmas are very strong. People don't read the Bible for themselves. They just believe whatever the priest says. So if the priest says something contrary to the Bible, how are you going to know? You don't know. You just believe it. When you confront people with the truth of the Gospel, it is difficult for them to accept because they will say, "This is not what our priest told me, I don't believe you." Even though you are quoting from the Bible, he or she would rather believe what the priest has said than what the Bible says. So, we have a lot of problems in spreading the Gospel in Italy. We have had Italians in our churches. They tell you that they have been born again, but they continue to pray with the rosary and to the saints.

It is in the light of the social, political, and religious power of the Catholic Church in Italy that I argue that Catholicism in Italy retains a significant portion of the hegemonic power that Antonio Gramsci described in his postwar analysis of Catholicism in Italy. The Catholic hegemony that Gramsci described is not a dominion but a highly persuasive and taken-for-granted horizon of a political and cultural project.³⁶ It is in this sense that one can regard Catholicism as a conception and perception of the world and of the sacred, with its own practices and rules for feeling.

The Subalterns and the African Charismatic Excess

For the time being, it is still reasonable to say that the only force really capable of challenging the Catholic hegemony in Italy has been folk Catholicism, the most profound and ancient expressions of popular religiosity, a form of Catholicism grafted onto pre-Christian beliefs and practices, one that the Catholic Church has never succeeded in eradicating completely. Gramsci described this religiosity as a counterhegemonic force, a form of embodied dissent against the Catholicism of the elite, of the official conception of the world, and of the ecclesiastical hierarchy that waged (but never quite won) a war against the structuring role of folklore and its legitimate power of control over the sacred.

The Italian anthropologist Antonio Cirese studied an example of this counterhegemonic force, namely, the now extinct funeral lamentations in central Italy that consisted in songs and chants of sorrow for the dead, accompanied by dramatic gestures that included women beating their breasts, pulling out their hair, tearing handkerchiefs and clothes, shouting, sobbing, and falling to the floor. These lamentations were also taking place during the official Catholic ritual. The Catholic Church was intolerant of such sounds, gestures, and embodied emotions of grief during its funeral rites and tried to eradicate the tradition, first by fining transgressors and then by threatening them with withholding from them the sacrament of the last rites.[37]

Modern-day Italy certainly differs from the one described by Gramsci, and the power of the Catholic Church has been reshaped by sociopolitical changes in Italian society. But rather than assuming Catholicism's disappearance, I prefer to highlight its new features. Changes that have occurred in the relationship between Italians, the religious institutions, and the empty churches are certainly clear signs of a significant new phase of the public life of Catholicism. However, those forms of folk religiosity remain components of the Italian religious life and history that have not disappeared but continue to live alongside official Catholicism and in the substratum of Italian society. According to the anthropologist Vittorio Lanternari, such forms of religiosity played an important role in what is known as the Milingo affair, the complicated case of the former Catholic archbishop of Lusaka, Zambia, who was removed from office after a harsh dispute concerning his healing and exorcism ministry.[38]

The inclusion of his story here has to do with Milingo's extraordinary success in Italian Catholic societies and in the clash between Milingo's religious practices and official Catholicism. Vittorio Lanternari, the Italian anthropologist who studied the Milingo case, writes that during Milingo's masses, he used to bless water, oil, clothes, and personal objects brought to him by the people. He also reported cases of people falling down and rolling on the floor, crying and shaking under the power of evil forces, along with scenes of collective hysteria as part of exorcism rites. Milingo's practices were not a novelty in Italian society but a reification of the popular religious culture that had been officially removed, yet nevertheless remained vividly alive in the substratum of Italian society. Lanternari wrote: "It is then appropriate to define the relationship between Milingo and the Italian popular culture as a 'short circuit' between two energetic wires that come into contact and emanate flares capable of producing a massive fire."[39]

Some questions concerning Milingo still remain open. According to historical records, testimonies, and even the ethnographic field notes of Lanternari, the exorcism practices by Milingo were in line with the Roman rite of exorcism. Then why was his healing ministry so disturbing for the Catholic Church? Why did the big crowd of Italians that flocked to Milingo's masses become a problem for the Vatican? As Lanternari aptly commented, Milingo brought back to the surface the vitality of popular religion. He brought back some of the embodied religious practices and material culture that the Catholic Church has long tried to control and repress.

After a long and strenuous battle, Milingo left the battleground, but his story remains an emblematic example of tensions and clashes between official Catholicism and another expression of Catholicism that comes from the heart of Zambia. The eruption of Milingo's practices in Italian Catholic society brought to the surface religious aesthetics of presence, and in this specific case, of evil presences, that official Catholicism has always treated with extreme caution.[40] His followers acknowledged and celebrated his healing power; yet for Catholic officials, this popularity became problematic.

According to African Catholic priests I met along my research journey in Italy, the Milingo case raised the alarm in the Catholic Church concerning "charismatic excesses" coming from Africa. During my fieldwork in Italy, I interviewed the African priest of a big Catholic Nigerian community in Italy. He asked to remain anonymous, and for this reason I will not disclose his name and his parish but instead will simply call him Father Marc. Father Marc is a forty-year-old Nigerian. He is a Catholic charismatic. His liturgy, attended only by Africans, is joyous and lively. The musical repertoire is in Italian and English, but also Igbo,

Yoruba, and pidgin English. Musical instruments include guitars, piano, and drums that energetically accompany the liturgy.

Father Marc also leads African charismatic prayer groups and passionately attends to the prayer requests of his parishioners, but he knows that the other Italian priests are carefully observing what he is doing. He said, "I do not feel free in my charismatic ministry. Sometimes, I do not have free access to spaces and the availability of the diocese's resources for my work. I think the diocese is afraid that another Milingo will come, sooner or later, and they don't want me to be this 'new Milingo.' That's why sometimes they are not very supportive about my charismatic ministry."

In Italy, African Catholics are the majority of the African Christian population. Despite the growing number of Pentecostal churches, they remain the most numerous in Italy. Although they might have frictions with Catholic hierarchies and structures, they are still part of the Catholic Church, although as Father Marc told me, their position seems to be peripheral. Their relationship with Pentecostal churches is limited to initiatives in support of the local African population. Sometimes priests and pastors attend meetings with local authorities to discuss projects of integration and aid devoted to the immigrant population, but apart from this collaboration, African Catholics keep Pentecostals at a distance.

On more than one occasion, Pentecostal pastors have said publicly that African Catholics have more access than African Pentecostals to social and material resources in Italy. Pastor Kalu, of the Deeper Life Christian Church in Italy, in one of his Sunday sermons said, "Sometimes I feel very sad when I see our fellow Africans wearing their rosary and saying they are Catholic just to get closer to Italians. I know they are not Catholic. They think that if they wear the rosary and baptize their children with Italians, they will have a better life. It is sad and, unfortunately, it is not true."

The relationship between African Catholics and Pentecostals is indeed complex and ambivalent. On the one side, they share the same condition of being immigrants and blacks in Italy. They suffer the same social discrimination and suspicion for their "charismatic excess." However, on the other side, Pentecostals are positioned in a diverse layer of the society. Although African Catholics are officially included in the Catholic order as Catholics with a potential risk of charismatic excess, Pentecostals remain suspicious Christian outsiders who openly question Catholic doctrine, power—and the focus of this book—its aesthetic order.

In the past, Milingo's alternative expression of Catholicism and the Catholicism of the subalterns described by Gramsci disturbed the official Catholic order and acted from the margin, creatively incorporating elements from the center.

Also African Pentecostals inhabit the margins of the Italian socioreligious and aesthetic order but, as this book discloses, they also try to incorporate elements from the center. How do they do this? Are the Pentecostals the new subaltern?

Are the Subalterns Back?

Some of the defining features of the relations between the Catholicism of the elite and the popular piety of the subalterns of Gramsci's time seem very similar to the contemporary power relations and the subaltern/agonistic condition of African Pentecostals in modern-day Italy. Gramsci accurately described this type of racism in 1926 in his writings on the "Southern question." He discusses the ideology (and elitist socialism) of the bourgeoisie of the North and describes the conditions of the farming communities of the South. His words on how Northern Italy's bourgeoisie viewed Southern Italians paint a picture that resembles the racist and colonial image that many Italians have of Africans today: a people who belong to an underdeveloped, backward land, a people who are victims of their own undoing and inferiority. Gramsci wrote:

> It is well known what kind of ideology has been disseminated in myriad ways among the masses in the North, by the propagandists of the bourgeoisie; the South is the ball and chain which prevents the social development of Italy from progressing more rapidly; the Southerners are biologically inferior beings, semi-barbarians or total barbarians, by natural destiny; if the South is backward, the fault does not lie with the capitalist system or with any other historical cause, but with Nature, which has made the Southerners lazy, incapable, criminal, and barbaric—only tempering this harsh fate with the purely individual explosion of a few great geniuses, like isolated palm-trees in an arid and barren desert.[41]

Italy was still in the grip of these racist ideas in the 1980s when the Lega Nord became deeply xenophobic and racist and started to adopt explicitly anti-African language. The popular Lega Nord slogan "Africa begins in Rome" puts in a nutshell the racist ideas that have been flowing through Italy's veins. African migrants, although enmeshed in diverse social relations of power in the hierarchical racialized Italian society, experience similar economic marginality to the peasants of Gramsci's time, exploited in the best interests of economic elites or, to use more contemporary terms, of multinational companies and corporations, from banks to oil companies. African Pentecostals also share with the Southerners described by Gramsci a profound discrimination, both socially and within their religion. As with the subalterns that Gramsci described, there is a significant imbalance of power between African Pentecostalism, which is the religion of the first-generation African migrants, and a powerful Catholic Church that claims to be the legitimate authority on how to be and behave as a Christian, how to engage the body and senses, objects, substances, and images to generate real presences. As Gramsci's subalterns, African Pentecostals arouse suspicion over their embodied practices and use of objects and words. Their worshipping, dancing, singing, praying, healing, and anointing, and their belief in the existence of evil spirits and forces raise doubts that in many cases recast Africans in a stereotypic world of superstition, ancestor worship, voodoo, and fetishism.

As emerged from the interviews I had with African Pentecostal pastors, in the public imaginary people speak of African Pentecostalism as a nonreligion, a "Black thing," as Phillip Jenkins reported on his study on the biggest Pentecostal church in London, led by the Nigerian Pastor Matthew Ashimolowo.[42] The Western imaginary of Africans and African religions also plays a significant role in the imposed position of Africans in the social hierarchy of Italian society. Africans or black people are often associated with the land of voodoo and fetishes, superstition and magical cults. In our interview, Pastor Sola gave his own account of the attitude of what he called "average Europeans" to African Pentecostals:

> All the stories coming out of Africa seem to talk about people living in trees. The average European does not see how Africans could possibly come and enlighten them. They expect Europeans to enlighten Africans. The thought process is: "What?! You come to preach the Gospel to me! We brought the Gospel to Africa!"

In the same vein, Reverend Adenitire said, "Here we are considered second-class citizens and second-class Christians. People think that nothing good can come out of Africa. They do not see us as a religious authority. They just look at our way of praying and worship and think that this is not Christianity!"

As we shall see, it is precisely in these churches that African Pentecostals—those perceived as a "dangerous race," as criminals, the unwanted survivors of the violence of the sea, street hawkers, and fetishists—find their way to tell their story and to take a stand against the official hegemonic narrative. While trying to navigate the web of connections and disconnections, the various relations of power, internal tensions, and divisions, African Pentecostal churches face the weight of their marginal positions imposed on them by a certain ethnoreligious stance. How do they escape this order to express their spiritual and political subjectivities? The following chapters respond to this question.

2

Contact Zones and Religious Short Circuits

And they were casting out many demons and were anointing
with oil many sick people and healing them.

—Mark, 6:13, NIV

CONTACT ZONES ARE spaces of encounter between people and groups
that were once separated by social, historical, and geographic barriers. According to Marie Louise Pratt, the scholar who coined this term,
in these spaces temporal, spatial, geographic, economic, political, and
bodily interactions usually occur in conditions of radical inequality and
conflict.[1] The people and groups who meet at a contact zone typically
hold asymmetrical positions of power in the hierarchical order of society. However, contact zones are also intriguing spaces of new possibilities and subjectivities that suspend divisions and established conventions. In this sense, contact zones are tumultuous and creative spaces
inhabited by transcultural subjects and objects that dwell in, cross, and
destabilize the boundaries that define identity and subjectivities. Contact
zones are social spaces that challenge consolidated hierarchies. All those
who inhabit a contact zone, regardless of whether their position is weak
and marginal or strong and central, have the opportunity to break away
from their role as mere passive spectators or supposed victims of conditions of marginality. In these contact zones, politics begin with the con-
figuration of a political space in which the role and capacity of subjects
and objects is generated and discussed.

In this chapter, I will focus on a particular micro contact zone
within the macro contact zone of Italy. This particular micro zone is a

Catholic parish building in which the local Catholic priest hosts several African Pentecostal churches that hold their Sunday services and prayer meetings there. I argue that through their aesthetics of presence, such as embodied prayers, body sensations, and use of sacramental substances like olive oil, the Pentecostals suspend the Catholic aesthetic order; temporarily disidentify themselves from their assigned marginal social, political, and religious power; and claim their equal right and authority to mediate divine and supernatural presence. I will analyze the politics of Pentecostal aesthetics of presence in this contact zone through Rancière's concept of dissensual communities and de Certeau's understanding of practices of everyday life. These two scholars' notions of political subjectivation, manifested through an apparently apolitical "consumption" of objects and spaces, are an especially intriguing lens through which to look at what African Pentecostals do in this Catholic parish.

Both Rancière and de Certeau investigated the constitutive relationship between people, gestures, spaces, and time that together form a certain imposed order; and both scholars referred to workers who rearranged proletarian space and time. Rancière illuminates the political act of the laborers who temporarily suspend the assigned role of their arms and gaze by experiencing their workplace in a new way and creating new possibilities for their freedom to expand beyond their assigned role.[2] This apparently apolitical moment is politically meaningful to Rancière because it redefines the place and role of laborers' bodies and creates a new aesthetic possibility for them. Similarly, de Certeau was interested in actions and procedures that people use every day on the micro level to subvert the disciplining powers from within, however briefly. De Certeau uses the example of *la perruque*, a tactic workers use at their place of employment to do something in their own interests by camouflaging it as work they are doing for their employer. De Certeau defines *la perruque* as follows: "It differs from absenteeism in that the worker is officially on the job. *La perruque* may be as simple a matter as a secretary's writing a love letter on 'company time' or as complex as a cabinetmaker's 'borrowing' a lathe to make a piece of furniture for his living room."[3] With this tactic, the worker reroutes time away from her work and uses it for her own activities that are "free, creative, and precisely not directed toward profit"—or at least not for the employer's profit.[4]

In the contact zone at the Tempio della Pace, as I shall disclose, Pentecostals use Catholic spaces for their Sunday services and prayers, and through their aesthetics of presence they also redefine the role and place assigned to them as African—black immigrant non-Catholics in a Catholic society. As I showed in Chapter 1, just as certain practices of popular Catholicism, such as the ritual of funerary lamentations that were frowned on years ago, involved bodies and sensations considered out of place, excessive, or primitive in Catholic ceremonies, so too do the African Pentecostals include embodied prayers, sensations, and objects in a space dominated by Catholic aesthetics.

In the previous chapter I focused on the socioreligious hierarchies of Italian society in which Catholic aesthetic and social power also defines the position and role of other religious expression. I will now briefly profile the Catholic economic power in Italy and its widespread presence in Italian urban spaces. This will shed some light on the asymmetric economic and social power of Roman Catholicism and African Pentecostalism.

In Italy alone, the Catholic Church owns almost one million properties comprising all sorts of buildings and land that, at a conservative estimate, are probably collectively worth more than 2,000 billion euro.[5] According to the property consultancy group of the Catholic Church in Italy, approximately 20 percent of all real estate in Italy belongs to the Catholic Church. This figure confirms a report published by a journalist in 1977 (that cost the paper's editor his job), from which it emerged that a quarter of the city of Rome was the property of the church.[6] This heritage extends from the capital city all over the country. These vast property holdings include 115,000 buildings, among them 9,000 schools, 26,000 churches, oratories, convents, sports grounds, and shops; and 5,000 clinics, hospitals, and health services, and other services of various kinds. The buildings that belong to Propaganda Fide (the Vatican's foreign ministry) alone are worth something like 9 billion euro. On top of this, in the city of Rome every year approximately 10,000 people leave their properties to the church in their wills. It is hard to say how many hotels, hostels, and other hospitality-providing structures the church owns because for the most part, they are the property of an order of monks or nuns, not of a diocese. Such properties are managed by a sizeable contingent of human resources. In fact, the Catholic Church in Italy has 107,000 people on its payroll (people working in services, schools, clinics, hotels, shops, and offices), making it the biggest employer in Italy after the State.

Several Pentecostal churches celebrate their Sunday services and events in rooms and halls of such real estate. Typically, local priests grant these Pentecostal churches permission to use for their prayer meetings some of the spaces left empty as a result of the dwindling numbers of their own Catholic parishioners.[7] These groups often start out with just a handful of members, then slowly build up their congregation and their finances, month by month, until they accumulate the economic resources they need to rent or buy spaces of their own. For the African Pentecostal churches, Catholic parishes are a great alternative to the expensive and inaccessible warehouses that often lie in the suburbs or the city's poorer districts. Catholic parish halls are usually in central urban areas that are well served by public transport, and they are generally in a good state of repair.

It is in these parish halls that Pentecostals and Catholics come into close contact and observe one another, sometimes overtly, sometimes secretively. The attitudes that I have encountered among the Catholic priests vary considerably. Some of them pay little attention to what happens behind the closed doors of the rooms they allow the Pentecostal churches to use. For instance, the Deeper Christian Life Bible Church in Padua holds its services in a charming hall loaned to them by Don Albino, a parish priest well known for his public spirit and for the pro-peace and pro-environment activities that he organizes through his association Beati I Costruttori di Pace (Blessed Are the Peacemakers). The hall hosts two Pentecostal churches that celebrate their Sunday services there, one in the morning and the other in the afternoon. According to what Pastor Kalu of Deeper Life told me, Don Albino does not seem to be particularly concerned about what the Pentecostals do when they meet. Pastor Kalu told me that he met the priest only once and that they had a brief and cordial conversation about the use of the space. Don Albino told me that he was happy to grant the use of the hall to both the Pentecostal churches and the city's Coptic community. He saw no reason to worry about how they worship.

For the Deeper Christian Life Church, being able to use the hall free of charge is important; it gives them some time to accumulate the finances they need to buy their own regional headquarters for their church, which is now a presence all over Italy. The Redeemed Christian Church of God in Padua likewise celebrates its Sunday service in the San Prosdocimo parish. Here again, apart from checking that the hall is left clean and tidy, the local priest does not appear to be particularly concerned about the activities that take place there. In fact, when I contacted him to ask if we could meet for an interview, he told me that he hardly knew the group that meets in the parish hall: "I just make sure they leave the room clean, and contribute to the electricity bill. Apart from that I don't know much about them," he said.

On the other hand, there are instances in which Catholics and Pentecostals have much more to do with one another, and in such situations we can see evidence of all the tensions, contradictions, and paradoxes that typically characterize the relationship between Roman Catholics and Pentecostals, especially the ones that come from Africa. Several of the Pentecostal pastors that I interviewed had countless anecdotes to tell about how their practices and prayers placed a strain on relations with the Catholic parish priests who had granted them the use of their buildings. One such instance in the city of Padua is the numerous congregations that meet at the church Tempio della Pace, to which I now turn.

The Tempio della Pace and the Shaping of Presence

Over the years, the Tempio della Pace parish has become an important resource, not only for its few remaining Catholic parishioners, but also and especially for immigrants. The parish is a place where Italians briefly stop by, especially if they are elderly and poor and seek charity. But it is also a place where the immigrant population has found a vital space in which to hold their religious and cultural activities.

African churches at the Tempio della Pace do more than merely change how and by whom the parish buildings are used. On Sunday mornings, the whole area around the parish, located near the railway station in the city of Padua, looks very different than on other days of the week. There is less confusion and hooting of cars, and fewer announcements of trains arriving and departing than on workdays; half of the coffee shops are closed, and so are most of the shops. There are fewer buses transiting through the area, and fewer taxis coming and going. In its place, a different kind of ferment fills the area.

On Sundays, the station becomes a hub for the local African population. Many of them arrive to attend mass or Sunday services in the thirty-two Pentecostal churches of the city area or in the English-speaking

Catholic parish, or the Methodist and Anglican Church located in the city center or inner suburbs. Scores of parked cars and minibuses await the arrival of entire families elegantly dressed in their colorful clothes, in *ankara* and lace, who arrive in the city for the Sunday services. Many of them walk along the road to the Tempio della Pace. They look as if they are making for the huge set of steps leading up to the main entrance, but then they take a few more steps, go around the great church, and disappear behind a gate. They pass by the now dilapidated basketball court and enter a small building behind the church where as many as nine different Pentecostal churches hold their services.

I conducted fieldwork at the Tempio della Pace over a period of al- most eighteen months, some time after returning from doing ethno- graphic research on Pentecostalism in Lagos in Nigeria and Accra in Ghana. It took me only a few months to get to know almost everyone, from the priest and his assistants to the Pentecostal pastors and their wives and children, and the majority of their church members. The fa- miliar ease with which I passed through the small courtyard after a few months was a far cry from the way I had felt the first time I had gone to the Tempio della Pace at the invitation of James, deacon of the Faith Tabernacle Congregation. His church did not have its own place, so its Sunday services were celebrated at the Tempio della Pace. I had met James as part of my previous research on the African diaspora in Italy. James was one of the elders of the church. He did the church's book- keeping and was intimately involved in a long legal battle to see his church officially acknowledged as a church by the Italian state. Like the other African Pentecostal churches in Italy, the Faith Tabernacle Congre- gation until then had been acknowledged only as a cultural association.

James is a forty-year-old Nigerian from Port Harcourt, Rivers State. He is married with two children in Italy and one in Nigeria. He works part time for an office-cleaning agency. He arrived in Italy in 1993 as an economic migrant. Both he and his wife have degrees in econom- ics awarded by the University of Port Harcourt, but neither was able to find employment commensurate with their qualifications. Over the years, they have both accepted much more menial occupations, work- ing as cleaners or as care workers for the elderly. At the time I met him, James's salary was around €1,000 a month, out of which he paid €550 for rent, and €100 for utility bills. With the remaining €350 he provided for his family (food, clothing, school for the children, and all their other needs); and he also paid his tithe of €100, that is, one tenth of his income, to his church. "I give €100 to my church every month because it was God who granted me my job," James told me during a conversation we had when I first visited him in his home.

When James met with economic difficulties because his employer reduced his working hours from full to part time, James turned to social services and was granted a small monthly contribution to help pay the rent. James told me that there had been some discussion with the social services because of his involvement with the Faith Tabernacle Congregation. I asked him to explain, but he was rather vague, and I realized that he preferred not to talk about it. Yet when we said goodbye, he made a point of asking me not to say anything to representatives of the social services, should I happen to meet them, about the tithe that he pays to his church. He said, "They don't understand. Here in Italy people do not believe in God. There are nearly two hundred people working for the cooperative society that employs me, but I don't know how many of them know God." The reason for the caution with the social services immediately became clear to me: The social service administrators would most likely not understand why, despite his difficult economic situation, James gives a tenth of his meager income to his church, and so James preferred to keep that information private.[8] When we said goodbye at the end of our first meeting, we agreed to meet on the following Sunday at the Faith Tabernacle Congregation.

When I arrived at the Tempio della Pace, I immediately saw that the courtyard leading to the church and parish buildings was a hive of activity, black children darting about every which way amid elegantly dressed black men and women. From the inside of the building came indistinct sounds of songs, drums, preaching, and handclapping. The people around me were all of African origin. I was the only white Italian person there. I soon saw that I was attracting half-curious, half-suspicious glances and began to feel slightly ill at ease. As I approached the entrance, I saw some men suspend their conversations to watch my movements. I responded to their stares with a "Good morning," but this did not distract them from monitoring my movements. I soon had the feeling that I was trespassing on territory in which the presence of someone like me was uncommon and unsettling. My impression was not far wrong: As one of the pastors I interviewed told me, many of those present thought I was either from social services or a plainclothes policewoman—the only Italians with whom Nigerians tended to have relations outside working hours. It would not have crossed their minds that I might want to attend worship services in one of their churches.

When I went inside the building, I tried to follow the instructions that James had given me to identify his church. Beyond the entrance, there was one room on the right and another on the left, and coming from both I could hear amplified voices praying. Somebody said, "Amen?" through a microphone, and a chorus of lilting voices answered, "Aaaameeeeen." But neither of these two rooms was the one that James had told me to find. The Faith Tabernacle Congregation was on the first floor, through the first door on the right. Their room was the first of six at which a further six churches were holding their services, all at the same time. I realized later on that the various congregations were competing with one another by raising their voices higher and higher, rattling the nerves of the parish priest who from time to time openly voiced his disapproval.

I finally located the room used by the Faith Tabernacle Congregation. As I was about to enter, the door opened and a woman coming out looked at me, stopped, and in English said in no uncertain terms, "You can't come in here, this is a church!" "I know," I answered calmly. "I've been invited by Mr. James." She looked me up and down before she replied, "Come in." Like the others in the courtyard, the woman probably thought I was there for quite other reasons. Between the lines of her unfriendly words, I seemed to hear an unspoken protest or even a threat: "You can't come to inspect us here. This is a church." Of course, she didn't actually say this, but several times over the course of my interviews with pastors I was told that such words had been used in vain to prevent the authorities from bursting in on their prayer meetings and detaining everyone assembled there until their documents had been checked.

I experienced one such police check myself. I was attending an annual harvest festival in one of the Italian branches of the Celestial Church of Christ (CCC) when the police showed up right in the middle of the celebration, ostensibly called by neighbors who were extremely disturbed by the noise of the drums and visibly worried about the massive gathering of Africans without shoes and dressed in white behaving in a "strange way."[9] The six "shepherds" of the CCC that came from some of the Italian branches of the church had to show their documents and to explain what they were doing and the importance of the annual ceremony. After almost forty minutes of discussion and examination of their permits, the police left with the request that the church not play the drums for the rest of the day. This of course did not happen; drum music was far too integral to the occasion to do without it.

When the Pentecostal churches were still new and unknown entities, the authorities were suspicious of Africans assembling in large numbers, day or night, in isolated parts of the city. That is why they would descend on these groups right in the middle of their prayer meetings and vigils, checking their documents and generating panic among the church members, who often did not have regular residence permits. It is important to note that this never happened in Catholic churches; police would have hesitated to do that.

After allaying the suspicions of the woman I met at the door, I was accompanied to one of the seats at the back of the room. A few minutes later, a young man came over and asked me whether I spoke English. When I said I did, he relayed this information to the pastor, who sent a church member to translate his sermon from Igbo into English. That morning, the sermon was the only part of the service that I was able to understand. It was followed by three hours of prayer in Igbo language, by the end of which I had learned my first sentence in Igbo, *Chineke idi mma*, which means "God is good."

A year and a half later I was there again, in the meantime having spent several months in Nigeria and Ghana. I had acquired quite a good vocabulary of pidgin English that was a source of great amusement to the members of the communities with whom I launched into brief conversations:

> *"How far! I dey ooo!!!"* (How are you? Fine!)
> *"Wetin dey happen?"* (How is life?)
> *"God don butta my bread ooo."* (God has been good to me!)
> *"Oyibo, you dey try oo!"* (Oyibo, you are doing well!)

I particularly remember attending a Sunday Pentecostal service of the Christ the Savior Church led by a woman, Pastor Stella. The service ended with a very long prayer time in which everyone became quite involved. One of the female members of the community, Ruth, was returning to Nigeria after nearly twenty years. The woman was sixty-five years old, short, slim, with a face marked by the passage of time. She had arrived in Italy as a student, had studied in Rome, and been awarded a degree in foreign languages and literature. After graduating, Ruth had decided to stay in Italy, refusing the offer of a job in Nigeria. She was from Imo State but had lived in Lagos for several years before departing for Italy on a student visa. When I first met her, she told me that Nigeria was not safe and that it was the political uncertainty, crime, and corruption of her home country that had induced her to try to make a future for herself in Italy. But things had not gone well for her. She had never succeeded in finding a job commensurate with her qualifications, and eighteen months after graduating, she was still harvesting tomatoes in Southern Italy. Ruth lived for years without a residence permit, sending home whatever money she could spare. For many years she was practically trapped in Italy, unable to travel because she had no regular documents. Thanks to an amnesty, she eventually managed to obtain a residence permit, but for her, Nigeria remained out of reach. A month before we met, Ruth had been told that her mother had died, and she had decided to go home for the funeral after being away for twenty years.

That day, Pastor Stella called Ruth to the front of the room to stand alongside her rickety lectern that served as a pulpit: "Come here, Ruth. We want to pray for you." Ruth left her place in the second row of chairs and slowly moved forward as the pastor announced to the congregation Ruth's imminent journey. "As you know," said the pastor, "a week from now Ruth will be returning home for the first time in twenty years. Let us pray for her and for her protection, so that she can return home safely, meet with no dangers, no evil, no attack from malignant forces." She asked the congregation to stand and form a circle around Ruth (who in the meantime was standing in front of Pastor Stella) and herself. I remained seated in the chair from where I had been taking part in the Sunday service, but the pastor asked me to participate, so I put down my pen and notepad and became part of the circle that surrounded Ruth and the pastor.

Ruth stood in front of the pastor with her head down. "Lord, this daughter of yours is returning to Nigeria after a long period of absence." As the pastor said these words, I noticed that two of the women standing alongside me had bowed their heads and begun to cry. They were probably thirty or thirty-five years old. I tried to imagine the reason for those tears: hardship, illness, poverty, or simply homesickness. Despite all the *wahala*, as Nigerians call their problems, I noticed that the very mention of Nigeria always fill the eyes of the men and women of the diaspora with a certain light and melancholic smile.

Their emotions seemed to infect the whole group, which became restless. Pastor Stella continued to pray, her voice gradually rising in volume, and the more she raised her voice, the more the men and women fidgeted. "I bind the spirit of death, armed robbery, and assassination, in the name of Jesus! Every evil power trying to attack you on your way back home, shatter in the name of Jesus!" Many members of the congregation began to shake their heads, make a fist, and walk restlessly around the circle. With each prayer uttered by the pastor, the "Amen" intoned by the congregation became louder. Handclapping and foot stomping accompanied their own prayers and entreaties. As the pastor prayed, she walked quickly around Ruth, miming the gestures of cutting away the air around her. At one point she stopped, grasped Ruth's head in her hands and began to blow on her forehead, as if she had seen something there that she wanted to blow away. Then she continued to walk around Ruth again several times before she stopped in front of her and asked a church member to bring her the bottle of extra virgin olive oil that she had placed alongside a chair. Meanwhile, Ruth had removed her beautiful *ichafu*, the head scarf that Nigerian women wear on their heads with their traditional outfits. Without it, her silver hair and wrinkled forehead now visible, she looked even smaller and more defenseless. The pastor prayed over the oil, saying words that I could not understand. With a practiced hand, she poured a considerable amount of oil into her right hand and used it to anoint Ruth's head. Then she pressed Ruth's forehead hard enough to make her stagger, and asked Ruth to give her a handkerchief. Ruth drew a white handkerchief from her pocket and gave it to Pastor Stella, who raised it high, praying all the while for Ruth's protection. She invoked the power of the Holy Spirit, named the prophet Elijah and his cloak; with a proud, decisive gesture, she returned the handkerchief to Ruth and said that it would serve her as a protective mantel during her return to Nigeria.

Ruth had remained immobile all this time, apart from staggering slightly under the forceful and oily hands of Pastor Stella, but all around her there was a veritable flood of sound, hands and arms in motion, and faces streaked with tears and perspiration. When she had finished with Ruth, the pastor turned to the other members of the church and invited them to move closer to be anointed. Pouring oil into her hand several times, she began to touch the heads of all the men and women. Some fell to the floor, some shouted, others fell into the arms of those standing alongside them, and others began to tremble like a leaf. While all this was happening, amid the shouted prayers that were resounding in my ears, the feet stomping on the floor and the handclapping, I could hear other pastors and congregations in adjacent rooms praying and singing, the whole building vibrating like the string of a guitar.

Moments of prayer like the one dedicated to Ruth are very common in the Pentecostal churches that meet at the Tempio della Pace, just like all the other Pentecostal churches elsewhere. There are always members who need special prayer. The pastors pray furiously with their oiled hands raised over the heads of men and women who have appointments the following week at police headquarters about their residence permits, or who expect a visit from the social services, or who have a job interview, or are awaiting news from Nigeria about their families' health or financial situation. There are even those like John, a member of the Redeemed Christian Church run by Pastor Augustine, who asked for prayer because he was awaiting trial for drug dealing, and whose story is worth telling in more detail.

When I met John, he was an active church member, married, and the father of two little girls. It was he who brought me copies of the songs that they would be singing in church—in English, Yoruba, and Igbo—when he heard that I would be attending their Sunday services for a while. He had written them out himself, in his own hand, to make sure that I could sing together with the rest of them. He told me, "We are happy to have you here with us, but you cannot remain silent while we sing." On the Sunday before his trial, John told the congregation his story, starting from when he left Benin City and up until the day when the police stopped him and found some "substances" (as he called them) on his person. Now, more than a year after his arrest, in the church he talked about his first year of law studies at the University of Benin and his decision to leave everything behind and join his brother, who planned to establish a shoe trade between Italy and Nigeria. Things went very badly for them. A dishonest Italian supplier tricked them; he took their money but then delivered only half of the agreed upon goods. All their plans went awry, and they lost most of the economic resources they had struggled to piece together.

The events in his life followed the same script as for many other young people who could speak not a word of Italian and had made the mistake of placing their trust in dishonest compatriots who exploited them in various black-economy jobs. The most common such job is called *shoroti* and involves selling various sorts of merchandise (household goods, socks, cigarette lighters, and counterfeit goods) at the roadside or door to door. The people who exploit the *shoroti* boys are Nigerians who own shops and warehouses where they amass these goods. In many cases, these warehouses are in suburban industrial zones, and quite often right next door to the industrial sheds where Pentecostal churchgoers meet and pray to God to wash away the *shoroti* boys' pains. The daily income from the sale of such products is a pittance, and the strain of selling door to door and on the road is tremendous, but immigrants who have no regular papers have little choice: It is either *shoroti* or drug dealing. John, who had married in the meantime and had a young daughter, opted for *shoroti*, but he found the experience devastating. Selling door to door exposed him to all sorts of unpleasant situations and even violence: people who insulted and mistreated him, those who set their dogs on him, and elderly men who wanted to pay him for sexual services. He said: "Those things usually happen to the *shoroti* boys and some of us are so desperate." John's story was interspersed with long silences during which his listeners would bow their heads and cross their hands as a sign of prayer and also sorrow for John's quietly voiced anger, a very personal protest that echoed the protest of the whole Nigerian diaspora in Italy.

John's story came to the day when he decided to try drug dealing. Within a very short time, the police arrested him and convicted him for drug dealing. Pastor Augustine met him during one of his evangelizing missions to the darker corners of the city where young Nigerians hang out and sell drugs, and succeeded in convincing him to attend the Sunday service of the Redeemed Church, where John was, as he put it, "born again." The expression *born again* is mentioned in the Bible in John 3, when Jesus talks to Nicodemus and tells him the way to enter the kingdom of God. Jesus said:

> Very truly I tell you, no one can enter the kingdom of God unless they are born of water and the Spirit. Flesh gives birth to flesh, but the Spirit gives birth to spirit. You should not be surprised at my saying, "You must be born again." The wind blows wherever it pleases. You hear its sound,

but you cannot tell where it comes from or where it is going. So it is with everyone born of the Spirit.[10]

To Pentecostals this passage of the Bible indicates a rebirth into a new life in which Jesus is the only personal savior. This rebirth implies a new lifestyle, new habits, new friends, and often an entire new community of born-again believers of which to be a part. It is a sort of personal and spiritual revolution, an event meant to change one's life forever.[11]

At the time when he told us his story, John was surviving thanks to support from social services and occasional part-time work. But he was still awaiting his trial for drug dealing and was expecting the sentence the following week. John did not want to go to prison and leave his family. He wanted to find a stable job and live with dignity. That is why he asked the pastor and everyone in the congregation to pray for him. Pastor Augustine invited him to come forward together with his wife and their two little girls, one five and the other two years old, and then he asked everyone to extend their hands toward them. In a prayer spoken with vehemence and energy, the pastor asked for a miracle for John. He asked God to send fire from the sky, to destroy walls, move mountains, and cleave oceans; he recalled all sorts of biblical images and metaphors of the impossible made possible, giving to these words the force and production of tangible reality, as Simon Coleman nicely showed in his book *The Globalization of Charismatic Christianity.*[12]

Pastor Augustine shouted like a furious man, the veins in his neck bulging, while his enormous hands rested on John's head, making him sway like a reed in the wind. The room where the church held its services was tiny, no more than ten meters square. It was fine for accommodating twenty people sitting neatly in four rows of five seats, but too small for twenty people engaging in fiery prayer. The ten square meters quickly became a casket dense with sounds, smells, and bodily contact. People rose to their feet and moved the chairs away. The pastor shouted, "Come close and pray, come close and pray, open your mouth and pray, pray loud and clear!" Not wanting to be the only person to remain seated alone amid the mess of chairs, I rose with the intention of remaining where I stood, in the background. But I found myself pushed this way and that, crushed against bodies that became warmer and warmer, bodies that smelled of soap and starch, bodies that pressed against me, bodies shouting in a jumble of words and languages. Before my eyes flashed the bright colors of the *ankara* fabrics, hands now tight fists, the faces of John and his wife and his two little girls. The confusion besieged me; I kept glimpsing images from John's story. All these images were steeped in a kind of bubble of sounds, smells, and heat. Surrounded by a fury of praying, I had the impression that the room had become smaller; the chaos of noise baffled me. The people around me were speaking in tongues, in Igbo, and in pidgin English. Men and women were shouting with rage and vehemence. Their eyes were closed but they were moving frenetically, nodding their heads nervously, pointing their fingers in an unspecified direction as if they were having one of the most important conversations of their life with something or someone I could not see.

I lost track of time. After a while it became so hot and airless in the room that I felt I was suffocating. The sound was puzzling, everyone was moving, it was hot, and the room was becoming small, too small. I started to lose my balance. I was suddenly overwhelmed by a tangle of emotions and before I knew it, tears were coursing down my cheeks. I wanted to escape from the tiny room and get away, for a while at least, but I felt unable to do so. I had to stay; I could not just walk out. I did not want to give the people the impression either that I was rejecting what they were doing or that I could not stand so much "power." So I bowed my head, shut my eyes, and tried to stand still, drowning in a sea of indistinct sounds and in the heat of feverish bodies. At that moment, I could not think; I could only dwell in the sensations. I did not want to go further than that, yet I wanted to stop what was happening to me. I was very uncomfortable with the idea of losing control of myself. I thought that maybe I would faint, or start to tremble, or fall to the ground as I had seen others do in the Pentecostal churches I had been observing over the last year. At that moment, what I always thought would be impossible for me to experience slowly became possible. The impossible possibility was slowly walking toward me. I did not want this; I was not prepared for it. I tried to regain full control of my mind and my sensations by concentrating on breathing and counting my breaths until I heard the last "Amen" that, as always, would mark the end of the prayers. When it finally arrived, the voices suddenly became calm again, like a pan of water taken off the boil, and the bodies stopped moving. I felt the air begin to circulate again and found myself still standing, feeling dizzy, between a woman who was drying her perspiring forehead with a handkerchief and a man in an elegant blue suit with his head down, still absorbed in his prayers.

Pastor Augustine asked us all to take a seat. As I took the few steps that separated me from my chair, I tried to seem as normal as possible. Yet I was exhausted. At the end of the meetings, I typically said goodbye to everyone, but this time I hurried away without stopping to chat. I wanted to be alone to gather my thoughts. But when I got home and tried to write about my experience, I realized that the dominant impression in my mind was not of explanations, theoretical reflections, or meanings, but just the memories of the sensations I had felt. I tried to think about what could have brought me to such a state. I could not make any sense of what happened and I could only remember what I felt, perceived, heard, and smelled. There was no story to listen to nor a particular sight I could stare at. There was no space in my mind to find a meaning for what had happened to me. I could only go beyond meaning and remember that intense indefinite moment that Mattijs van de Port calls "the rest of what it is," or the "absurd," for our world view to make sense.[13] But over time, I came to understand that the answer to the questions I was asking myself about that moment formed the very core of this book, namely, aesthetic moments of being that generate a presence, a being here and now through the wholeness of the body, the abundance, as Orsi puts it, the saturation of the senses and the uncomfortable overlapping of sensations.

Wariboko analyzed these moments of "manufacturing the spirit" in Nigerian Pentecostalism by focusing on the emotional energy that fills this "being exposed," coming to existence, or a coming into presence.[14] Following Collins's approach on the ritual chain of interactions and his thesis on the generation of emotional energy, Wariboko argues that emotions are the engine of these manufactured moments.[15] I agree that emotions are certainly crucial components of these moments, as important works in the field of religious emotions have also demonstrated.[16] Yet I argue that what also profoundly shapes certain perceptions of presence is an excess of life that cannot be contained. It is the saturation of sounds, smells, sensations, and sights that generates a sense of overabundance that redefines even human beings' power over their own bodies.

The ensuing week passed quickly, and the following Sunday I went back to Pastor Augustine's church. The Sunday service began as usual—adoration, prayer, sermon, and offerings. John was there, smiling and more than happy to talk about his situation. He said the trial had been postponed because the judge had suddenly fallen ill. As soon as he said these words, the approximately thirty church members rose from their seats and, with their hands raised shouted, "Praise the Lord! *Alleluya*! *Na God oooo*! *God dey ooo*!" They were delighted that their prayers had worked somehow. The joy experienced by the congregation was like an eruption, and to my surprise, I suddenly found myself standing, clapping my hands, and smiling along with all the others. The trial had only been postponed, but for John and this congregation it was enough: It confirmed the power and efficacy of their prayers and the mercy of God. Strong in these convictions, Pastor Augustine prayed again for John, asking that all the evil forces that had arranged for John's imprisonment fail miserably.

It was just at this moment of fervor that the Catholic parish priest burst through the door and, his face dark and his eyes wild, said, "You can't carry on like this! You are driving us crazy with your shouting and noise!" Pastor Augustine quietly apologized, but when the priest left he exclaimed, "These Catholics really don't know how to pray!"

Prayers in the Contact Zone

At the Tempio della Pace, Pentecostals' embodied religious practices become signifiers of their diasporic experience in Italy—of their sorrows, memories, and homesickness, their anger and hope, but also of their claims for dignity and an equal share in the mediation of real presences. Through their bodies they do more than just tell their stories. As the anthropologist Michael Jackson argued, the body is not secondary to verbal praxis: "The body precedes and, to a great extent, always remains beyond speech."[17] Their movements do not illustrate or represent their story. They *are* their story, together with the objects they bring to church. They are, as Bourdieu would put it, "a political mythology realized, embodied, turned into a permanent disposition, a durable manner of standing, speaking and thereby of feeling and thinking."[18]

While conducting my research in Nigeria and Ghana, I saw these same impassioned gestures and prayers many times. In Italy at the Tempio della Pace I saw them presented in just the same way. Nothing appeared to have changed en route from Nigeria and Ghana to Italy. Yet Pentecostals in Italy experience the weight of an imposed racialization of their bodies. Pastor Augustine in our interview told me: "When I was in Nigeria I never thought about myself as a black person. But here I am aware of my black skin every day."

Within a Catholic space Pentecostals narrate stories about their roots, their displacement, their encounter with Italian society, their struggle, and their weapons. They also talk about their alienation and fear, and their anger against the social oppression they experience as African, black, working-class, Pentecostal migrants. Their raised arms speak of their freedom and their will to give themselves to the power of the divine. Their fists talk about their willingness to battle for their dignity; their tears are their pain; their sweat is their tenacity and resilience; and the overwhelming soundscape of individual and collective praying, crying, and speaking in tongues that fills the little room is a river of sensations that washes away Ruth's and John's fears.

As Ruth's and John's stories show, it is in the half-hidden spaces lent by a Catholic parish, alongside a handsome church containing a magnificent altar with statues of Christ on the cross and the Madonna adorned with flowers and candles, where Pentecostals speak of their social and spiritual world and their experience in Italian society.

At the Tempio della Pace, Pentecostals manifest their own manner of praying, healing, anointing, and delivering from evil; of understanding and making sense of divine presence and power, of its forms and possibilities. This way of praying and relating to the divine and the supernatural appears to be quite different from the way the priest of the parish loves to engage his parishioners in the Sunday Mass or in other moments of prayer. The priestly style, as I described in the introduction, emphasizes silence and meditation, and physical stillness.[19] While he and his parishioners dwell in the most absorbed, quiet atmosphere, a few meters away in the various rooms of the parish hall, Pentecostals engage in vibrant, loud, and at times desperately overwhelming prayer.

The scenario seems to capture two apparently irreconcilable diversities. Yet I suggest this apparent diversity hides the profound and shared visceral allure of real presence for both Catholics and Pentecostals.

Pentecostals have their own way of perceiving the real presence of the Holy Spirit and of accessing divine power as well as chasing away and defeating the real presence of evil forces that possess human bodies or, as I will discuss in Chapter 6, that hide in images, statues, and relics. In a still sensuous but different way from the Catholics,

Pentecostals' prayers invoke and access the real presence and power of the divine when they turn their bodies into multisensorial devices that perceive the touch of the divine through the pastor's hand and through the olive oil, or through the vibrant sound of glossolalia, music, and powerful words.[20]

Don Elia's prayer style is certainly different from that of Pentecostals, but like the Pentecostals he too leads his parishioners to engage the body and the senses. His sensual engagement with the divine has its own hierarchies and intensity of the senses. It invokes divine presence through the sweet taste of the host, the "sound" of silence and stillness, the sight of holy images and crucifixes permeated by the typical scent of Italian Catholic churches interiors—a mix of incense, candlewax, flowers, and old wood.

Catholics and Pentecostals each have their own aesthetic regime that determines how, when, and where bodies, sensations, and objects can access the divine and the supernatural. They both acknowledge the immanence of God and the Holy Spirit as well as the tangibility and real presence of evil forces that can possess human bodies. However, they disagree about the way in which this occurs, along with the time, space, and authority through which the supernatural, be it divine power or evil forces, becomes tangible, visible, and accessible.

At times, at the Tempio della Pace, Pentecostals' prayers are perceived to be excessive: too much sound, shouting, and sweating. The clash between Pentecostals and Catholics appears to be essentially somatic and concern the very use of the body and the senses. It is an aesthetic clash indeed. As for the mediation of divine real presence, conflicts arise also for the mediation of evil real presence. During one of our interviews, Don Elia told me,

> I am always amazed when I see [Pentecostals] throw themselves down and roll around on the floor. They shout a lot, do a lot of exorcism, and things like that. They see evil everywhere! I even consulted a Catholic priest who practices exorcism to try to [better] understand the question of devil possession. Of course, evil exists and we must combat evil, but it is not by dint of shouting and rolling around on the floor that we can defeat the devil. Here we need to understand how African Pentecostals see the battle between good and evil, otherwise we are like married couples who are separated but continue to live under the same roof. We might even live quite well like such couples, but we are still separated nonetheless!

Intriguingly, despite the fact that Don Elia identified the question of evil and good as a crucial matter that defines the boundaries between "us" and "them," deliverance or exorcism is also a complicated question within the Catholic Church, a church that has always been extremely cautious about evil manifestations, demon possession, as well as about practices and rituals of exorcism. The case of Milingo that I introduced in the previous chapter is an example of the tensions that often arise even within Catholicism about the authority over and legitimacy to control evil presences. Certainly the Catholic Church acknowledges the power of evil and has consolidated practices of exorcism and healing.[21]

As I observed in my fieldwork and as Don Elia also noted, Catholics and Pentecostals do not disagree about the existence of evil or about whether evil can possess human bodies. The conflict is about the authority, legitimacy, and power to operate against Satan. In other words, the conflict is again over the control and power over the—this time evil—real presence. At the Tempio della Pace, for instance, the priest is not denying the presence of evil. A number of things make him extremely uncomfortable about Pentecostals' practices of deliverance. According to him Pentecostals are not well trained in theology and consequently do not have the legitimacy to operate against Satan. He said, "I am trying to understand, but for the moment I probably lack the means. I find it very difficult. I have asked the pastors about their studies and who sent them. But I can see that it is something more personal, something that comes from inside [that motivates them]." Then he added, "Priests like me have a solid training that doesn't make us heroes, but it does make us competent. Here in Padua, for example, we have schools of theology dating back to 300 AD, and a powerful organization of the parishes all over the territory. I don't think they have all this in Africa, or in other countries either. Wielding the Bible isn't enough."

On top on the pastors' poor training, to the Catholic priest, Don Elia, the other disturbing issue is that Pentecostals are materializing and chasing evil forces in his parish hall and during the weekends and sometimes on Sunday mornings when he is celebrating the Mass. For Don Elia, the Pentecostals' intensely physical, bodily experiences under the effect of either the Holy Spirit or of some evil force that struggles to avoid being driven out of their bodies, is excessive and inappropriate. In other words, according to him, this is not how Satan works. Don Elia admits that evil and the devil exist, but not in the way the Pentecostals mean nor in the way they try to defeat them. In our interview he added: "Exorcism is a prayer that the community makes for people who are possessed by evil forces, but Pentecostals see evil everywhere!"

Many Catholic priests who host these Pentecostal churches on their premises feel caught between the Catholic tradition of offering charity and hospitality and a certain discomfort over the irruption of such embodied practices that invoke a disturbingly real presence. The stories of other pastors are examples worth mentioning in order to better illuminate this scenario. In an interview, Reverend Michael, the pastor who founded the Zoe Pentecostal Mission in Italy, talked about the parish priest who had granted them the use of a chapel but became concerned when he actually saw them praying there. Rev. Michael had begun his pastoral activities when he first arrived in Southern Italy as an economic migrant. He had approached the local priest and asked for a place to pray. The priest kindly granted him the use of a little chapel in the parish church without knowing how it would be used. Reverend Michael said, "He let us use the chapel in the church, but one day he arrived while we were worshipping. He saw us falling down and rolling on the floor. When we finished worshipping that day he told me, 'I see now what you do. You can't gather to pray in the chapel. I will give you another place instead.' I remember he was red in the face. From that day on, he let us use one of the parish halls outside the church. He was not comfortable with us."

Pastor Adebamdo of the Mountain of Fire and Miracles Ministries (henceforth MFM) had a similar experience, although with a different outcome, when he set up the first MFM church in a room in a Catholic parish in Rome. The pastor said, "I started the first Mountain of Fire and Miracles branch in Rome. A Catholic church gave us the space. At the beginning, the priest was nice to us. We used the room he gave us for a while. Then one day the priest came while we were holding one of our deliverance services. We were praying as we usually do. I was praying for two of my members, stretching my hands over their heads. The priest saw them shout and tremble and fall down. When we had finished, I went to say hello to him and shake his hand as I usually did, but he did not want me to touch him. He said: 'Don't touch me, don't touch me! What are you doing here? You do exorcism! You can't do this here: you must leave this place!' And so we had to find somewhere else. He gave us only a week to leave the place."

From Don Elia's words and the accounts of the pastors it is clear that onlookers have not underestimated the power of African bodies collapsing on the floor and trembling in the grips of the Spirit. Quite the contrary: Onlookers perceive the Africans' power to be real; otherwise, why be scared of touching them? Why relegate them to out-of-the-way spaces?

While talking about evil, another religious entity popped up in the conversation at the Tempio della Pace. Paradoxically, although Don Elia negatively associates certain Pentecostal practices with traditional African religions, the Pentecostal pastors note how certain Catholic devotional practices resemble the veneration of idols of those traditional religions. During an interview with Pastor Clement, a pastor who celebrates the services of his new church at the Tempio della Pace, I was told:

> Italians must repent! They are idol worshippers! Catholics worship idols. They worship images and statues molded in various forms. Sometimes you see them worshipping Mary. This is dangerous! God doesn't like it. We should not worship anything molded. We should not allow anything to distract us from God. I do tell Catholics that what they do is not biblical. The Bible says: "You shall have no other gods before God. You shall not make for yourself a carved image, or any likeness of anything that is in heaven above. You shall not bow down to them or serve them, for I, the Lord your God, am a jealous God!"

The reciprocal suspicions and accusations of idolatry show that along with Catholics and Pentecostals, other religious "entities" also dwell in this contact zone. The specter of African traditional religions haunts the Western imagination and African Pentecostals' daily life. In the Western imagination African traditional religions are relegated to peripheral spaces of the religious imaginary. These are confined spaces, the realm of the "primitive," just as some deemed the practices of popular Catholicism to be, but in this case a primitive realm deemed inferior, associated with magic and voodoo from Africa and, as Fanon also described, with blackness. Such a world is located on the periphery of the Western imaginary. It is inhabited by the savage, the "exotic," and is associated with grotesque imagined rituals of blood and sacrifices, such as have long been portrayed in film, popular culture, and the news media. Here, Fanon's words are particularly apropos:

> I was all at once responsible for my body, for my race, for my ancestors. I ran an objective gaze over myself, discovering my blackness, my ethnic

characteristics; and then I was deafened by cannibalism, intellectual de-
ficiency, fetishism, racial defects, slave-ships.[22]

It is significant that Don Elia construed as suspicious what he considers to be the excessive use of the body and emotions, something
ancestral that resonates with a primitive world. He said, "They mix
Christianity with their traditional religions. They see evil and the devil
everywhere, and I think that they suffer a lot of this but they are afraid
of talking about it. One of them once told me, 'There are those amongst
us who practice voodoo,' but I saw that his companions promptly made
him drop the subject. Why don't they want to talk about these things in
front of me? I certainly don't know. But there must be a reason, don't
you think?"

The suspicions raised by the idea that Pentecostals mix Christianity with traditional religions, something that Don Elia seems to look at
with a certain measure of disapproval, goes along with questioning the
authority of the pastors. When I interviewed Don Elia, he told me that
his mind was buzzing with questions that he had several times asked
the pastors to answer. Don Elia is very curious. He pays attention to
what goes on in these churches, asks for explanations, and exchanges
views with the pastors. He is a man with an ingrained sense of tradition,
strong in his convictions, experienced and well versed in the history and
rigorous teaching of Catholic doctrine. He received a strict education
at seminary and then continued to study, graduating in social sciences
with a dissertation on Italians abroad. He certainly would have liked to
know more about the Pentecostal churches that he "inherited" from his
predecessor, Don Angelo, when the latter retired. In fact, Don Elia was
faced with a reality completely unfamiliar to him when he first arrived
at the Tempio della Pace. He told me, "I knew about these great American evangelical preachers, of course. I was aware of the phenomenon,
but here . . . Well, I don't know. I lack the means to understand."

One of his concerns was the pastors' formal training and theological
knowledge—or rather, what he perceives as the lack of it. To his mind, a
certain kind of training is an essential condition for someone to be able
to stand in the pulpit and claim to be a minister of God.

In this parish hall, Pentecostals are disturbing Catholics' aesthetics,
a mix of conventions, different approaches to the sensuous and to the
possibilities and power of bodies and objects, as well as consolidated

rules of mediating and accessing the supernatural. African Pentecostals are also suspending the role that the ethnoreligious politics of the Italian Nation State has by implication assigned to them.

Women in the Contact Zone

Particularly provocative of the Italian ethnoracial order and Catholic aesthetic order is the presence of female pastors. Nigerian women migrants in Italy outnumber men, and although they represent a significant workforce, they are overwhelmingly concentrated in service occupations, primarily street vending and domestic service. Many Nigerian women migrants are single mothers with children to support. Many cannot count on their husbands, lovers, or the fathers of their children to provide income or domestic support. Their nuclear families are greatly challenged by the migrant conditions of unemployment and underemployment, and the lack of adequate housing and family support. They also experience particularly acute class, gender, and racial discrimination.

But in Italy, where women do not have access to religious power and authority, these female pastors are remarkable sights. Female pastors in Italy receive a great deal of visibility and exercise a certain degree of power and authority within their religious communities. Particularly emblematic is the experience of the Ghanaian Bishop Diana. She claims to be the first female African ordained as a bishop in Europe. In her public speeches, she always expresses the will to reach out to men to accept the calling of God on women and treat them as such since "in Christ there is no male and female." She also expresses the hope that the ordination of a female bishop will encourage other women to take the right path and bring honor to African women. After her ordination, she started ordaining women, and greatly increased the number of women pastors in Italy.

In our interview she said, "I remember the first time I put on my white collar, I was traveling with my husband. At the airport all the police officers came around and asked me: 'Is this your husband?' I said 'Yes!' 'Are you a priest?' he asked me. And I said 'Yes!' And then he added, 'And why are you married?' They were totally confused. They had never seen a female priest in the first place, but a black priest to boot! It is two problems in one!"

I witnessed for myself how Italians reacted to the sight of Bishop Diana in her religious regalia. One Sunday morning we walked together from her place to the car park to go to her church located in the industrial zone of the city of Brescia in the northeast of Italy. We passed by a café where people were sitting outside enjoying their Sunday morning coffee and croissant, and I noticed that people were unable to stop staring at her. To a certain extent, I could not blame them. Bishop Diana was dressed like a Catholic cardinal, wearing a black robe with a red cincture, and high-heeled red stiletto shoes. Adorned in her regalia, with a proud bearing, she walked down the street, her black-and-red robe fluttering in the light morning breeze. Even to me, at times she looked like an otherworldly apparition: a black female Catholic cardinal walking down an Italian street.[23]

The story of Pastor Patience is also worth narrating. She arrived from Nigeria as an economic migrant. She works as a domestic maid and also leads a small charismatic church called Captain Jesus Power Ministries. According to Pastor Patience, she received the call of God when she was in Italy. She usually wears her pastoral vestments, especially when she visits her church members. But the first time she wore her vestments she faced some unexpected reactions from the local people and the authorities.

> My first two years in the ministry here were very, very tough. The first time I wore the pastoral clerical uniform, I was traveling to Rome. I sat in a coach compartment of the train and people ran away from that coach. Some were crossing themselves because they had never seen something like that before. One woman, who was obviously bored, asked me if I was a pastor. When I said yes she was very surprised. I told her I was a Pentecostal pastor and she said: "In Italy?" because she couldn't believe it! When I told her she said: "God forbid!" I said that I wasn't a Catholic but a Pentecostal, and I told her it was normal. When I arrived in the hall of the train station at Rome, a policeman asked me to follow him into the police station. He invited other policemen to come and see how I was dressed with the pastoral uniform. And this is just because I was wearing it. They asked me so many questions, and after about two and a half hours they let me go. I know they thought I was crazy.

Women pastors work intensely on campaigns to promote religious leadership by women. They use conventions, workshops, gospel concerts, and write articles in a Pentecostal bimonthly magazine entitled

The All Christian Magazine. The stories of women pastors and their increasing ordinations are documented with pictures, testimonies, life stories, and travelogues between Italy and the United Kingdom, the United States, and West Africa. Nigerian and Ghanaian women pastors present themselves in all their splendor on the magazine's cover. Captions such as "Bishop Diana—the woman with the kingdom heart," "Bishop Diana, her 10 years as a Gospel artist celebrated with her new album 'God is able,'" "Pastor Ehighe, the woman with good understanding"—adorn the glossy magazine's pages. Dressed in traditional ceremonial clothes, photos show them praying, singing, healing, and preaching.

One of the most remarkable features of these female Pentecostal pastors is their dissenting role within a Catholic aesthetic order, where there is no place and no opportunity for women to become priests. Some of the narratives I collected are emblematic of the surprise they arouse when they walk down the street or take public transportation. In the Tempio della Pace, the presence of women pastors is particularly intriguing. They are religious leaders, healers, and exorcists. They baptize, ordain other pastors, celebrate marriage, and anoint people in a Catholic space. However, Pastor Stella's dream is to have her own church. She is looking for a space to rent where she can freely conduct deliverance sessions and Sunday services. She told me she is limited in her pastoral activities because the Catholic priest does not permit her to use the space freely. For instance, she would like to have night vigils, but the priest does not let the Pentecostal churches use the space at night. She told me, "I am sure I will find my own place, but for now I celebrate my Sunday service here. My church is growing, and little by little we will have enough money to leave. But for now, I stay. I do not leave."

Like Pastor Stella, other pastors also complain about their limited access to the space. They protest that they have to empty the room assigned to them at the end of every service and dismantle their improvised altar, the band instruments, and the decorations. They also object to the restrictions imposed on the volume of the music and the liveliness of the service. But despite these uncomfortable conditions, there is a long list of pastors waiting to be assigned a room to start a new church.

The Catholic priest tried to engage Pastor Stella in order to understand more about her and her services. He told me, "I do not have problem with her, but I think that women pastors should be trained, go to theological schools, and have a solid preparation. I am wondering what kind of training she has. I tried to ask, but her answers are vague."

Pastor Stella did not attend formal theological school, nor was she trained by her church's pastors, but she acted in response to the needs of her community and her God-given skills and powers, she said. She is inhabiting and using the Catholic spaces to develop her emancipatory desires and her embodied critique of the Catholic and Pentecostal power structures and her subjectivity. In Nigeria and Ghana, for instance, female religious leaders are part of the ongoing process of continual transformation and redefinition of their societies and religious spaces.[24] Previous research also highlights the ambivalent attitudes of Pentecostal Africans toward women. In Italy, they are a novelty in the context of the Italian Catholic patriarchy where women are not allowed to be priests. In Italy, these women pastors continue to challenge the role they are ascribed as domestic workers, street sellers, sex workers, and muted black migrants.

Objects and Substances in the Contact Zone

At the Tempio della Pace in Padua, Pentecostals' practices also involve objects and substances, such as the olive oil that Pastor Stella used to anoint Ruth. In such contact zones, these material forms pass through the gaps of theology, and cultural and community boundaries, channeling the flow of power between individuals, communities, and supernatural presences. In these spaces, objects not only mediate divine power but also question hierarchies and the legitimacy to mediate divine presence and power. They channel transitions of power from the divine to individuals and communities, and also, as in this case, from individual to individual and from communities to communities. The olive oil is an example of this. Pastor Stella used oil to anoint Ruth and protect her against evil forces. Her hand dripping with oil, Stella touched Ruth's forehead and prayed for her physical and spiritual safety. Pastors use anointed olive oil to heal and deliver people from evil spirits, to seal the ordination of pastors, to bless and protect places and people, and to help them attain breakthroughs in life. The oil is anointed by the pastors by means of a series of prayers and gestures, as well as through contact with a sacred place or an anointed person, such as a pastor, a prophet, or a healer, as Bruno Reinhardt extensively discussed in his work.[25] These prodigious men and women have "the unction to function," as Asamo-ah-Gyadu put it.[26] As both scholars argued, the term *anointing* in African Pentecostalism is also closely related to the idea of personal charisma. The anointed pastor is a person to whom people attribute extraordinary gifts, made visible by their personal success, the success of their church, or the miracles they are able to perform.

I was able to see a case of this on one particular occasion. There was a special three-day convention organized by a network of African Pentecostal pastors in Italy. The convention was held in the auditorium of a parish run by the Salesians of Don Bosco. One of the special guests at the convention was Pastor Ayo Oritsejafor, president of the Nigerian Christian Association. His participation attracted many Nigerians eager to meet the popular pastor and tap into his anointing. That night Oritse-jafor delivered his speech to the people in the audience and ended with his special anointing. There were no Italians attending the prayer service that night, although at one point a nun made an appearance and stood for a while at the entrance to the auditorium, staring wide-eyed at the anointing ceremony.

The pastors and the Nigerians who came to attend the event were visibly moved by the man's presence. The stage was carefully prepared by other pastors who continued all through the night to say prayers of thanksgiving to God for Oritsejafor's visit to Italy. When he eventu-ally appeared on stage, in his shining, elegant green Nigerian traditional dress, many people in the theater burst into tears. Some fell to their knees, and others waved their hands toward the stage as a sign of grati-tude. The other pastors gazed at him with reverence and admiration, welcoming him with bowing and applause as he walked regally to the center of the stage. For the sixty-five minutes he spent on stage, Pas-tor Oritsejafor was every bit as captivating as the liveliest showman. He made the audience laugh, cry, sing, pray, shout, jump, fall, and tremble in a vortex of emotions. At the end, he solemnly announced the mo-ment of anointing:

> I tell you, I feel the spirit of God in this house. When I finish preaching tonight I will anoint you with special oil. Do you see this thing I am wearing around my neck? It has oil inside. I am going to ask the pastors here to bring one or two containers of oil. I will take a little bit of my own oil and I will put it in the containers. I will pray over the oil. Then you will come and touch the oil and put the oil on yourselves. A man can't

give what he doesn't have. I have never celebrated anything in my life, but this year I will see the celebration of forty years of my ministry. My people are trying to give me a good celebration. In these forty years, I have seen God many times. I have seen God in my life. Can you imagine? God found me on the street and today I am the leader of nineteen million people![27]

Pastor Oritsejafor used the oil that was presumably contained in the big, gold cross that hung from his necklace as a sacramental substance charged with his personal charisma and power. He said the same power that had changed his life was now dwelling in him and in the oil that had been in contact with his body. That power could be moved and transferred to other substances (olive oil, in this case), and simply touching it could have an impact on the life of the people who came to listen to him, he alleged. The olive oil was considered to be the material expression of the charisma and power that people attributed to Pastor Oritsejafor. In this sense, the oil acquired sacramental power.

Olive oil is mentioned in the Bible as many as thirty-three times. It is described as a precious substance, a sign of wealth, a pure substance for use in anointing, and it is often associated with bread, wine, milk, incense, and gold. Pentecostals and Catholics both use olive oil. It takes pride of place in important Catholic religious functions and it has always been used to celebrate certain sacraments, such as baptism and confirmation, anointing the sick, and consecration to holy orders. The Oil of Catechumens is used for baptisms, for anointing a child's forehead with the sign of the cross as visible evidence that he or she belongs to Christ. The Holy Chrism, a blend of olive oil and a fragrant balm, is used at confirmation ceremonies: Here again the priest anoints the person's forehead with the sign of the cross. Anointing of the sick is done with Oil of the Infirm, considered to be a sign of grace and strength; the oil is applied to the forehead and hands of the sick by making the sign of the cross. When a priest is ordained, a bishop applies the Oil of Catechumens to the hands of the future priest, who will then use his hands to give blessings. When a bishop is consecrated, the Holy Chrism is used instead. All these different oils are blessed during a Mass of the Chrism celebrated on the morning of Holy Thursday, the day when—according to the Bible—Jesus Christ ordered the apostles to take holy orders.

Alongside these oils, there are also other "unofficial" oils, such as those that allegedly ooze from statues of the Madonna that have attracted thousands of pilgrims in recent years. At the places where this happens (some of them acknowledged by the Catholic Church, others rejected, and others under observation), the faithful can obtain tiny samples of oil, usually preserved in little ampoules. These oils are attributed a healing and protective power that the Catholic Church only acknowledges in some cases. However, whether the Catholic Church authorizes it or not, people fully engage their moments of freedom and flock to these places to experience their aesthetic encounter with the miraculous statues and their oils.

Pentecostals at the Tempio della Pace make ample use of oil in their prayers, but this meets with the disapproval of Don Elia. When I interviewed him, he said, "I see that they waste so much olive oil! And this is their way to do exorcism. I told them that they can't do it in my parish."[28]

Oil has a place in both Catholic and Pentecostal aesthetics. For both of them, it channels the flow of power between people and the supernatural being. But in the contact zone at the Tempio della Pace, it is also a focus and locus of dissent through which Pentecostals redistribute the power and authority to mediate the divine presence. For Catholics and Pentecostals alike, olive oil is a crucial medium for the sacramentalization of holy power. As I briefly explained above, in Catholicism oil mediates healings and blessings as well as the comforting and authoritative power of the Holy Spirit. The only religious authorities who can sacramentalize the oil are the bishops, whereas the priests are authorized to make use of the holy oils.

The Pentecostals' use of olive oil to bless, protect, heal, and to ordain pastors is founded on the sacramental principle through which this substance can be filled with divine, healing, and blessing power. The pastor has the power and authority to anoint the oil, and the more anointed the pastor, the more powerful the oil. Contrary to what happens in Catholicism, the anointing of the pastor is a spiritual gift, not a power and authority given by the position held in the hierarchical ecclesiastic order.

Despite Don Elia's requests that they stop using the oil in his parish, the Pentecostals continue to hold their services and prayer meetings using the precious Italian olive oil. When I visited Pentecostal churches in Nigeria and Ghana, Italian olive oil was one of the most expensive items the church purchased. Imported Italian olive oil was considered to be a "spiritual luxury." But in Italy, that same oil is available at a moderate price in every supermarket, so what reason is there to be stingy with it during the prayer meetings? To Pentecostals, abundance of oil will attract abundance of grace, despite Don Elia's concern about the waste.

From Relegation to Emancipation

The Tempio della Pace is just one of many parishes in which Pentecostal African churches celebrate their services on Sundays. Its peculiarity lies in that there are as many as nine Pentecostal churches that all meet in the same building, but in nine separate rooms. From the time when the former parish priest, Don Angelo, first hosted these churches up to Don Elia's time today, at least thirty different churches have found hospitality in this parish. It has served as a sort of incubator, a convenient place where these churches have been able to consolidate and grow their congregation and their financial resources, and then leave for a better location, somewhere where they would be freer to do as they pleased in a space of their own.

The Tempio della Pace is an emblematic contact zone were Catholic and Pentecostal aesthetics of presence meet and clash. In my fieldwork I observed them clashing over religious practices, prayer styles, engagement with the bodies and the senses, and the use of sacramental objects and substances. They clashed over the embodied practices, gestures, intensity of sounds, time, space, and authority involved in the mediation of divine presence, as well as over deliverance or exorcism.

Interestingly, they do not clash over the very possibility of generating real presence.

Yet with their aesthetics of presence, the Pentecostals burst in on the Catholic aesthetic order, introducing their own sounds of prayer, their gestures, their own sacramental objects, and their own spiritual and charismatic power and authority. They behave like guests who move the furniture around and turn lights on and off without asking for their host's permission.

At the Tempio della Pace, the Pentecostals are well aware of being temporary guests in a space dominated by Catholicism. Yet they would hardly tell Don Elia that they see Catholicism as being close to idolatry, or remind him that despite the Catholic Church's authoritative presence, his Sunday services are scantily attended. During our interviews, many pastors made such comments to me, but none of those celebrating their services at the Tempio della Pace has ever pointed out to Don Elia that it is mainly people over fifty years old who attend his parish and others like it, but it is the Pentecostal churches that meet in the Catholics' buildings that make the space come alive.

Pentecostal churches occupy rooms borrowed or rented in Catholic parishes for as long as they can, and they see these limited spaces as an opportunity to become established and expand. Inside the Catholic building, they consolidate their membership and gather sufficient economic resources to move elsewhere. They occupy and manipulate the space, turning this parish hall into a vibrant praying ground in which to experience, in their own aesthetic styles, the supernatural presence and power. The African Pentecostals who celebrate their Sunday services and meet to pray at the Tempio della Pace emerge from the backseat position to which they are relegated as black African economic migrants and religious leaders with no power or authority and instead become legitimate storytellers and translators of embodied stories. They become actors and spectators of intense aesthetic moments, mediators of supernatural and divine powers, as well as skillful deliverance pastors. In a word, they move from relegation to emancipation. In contact zones like the Tempio della Pace, the Pentecostals and the material world they bring with them undergo a resignification from being prickly guests occupying the lowest step in the social hierarchy, obliged to accept peripheral and embarrassing jobs, kept at arm's length on buses, exposed to harassment and racism, and instead, to paraphrase the words of Jean Comaroff, become bodies of power.[29] It is especially in such contact zones that one can see how these communities, although protesting against the overwhelming Roman Catholicism, like the laborers' dissenting gestures and tactics of Rancière and de Certeau, tactically appropriate its resources. The irruption of African women pastors and bishops dressed like Catholic priests or cardinals in the Italian religious field, the use of olive oil as a sacramental substance, the breaking in of the sounds of speaking in tongues, stomping the floor, or singing in Catholic spaces and liturgy are, I suggest, moments or events of spiritual and political subjectivation that take place in a very intriguing way. They happen from within the very aesthetic order that marginalizes them. These acts of political and spiritual subjectivation do not deliberately or consciously intend to overthrow Catholic priestly authority. Neither are they mere acts of disobedience or provocation. They are political events, such as the rare and exceptional situations of coming into being, as Alain Badiou argues in his work on political subjects.[30] To Badiou, an event happens when the excluded and marginalized subjects suddenly appear in the social scenario and with their doing and being break the dominant social order. The event opens a space to rethink reality from the standpoint of the excluded. Those events suspend the social order that determines the relations of power between people, groups, and as this book intends to disclose, also between people and things. In the contact zone at the Tempio della Pace, the irruption of Pentecostal religious aesthetics redefines the order and aesthetics of presence of this Catholic-dominated space.

The Tempio della Pace can be seen as an emblematic example of a contact zone in which two aesthetic communities meet and clash over the very rules, practices, and authority to administer and control the corporalization of the sacred, as Orsi puts it, or to mediate the presence and power of the divine flowing, as this chapter disclosed, in the olive oil or in handkerchiefs.

Their actions are not subversive but they are terribly disturbing. Their aesthetics are moments of dissent, temporary suspension of hierarchies, rules, and conventions through which Pentecostals step out of the straitjacket imposed on them by the dominant ethnoreligious order and don new clothes, here and there borrowing from the "closet" of the Catholics too. The divine presence and power they invoke becomes a constitutive force of temporary egalitarian moments that paradoxically illuminate both the separateness and the communion of Pentecostals and Catholics. The friction caused by their aesthetics illuminates ambiguities and contradictions that inhabit the relationship between Catholics and Pentecostals. If Pentecostal pastors have no authority and power to mediate the sacred power with oil, then why is their oil a problem? Why are their rolling and trembling bodies so disturbingly intimidating?

I argue that the issue lies not in the acknowledgment of the possibility of materializing the presence of divine power through bodies, objects, and substances, but in the question of the authority to mediate this power. Who has the authority to turn the oil into a sacramental substance? Who has the power to deliver a possessed body from evil spirits? Who defines the rule?

Ambiguities and contradictions arise when the two aesthetic communities and their way of doing and dwelling in the presence of supernatural powers come into contact. By doing so, the Tempio della Pace becomes a place of religious short circuits. At the Tempio della Pace,

Pentecostals and Catholics are like two wires that convey a current and inadvertently come into contact with each other: Sparks appear in the form of conflicts and smoke arises in the form of ambiguities. In some parishes, priests take the more radical step of tripping the circuit breaker, as it were: They ask the Pentecostal churches to leave, or they move them to a more remote, out-of-the-way location where the two religious communities' worlds do not have to come into contact.

Interestingly, when these two religious wires come into contact, others religious entities suddenly appear on the scene, in this case African traditional religions. The priest said that Pentecostals mix Christianity with African traditional religions, and Pentecostal pastors said that Catholics are idol worshippers like their forefathers. Paradoxically, they see in each other something that is intrinsic to their own history and religious worlds and that apparently they refuse to acknowledge. Catholicism is indeed the fruit of multiple encounters of diverse expressions of paganism and Christianity. As I will discuss in Chapter 3, in the Catholic churches one can observe the signs of these diverse religious encounters that shaped contemporary Catholicism and that appear in the stunning works of art depicting the deities of the Roman idols along with Christian figures and symbols. So why look with suspicion on the supposed signs of African traditional religions in Pentecostal aesthetics? Moreover, if Pentecostals also use sacramental substances and images, as I will discuss in chapter four, why do they continue to condemn Catholic paraphernalia and Catholics' use of images and statues? The truth of the matter is that Pentecostals paradoxically reject objects and substances, but the more they reject matter, the more matter becomes constitutive of their subjectivities and immanence.[31]

The Tempio della Pace is a cradle of ambiguities, contradictions, and short circuits. Yet, like other Catholic churches in Italy, it is one of the safe incubators of African Pentecostalism in Italy. From being the ones who have no place, in the Tempio della Pace Pentecostals tactically benefit from the empty spaces once populated by Catholic parishioners and local Catholic associations. In these empty spaces, the fruit of the unchurching of Italian Catholicism, the African Pentecostal churches have cleverly found ways of operating. They have used their creativity to push the boundaries and disturb the aesthetic order set by the Catholic Church. They find life-giving space in the very structures of power that limit their religious authority and power.

3

Holy Bones

Desire and Disgust of Real Presence

*And it came to pass, as they were burying a man, that, behold,
they spied a band of men;
and they cast the man into the sepulcher of Elisha:
and when the man was let down, and touched the bones of Elisha,
he revived, and stood up on his feet.*

—2 Kings 13:21, KJV

THERE ARE FEW religious objects able to arouse the mix of devotion, desire, and disgust that relics do. Across the globe from ancient times to the twenty-first century, relics have been the focus of veneration, inquisitiveness, and dispute and have elicited religious emotions, intellectual curiosity, and historical interest. Because of their fluid and ambiguous nature, relics elude easy definition, which makes it problematic to establish precisely their distinctive nature.

Different societies invest relics with diverse functions, meanings, and powers according to their religious habitus and semiotic processes as well as their collective preoccupations and hopes.[1] Exhaustive scholarly debate on the nature of relics and comparative analysis of these material forms in various religious traditions is beyond the scope of this chapter, in which I examine more narrowly how Catholics and Pentecostals perceive the real presence of divine and supernatural power in relics within their own religious aesthetics.

Despite this fluidity of meaning, here I focus on some of the properties of relics in the Roman Catholic tradition according to which they are either the mortal remains of honorable individuals, saints, and venerated martyrs; the clothing or other objects that belonged to them; or the instruments of their martyrdom, all things whose contact with the individuals when they were alive or dead makes them precious to believers.[2]

Carolyn Walker Bynum suggests that the power of the relics was associated in medieval Europe with their capacity to survive the normal course of nature and to translate the anxiety about decomposition and fragmentation of the human body into the sublime victory of the resurrection of the body in its entirety.[3] This holy matter, as Bynum writes, in displaying its eternal life and its power over evil, death, and putrefaction, aroused devout and deeply felt religious emotions.[4] Intrinsic to the veneration of relics is the doctrine of concomitance, according to which each fragment of the body of a saint carries the fullness of the power of the saint's whole body. This understanding, Bynum argues, is a "habit of mind" that has remained unchanged, even where it seemed incoherent, ambiguous, or even aesthetically offensive.[5]

The sacramental logic implicit in the cult of relics renders this peculiar matter not merely a representation or a symbol but an actual, real presence—a power made tangible, visible, and real. This power needs neither a ritual nor contact with other material forms to be mediated. It is inherent in the relics. Believers access this power by seeing or touching the relics or their precious reliquaries.[6] Touching and venerating the relics is an act of intense devotion through which believers access and experience the power of the saints or the martyrs.

Yet although this power inheres in each fragment of a relic, not all relics have the same value and status. Different relics of the body of the same person can have greater or lesser worth. According to the Roman Catholic Codex Juris Canonici, the most precious bodily relics are termed *insigni*, defined as the entire body or the head, an arm, a forearm, the tongue, a hand, a leg, or the part of the martyr's body that was tortured. Over the years, the huge demand for relics prompted a widening of what is understood to be a relic. Now relics *ex contactu* (typically, pieces of cloth that have been in contact with the venerated tombs or steeped in the oils that burned in their sanctuaries) in addition to the body parts themselves are included in the term—largely in order to satisfy the demand for relics. And the demand continues to be remarkable. Even today, the vicariate in Rome supplies hundreds of relics to churches all over the world for public veneration.

The presence of relics in Rome has always had an enormous power of attraction. Ever since the Reformation, every year thousands of pilgrims have flocked to Rome to come into contact with the power of the city's relics, most often to earn indulgence, such as forgiveness for their sins.

In his book *The Renaissance in Rome*, Charles Stinger writes:

> The impulse that drew . . . thousands of humbler people to Rome stemmed, as it had for centuries, from the desire for immediacy of contact with the more than earthly heroism of the Apostles and martyrs. Here pilgrims could behold directly the places where the saints had remained steadfast in their faith in the face of such spectacular tortures. Here, too, they could gaze upon scenes where so many miraculous signs of divine intervention had been manifested. In the pilgrims' eyes, the Eternal City became in fact a vast repository of sacred relics. To the devout visitor, these did not exist merely as symbols or commemorative tokens. They retained the spiritual potency of the Apostles, martyrs, and saints, and their power proved tangibly real.[7]

In this chapter, I show that the real presence of divine and supernatural power in the relics extends beyond the sacred realm. In fact, this presence can be instruments of religious and social authority as well as the focus and locus of relations of power between people and sacred powers, between people and religious authorities, and between opposing religious authorities or social powers. Relics can act as signs of power and authority for those claiming their possession and control and they can also become political devices and instruments of political power, as several scholars have shown in their works and as we shall see in the case of the "kidnapping" of the tongue of Saint Anthony from the city of Padua.[8] By looking at how Catholics and Pentecostals aesthetically engage relics and their power, I will highlight how Pentecostals' aesthetic response to relics embodies their dissent against the aesthetic and spiritual order of the Catholic Church.

To start, I offer some detailed historical accounts on the role of relics in the building of the religious and social power of the Eternal City, the seat of the papacy, and on the emotional response the relics still arouse in contemporary Italian society. I will start by recounting the conversation I had with a pastor of the Mountain of Fire and Miracles Ministries in Rome.

Inhabiting the Eternal City: Gods, Martyrs, and Bones

The Headquarters of the Mountain of Fire and Miracles Ministries (MFM), one of Nigeria's Pentecostal churches, is in Rome. Pastor Wole, a forty-year-old graduate of the University of Lagos, heads up the MFM in Italy. He and his wife, Ruth, coordinate the activities of MFM's various Italian branches.

During my first interview with Pastor Wole, he told me the story of how he was sent to Rome by the founder of the church, Daniel Kola-wole Olukoya, who holds a PhD in molecular biology, and is currently the most popular deliverance pastor in Nigeria.

> One day Dr. Olukoya called me into his office and said, "Please close the door and sit down. I have something to tell you. Would you like to go to Rome?" When I answered, "To Rome!?" he said, "Yes." I said again, "Rome!?" and he said, "Yes! Why do you keep repeating 'Rome' as if you don't understand what I am saying? I want to send you to Rome." I said, "Rome, no . . . I don't know . . . Rome . . ." He said, "No! I am sending you to Rome for a reason. It's a country where they need somebody like you."

Pastor Wole told me he was very hesitant to accept this assignment because he had an idea of how spiritually challenging Rome might be. He was well aware of the religious history of Rome and of the power of what Pentecostals call the *spirit of religion*, such as the spirit that pushes people to follow practices, strict dogmas, and doctrines, which to his mind creates confusion and overshadows what Pentecostals consider the true faith. Some Pentecostals also refer to the spirit of religion as Babylon, including, among other spiritual bondages, religious coldness, false oaths, rigid theological constructions, the authority and supposed infallibility of the Pope, fear of priests and nuns, confession to priests, and forced celibacy. Pastor Wole's church, MFM, has a special deliverance prayer for the spirit of religion, which includes a long list of spiritual issues related to this spirit.[9] In our interview, Pastor Wole said:

> You see, this is the place where the Apostle Paul was killed. The Bible says that if you preach to people about Jesus Christ and they accept you, then peace will come upon them, but if they reject you, shake off the very dust from your feet for a testimony against them. Paul was killed here. They did not just send him away. They killed him! This country has a lot of spiritual problems! It is a foundational problem. Italy is afflicted

with the spirit of religion: Catholicism! The very foundations of Catholicism are here, in Rome. This is where we have to start!

With these words Pastor Wole explained how, having accepted the invitation, he began his experience as a missionary in Italy, a land where the blood of the Apostles had been spilled, a land that to him is polluted by the presence of the idols of the Roman Empire, its images, statues, symbols, and above all, to his mind a land polluted by dead human bodies and bones jealously preserved as relics in Italian churches and basilicas.

In this context, one can understand that to African Pentecostals the city of Rome, the seat of Roman Catholicism, the capital of the Vatican State, and the home of the papacy, is the metanarrative of the power of Catholicism that has become consolidated over centuries of history. To Pentecostals Rome is like an immense altar raised to venerate idols of the past and present, idols whose presence is still visible and tangible in the various temples and churches where the gods of the Roman Empire cohabit with the Christian God. Because of all this, Rome to them is anathema and hence a spiritual battlefield.

This battlefield was of course in the making long before African Pentecostals came along. For the story of Rome is a narrative of many religious cohabitations and juxtapositions and adaptations. In its two thousand years of history, Rome has gone from being the capital of a pagan empire with its gods and temples to being the capital of one of the largest and most powerful Christian faiths. Many of Rome's churches were built on the foundations of temples dedicated to gods of ancient Rome. Atop altars to those gods there are now altars dedicated to Catholic saints who, rather than obliterating their predecessors, have simply taken their place.

The presence of the pagan gods is still visible in the architecture and symbols hidden within the churches of Rome. The Pantheon, for example, was once a temple dedicated to all the gods of the Roman Empire, and in the seventh century was reconsecrated as a Christian church dedicated to Saint Mary and all the Martyrs. Other emblematic examples are the churches of Saint Clement and Saint Prisca, where Priscilla and Aquila lie buried, as does the apostle Paul. Both churches were built over temples dedicated to the god Mithras, one of the gods of the ancient Romans. In the church of Saint Prisca, one can still see the altars where sacrifices were made and the typical tauroctony showing Mithras killing the bull, and a dog and a snake drinking its blood while a scorpion stings the bull's testicles.

Likewise, even today the places where Christian martyrs died are an important part of Rome's sacramentalization. Saint Peter's Basilica was rebuilt in its current dimensions specifically to host the masses of pilgrims coming to venerate the martyrs, to see or touch their relics, and to visit the places where their blood was spilled. Here, the story goes, is where Peter the apostle was crucified and his body buried during Nero's great persecution of the Christians in 64 AD. Where the basilica now stands there once stood the Circus of Caligula, where the emperor watched brutal entertainment. Many Christians were persecuted and killed in this arena, in the shade of the same obelisk that still stands forty meters high at the center of what is now Saint Peter's Square.

The basilica was thus designed to safeguard the relics of Saint Peter (now kept at the Vatican necropolis, a building aligned with the basilica's high altar). But there is more. Inside the four pillars supporting the dome at Saint Peter's there are niches opening onto chapels that were built to contain the most important relics, such as the veil that Veronica used to wipe Christ's face, a piece of the cross on which Christ was crucified, the sword that pierced his body, and Andrew the apostle's head.[10] An enormous statue more than three meters high occupies each of these niches in the basilica.

Consecrated in 329 by Constantine, Saint Peter's Basilica acquired its current size and shape in 1626. The massive cost of its reconstruction was raised through the selling of indulgences and relics, which the Church of Rome had always controlled. The basilica is approximately 190 meters long, the three naves 58 meters across; the central nave is 45.5 meters high at the top of the vault, and the dome soars to approximately 136 meters. From 1626 onward, the basilica could accommodate twenty thousand faithful. The present-day dimensions of the church were reached after approximately 130 years of restoration work that began in 1500, when the winds of the Reformation were already blowing and Luther was circulating his 95 theses expounding his revolutionary doctrines. Among his numerous critiques of the Roman Catholic Church, he included the abuse of indulgences (often associated with pilgrimages) and the veneration of relics that to him were just symbolic mementos and did not impart miraculous divine presence.[11] The fact that Martin Luther nailed the 95 theses on the door of the Castle Church in Wittenberg is quite significant. The Castle Church held the largest collections of relics outside of Rome; by 1518, 17,443 pieces were on display in twelve aisles, allegedly including bones of saints, a piece of the true cross, locks of martyrs' hair, bread from the Last Supper, a twig from Moses's burning bush, and a veil spattered with the blood of Christ. Not only was the collection enormous, it was also elaborately displayed in special reliquaries ornamented with gold, silver, and precious stones.

Italy had always exerted a considerable degree of control over the trade and circulation of relics. Those relics constitute a considerable symbolic capital for the city and are a means of legitimizing the authority and spiritual power of the whole Catholic Church.[12] More than five hundred years later, today countless relics continue to travel back and forth from Rome to the rest of the world, so much so that Alitalia, the Italian national airline, has special procedures in place for carrying relics. The last time was when Alitalia flew the heart of Saint Camillus from Rome to Brazil, on which occasion Alitalia released a lengthy press communiqué that began as follows:

> Next June 30, Alitalia will be carrying the holy relic of the heart of St. Camillus on board one of its Boeing B777s on a journey from Rome Fiumicino to Sao Paulo in Brazil. Alitalia is proud and honored to take the holy relic of the heart of St. Camillus, patron of the sick and of hospitals, on board one of its airplanes for its journey from Italy to Brazil, where it is going as part of a month of celebrations commemorating 90 years of the Camillian religious order's presence in Brazil. The holy relic will embark on a long pilgrimage, passing through as many as ten dioceses dotted all over Brazil. This pilgrimage of the holy relic is one of the activities organized by the order in preparation for its jubilee in 2014, when they will commemorate the fourth centenary of the death of St. Camillus de' Lellis. The holy relic of the heart of St. Camillus will be collected on June 30 from the General House of the Camillian order, where it is on display for people to visit and venerate in the "Cubiculum"—the room where Saint Camillus lived the last months of his life. Camillus de' Lellis died on 14 July 1614 and was canonized on 29 June 1746 by Pope Benedict XIV, when the Holy Father said, "Camillus was the founder of a new charitable order." All the Alitalia flight personnel on board its Boeing B777 will have been trained specifically to look after the holy relic of the heart of St. Camillus and supervise this special delivery from Rome to Sao Paulo.[13]

To Roman Catholics, relics are a source of divine power, as well as vehicles of the creation and circulation of social memory, and as the official statement of Alitalia says, a source of considerable honor and pride. In reality of course not everyone and even not all Catholics venerate the relics, and the attitude of the devout toward relics has changed over the years too. But touching and venerating the relics is still seen as an act of intense devotion, and a means by which to access the divine power and favor of the saints. But as I shall disclose in this chapter, the power of the relics also extends to the social and political realms.

The Tongue of the Saint

Emblematic of relics' social power and deep devotion are the processions of relics that take place every year in several Italian cities. These processions are religious, urban, and civic events. They are not only a spiritual exercise, but also a confessionalization of urban spaces and a reiteration of the power of the church and the saints in a particular territory. One of the most popular processions of relics in Italy is the procession of the relics of Saint Anthony of Padua. The relics—his tongue, his chin, and part of his voice box—are preserved in the basilica of the city along with his skeleton and some of his belongings. The Basilica of Saint Anthony of Padua is one of the largest churches in the world, visited every year by more than six million pilgrims, which makes it one of the most revered sanctuaries in the Christian world.

The relics were discovered in 1263 in a pile of ashes and bones thirty years after Saint Anthony had died. His tongue was still intact (although this is ordinarily one of the first parts of the human body to decay after death), and this was interpreted as a miracle that confirmed Anthony's saintliness.

The skeleton is exhibited to the public every twenty-one years. The last time this happened was in 2010; the ostentation lasted for a week and approximately two hundred thousand people came to see the skeleton, at a rate of 2,500 visitors per hour. The pilgrims deposited 150,000 written prayers and appeals for help during their visit. Besides this exhibition of the skeleton every twenty-one years, there is a big annual procession of the relics streamed live by several TV and radio stations. Representatives of the Curia in Padua and of the various religious orders; as well as the mayor, the local authorities, various Catholic confraternities and associations; along with a large crowd of pilgrims and faithful, accompany Saint Anthony's relics in what is a very stately procession. Flags, standards, candles, flowers, and a sizable band follow behind a statue of Saint Anthony and the jeweled caskets containing the relics. Each year, close to sixty religious and public authorities, religious groups, associations, charitable organizations, and brotherhoods march in procession with relics and the statue of Saint Anthony. As the procession passes through the city's main streets, decked out for the occasion with Italian flags and the red standards of Saint Anthony's Basilica, people make the sign of the cross, clap, and blow kisses to the relics. The windows of Padua's ancient palaces, shops, and bars are draped with the colors of the saint, worn by the town like religious high-ceremonial garb. The procession moves through the heart of the city and ends in front of the basilica with speeches by the mayor and the rector of the basilica, and with the blessing of the relics and of the numerous congregations.[14]

The social and religious power of the relics became sharply evident when the relics were stolen in 1991. It was just after six o'clock in the evening and in the basilica there were the people who had attended five o'clock mass, as well as the usual crop of tourists. Three thieves wearing masks over their faces entered Saint Anthony's Basilica armed and headed straight for the chapel containing Saint Anthony's relics. One thief made three tourists lie down on the floor and kept his gun aimed at a monk who was distributing blessed images, while another broke into one of the cabinets containing some of the relics, notably, the tongue and the chin. He seized the chin, and the three escaped through the sacristy.

The newspaper headlines next day screamed: "The World's Emotion over the Sacrilege in Padua," "The Saint Held Hostage," "Manhunt for Relic Thieves," and "Powers of Satan in Action."[15] Articles followed with hypotheses, inferences, and appeals, and vigils were held to pray for the relics' safe return to the basilica. The Vatican was mobilized and it subsequently issued a statement that it was willing to negotiate with whoever was responsible for the theft. For seventy-one days, from October 10 to December 20, 1991, people devoted to the saint and millions of faithful in five continents held their breath. Who had taken the relic, and what did they plan to do with it? Some priests spoke in hushed tones of satanic rites and occult powers; others assumed the thieves wanted money.

The truth of the matter—discovered three years later—was that a local boss named Felice Maniero, whose mafia organization was active in the northeast of Italy between the 1980s and early 1990s, had organized the robbery. Maniero, nicknamed Angelface, Felicetto, or Felix, boasted a long list of crimes: drug dealing, prostitution, billion-dollar robberies, usury, gambling, weapons dealing, and abduction. He had also made some remarkable escapes from jail, the most surprising of which was from Padua's high-security prison, when six of his men turned up at the gates in police uniforms, bribed one of the prison guards with a billion Italian lira to hold the door open for them, and simply took their boss away; not a shot was fired during the escape. Maniero was particularly well known for his ironic sense of humor and the way he played games with the police. He would often send them postcards from his various hiding places saying, "Wish you were here in Dalmatia," or "Warm regards from Austria," or "Yours, as always, Felicetto."

Maniero ordered the relic to be stolen because he wanted to force the authorities to come to terms with his local mafia and comply with his demand that a cousin imprisoned for drug dealing a few months earlier be released. Maniero himself confirmed this story in an exclusive interview reported in a special edition of the *Messaggero di Sant'Antonio* (a magazine published by the confraternity of Saint Anthony's Basilica), in which he apologized "for the distress he had caused to the faithful."[16] This is how the mafioso tells the story:

> I had a serious problem to solve at the time: my cousin Giuliano had just been arrested and risked at least 10 years in prison. I couldn't allow that to happen. I had to get him out of there somehow. I had thought of everything: helping him to escape, going in to release him, and stealing something exceptionally important to offer in exchange, corrupting a judge . . . and I had to decide quickly. I felt responsible and the idea was making me feel suffocated. One day, while we were talking, one of my men said, "Feli, how about the Saint in Padua?" The idea made my eyes sparkle! This was more than just a rare work of art, people come to see it from all over the world, so it would be perfect for an exchange. We wasted no time. I called another cousin of mine, and some other men, and within days the theft was planned and implemented. I got what I wanted: Giuliano was released when I handed the relic back. Actually I had told my men to take St. Anthony's tongue, it would have been a much more important item to exchange. The fools turned up with his chin instead, but I didn't make a fuss about it. I thought to myself, they must have mistakenly believed—like the rest of us—that the Saint's tongue would be inside his mouth! As soon as the relic was stolen, it was taken to one of our hiding places. My cousin and I went to collect it straight away to put it somewhere safe. We wrapped it up carefully to protect it against the damp and buried it along the banks of the Brenta

River, and that is where it stayed until we handed it back. One thing is for sure: even if I hadn't got what I wanted, the relic would have been given back to the monks. I would never have sold it to take home a pile of money. That wasn't my objective. Holding the authorities to ransom to get what I wanted was pretty exciting, to say the least. My family and relatives are all practicing Catholics, but that had nothing to do with it. I am an art lover and I had already been to the Basilica three or four times to see its architectural and artistic treasures. Anyway, when I had the relic stolen it was light years away from my mind to do anybody any harm. At the time, it was the only solution I could think of to get what I wanted.[17]

Eight weeks after it was stolen, the deal between Maniero and the State was done; Saint Anthony's chin was returned with only minimal damage to the casket (a tiny inlaid bronze lion was missing) and the boss's cousin was released from prison. The recovery of Saint Anthony's chin was presented to the public as the final act of a risky operation conducted by the carabinieri, but in actual fact the relic was delivered back into the hands of two police superintendents by one of Felix Maniero's men. The story ended as planned with the relic returned in exchange for the release of Maniero's drug-dealer cousin.[18]

The return of the relics to the basilica was celebrated with great pomp and ceremony. The relics crossed the threshold of the church in the hands of two policemen who walked through an ecstatic crowd of the devout. The city's public authorities, the Vatican, the devotees of the saint, and Felix Maniero and his cousin were all happy, and the social and political power of the tongue of the saint was confirmed by the fact that its theft forced the Italian State and the Vatican to negotiate with a criminal.

Sacred Presence, Mediation, and Sacramentalization

Interestingly, there is another place where people venerate the remains of a very old clay statue of Saint Anthony of Padua, attributing to those old pieces of clay a power similar to the one that Catholic devotees attribute to relics of the saint himself. The place is a little fishing village in Ghana called Elmina. The people who take part in religious rites dedicated to Nana Ntona (the local name for Anthony) call themselves Santonafo.[19] A second wave of Catholic missionaries that arrived in Elmina discovered the Nana Ntona cult, to their great surprise, at the beginning of the eighteenth century when they came upon a little shrine at which the local people venerated the remains of an old statue of Saint Anthony. The missionaries who discovered the cult did not speak out against it. Instead they tried, in vain, to reclaim their authority and the authority of "their" Saint Anthony over the statue by attempting to convince the locals to venerate the Catholic saint instead of Nana Ntona. The locals flatly refused and claimed the statue as their Nana Ntona, whether the missionaries liked it or not.

During my visit to the Nana Ntona shrine in May 2010, I interviewed the local priest of the little shrine whose family, from one generation to the next, performs the rites relating to the god Nana Ntona. He told me that the statue moved from the Portuguese chapel to the local shrine when the Dutch toke over the town of Elmina.[20] According to historian Larry Yarak, during the Dutch colonial time, the shrine became well known for giving shelter to runaway slaves. In late 1836, a harsh confrontation between the Ntona priest and the Dutch ruler ended up with the Dutch attack of the shire and banning the priest.[21] In 1928, Craft Johnson wrote that in the shrine there was a crucifix, a baptismal bowl, and all the symbols of the Catholic Church of Elmina under the Portuguese.

Currently, the devotional practices of the Santonafo toward Nana Ntona include washing the remains of the statue with water and then sprinkling that water over their fields, purportedly to spiritually clean the land. According to the local people, because it has come into contact with the statue, this water has the power to keep evil spirits away and improve their crops.

Even today, this ritual is still repeated once a year. It used to happen on June 13, just like the celebrations dedicated to Saint Anthony in the city of Padua, but now the family in charge of the shrine decides the date of the celebrations, and it varies year to year. During the celebrations, the Santonafo organize a procession: The water used to clean the remains of the statue of Saint Anthony is carried with great pomp and ceremony, followed by the local leaders, priests, and priestesses, and accompanied by music and dance.

The described practices of veneration of relics in Elmina and Padua seem intriguingly similar. In fact, they both apply a similar sacramental principle and sacramentalization of the land. In Padua and Elmina, these two diverse relics–the human remains of Saint Anthony and old pieces of clay of a statue of Saint Anthony renamed Nana Ntona—are perceived as the incarnation of a healing and blessing power that can be accessed through sight and touch. Both sacramentalize the land by parading the relics and the water in the streets, and they mediate the power of Saint Anthony and Nana Ntona through tactile contact with the relics. The Catholics touch the reliquary of Saint Anthony's relics, send kisses to them, and clap their hands when they make visual contact with the relics at the processions; and the Santonafo sprinkle on their fields the water used to wash the remains of the statue on their fields.

Deadly Passions and Bodies Fragmentation

The cult of the relics, throughout its evolution and change, has always attracted criticism from skeptics, who see in this cult superstition and irrationality. But Pentecostals do not share this attitude. To them, relics are not the fruit of superstition or mere meaningless substance. To them relics have real and immanent power: an evil power, but power nonetheless.

During my fieldwork in Italy, I visited Saint Anthony's Basilica in Padua with Ola, a forty-year-old Nigerian man who had been living in Italy for about eight years. He is a very active member of a Pentecostal church that I often visited in Padua. We frequently chatted after the Sunday service and in time became good friends. One day, Ola stopped by at my workplace not far from Saint Anthony's Basilica. We went out together for a little walk and a chat, and I invited Ola to go inside the basilica with me. Ola was a little doubtful, but curious too, and he agreed to visit the church because he had heard a great deal about it. It was the first time he had entered the building. Saint Anthony's Basilica is one of three papal basilicas outside Rome. It has a history very similar to that of other important churches in Rome. According to the historians, it was built on the foundations of a temple dedicated to Juno, queen of the gods, protector and special counselor of the Roman State, in the old citadel of the Holy Roman Empire.

When we entered, I saw immediately that Ola was amazed. Even at first glance, Saint Anthony's Basilica is clearly magnificent. It is one of the largest basilicas in the world and contains artistic treasures of immeasurable value. The paintings, frescoes, statues, sculptures, and monumental tombs tell the story of the people of Padua, their heroes, and the notable personalities of the city's political, cultural, and religious history. As we walked along the right nave, I saw Ola look very carefully at the marble statues and various images that decorate the walls of the altars. He stopped to look at one or two in particular but made no comment.

When we arrived at the altar containing Saint Anthony's tomb, we stopped to look at the hundreds of photographs left by the faithful in thanksgiving for miracles received or in supplication for healing and miracles of all kind. There were numerous people praying and resting their head or hands on the marble surrounding the tomb. Ola stopped briefly to look both at the photographs left by the devout and at the people's gestures of devotion: signs of the cross, genuflections, and their kissing and touching Saint Anthony's marble tombstone.

When we left the altar, we moved toward the Chapel of the Treasure. As we covered this short distance, Ola focused on the enormous fresco of the *Tree of Life with the Prophets*. "Beautiful," said Ola, "Magnificent! All the prophets are there." He was able to identify the visual narrative of the Bible illustrated in the frescoes inside the basilica. He only needed to see a detail alongside a character to identify the corresponding biblical passage. His knowledge of the Bible astounded me. He stopped to look in silence at the images of Saint Anthony of Padua and various other historical personalities of the city.

We then came to the funeral monuments dedicated to Pietro and Domenico Marchetti, professors of medicine and surgery at Padua University's Faculty of Medicine, which already in the seventeenth century was highly renowned. The Marchettis' monumental tomb was built between 1678 and 1690; it is an excellent example of the baroque monument, magnificently interpreted by the sculptor Comini in polychrome marble. The monument has a great scenographic effect, culminating in a Bernini-like memento mori, a flying skeleton, at the top of the monument together with the classic trumpet symbolic of the Last Judgment. Within the monument there are busts of Pietro and Domenico Marchetti atop piles of books being held by Hippocrates, Galen, and Aesculapius. The latter was the god of medicine in ancient Roman times, whose extraordinary expertise as a physician enabled him not only to cure the sick, but even to reawaken the dead. Alongside Aesculapius stands his cockerel, a symbol of the day and of life reborn. Rising above the monument there is a black pyramid with flames at the top, from where the immortal phoenix, symbol of death and resurrection from the ashes, takes flight.

Standing in front of this monument, Ola asked me for some explanations. I told him about the doctors of medicine and about Hippocrates,

Galen, and Aesculapius and his cockerel. "Roman pagan idols!" he said. "How can they possibly have such idols in a church? The idols of the Roman Empire in a Christian church!" To which I responded, "But they are part of the story, the memory of our past!" Ola shook his head and moved on until we came to the Chapel of the Treasure where the relics of Saint Anthony and other treasures are on display. The building of this chapel began in 1691. It is a baroque work by Parodi, a pupil of Bernini's. The passage through which one walks to admire the treasures and relics is crowned with rows of stucco festive angels and musicians. In specially made glass cabinets there are the fragments of his clothing, the wooden case that once contained his bones (subsequently placed in a glass urn in the tomb), the cloth in which the case was wrapped, and an inscription that dates from 1263 which attests to when the saint's body was first transferred to the basilica.

When we came to the relics, Ola asked me, "Exactly what lies behind these panes of glass?" I answered, "The relics of the saint, his tongue, his chin and teeth, and his vocal cords." "The real ones?" he asked. "Yes, of course. Original parts of the saint's body." By now, what I saw on Ola's face was an expression of utter disgust. When I next turned to him, he was gone, headed for the exit of the chapel. I followed him out and said, "I wanted to explain the relics to you better." But he answered flatly, "I don't want to see the relics. I don't want to see all this again in my dreams tonight. There is nothing biblical in the things I see here. Those are fragments of a dead human body. This is worshipping of the dead!" We left the church and, once in the square outside, Ola said, "Do you see why this country has so many problems? The problem with Italy is the spirit of religion that is the great bondage of Italy. Here in this beautiful church there are so many beautiful works of art, but I don't see the presence of God. I see worshipping of the dead!" Ola was visibly disturbed and even disgusted by the exhibition of the relics in the church.

In the basilica, Ola saw the deep connection between the living and the dead, which is certainly part of the Catholic doctrine of the communion of the saints. In this regard, Pastor Sola, told me, "This is ancestor worship!" Interestingly, this similarity has been acknowledged and even celebrated by the Roman Catholic Church. In 1995, John Paul II in his apostolic exhortation "Ecclesia in Africa" included several positive comments on the practices and practitioners of the indigenous African religions, including their veneration of the dead. He wrote: "Ancestral veneration is intrinsically linked with a profound religious sense. A sense of the sacred, of the existence of God the creator, is implicit in African belief in ancestral mediation and in God as the great Ancestor of a spiritual world." As reiterated in "Ecclesia in Africa," ancestral forms of worship are closely related to the love of life: "It is precisely this love of life that makes Africans give such great importance to the veneration of their ancestors."[22]

Despite the fact that ancestral veneration takes different forms in different African societies, the cult of the ancestors has been an important element of African cultural and spiritual heritage, and as Alisa La Gamma also showed, in some cases it also included a form of relics veneration.[23] The cult consists of honoring the spirits of the dead that are believed to survive after corporeal death. Believers view ancestors as the living dead who have achieved a higher status by being closer to God. With this status they are believed to be able to play an intermediary role between God and the living. Such a belief in intercession is also very central in the Judeo-Christian faith, especially in the Catholic and Orthodox Churches.

Ancestral veneration is not a religion in itself but one aspect of a composite religious cultural system that usually has God as Supreme Being. The ancestors are women and men who lived exemplary lives, died natural deaths, and had proper funerals and burial rites. They are vested with mystical supernatural powers and authority, and have a peculiar role in the life of their living kin. They look after their descendants and they can dispense both favors and misfortune according to the respect and attention they receive from their kin. They protect them from sickness and evil, inspire and empower them, reward and discipline them, and above all mediate between humans and divinity; but they can also disturb their kin if their kin fail to pay them respect or do not comply with their requests. The ancestors communicate with the living through dreams, animals, signs, and also diviners but are believed to be everywhere, freely inhabiting the world of the living.[24] Moreover, the spaces where humans communicate directly with the ancestors and offer animal sacrifices and gifts, places such as shrines, cemeteries, and tombs, are believed to be charged with a special power.

Ancestral veneration is based on the understanding that life and death are a continuum in which death is just a change of state. Ancestral veneration celebrates the existence of the Absolute Being as the only source of life both for the living and for the dead, and continuous communion between the living community in the world and the living dead in the beyond. The belief that the living Christians on earth and the blessed Christians in heaven are in communion undergirds both these ancestral practices and Catholicism. Contrary to Protestants, Roman Catholics believe that the communion of saints is the church itself, consisting of the faithful on earth, in purgatory, and in heaven.[25] The Church on earth can pray for those purified in purgatory and venerate those in heaven, and can invoke their intercessory prayers.

The similarities between Catholicism and African traditional religions, their practices and beliefs regarding the place and role of the dead, did not pass unnoticed by Pentecostals, as Pastor Sola told me in our interview: "The worship of the dead is wrong! It is idolatry! The Bible said this. There is no difference between Africans worshipping the ancestors and the Italians. It is just that the Catholics are more refined! This is idolatry. God hates idolatry with perfect hate! Psalm 16, verse 4 says: 'Their sorrows shall be multiplied that hasten after another god: their drink offerings of blood will I not offer, nor take up their names into my lips.'"

However, those similarities do not reduce the complexity of relics, which pose several challenges also to African Catholics. During one of my ethnographic field studies in Saint Anthony's Basilica, I had a brief conversation with a Kenyan priest, a student of the Gregorian University of Rome, who was spending three months of spiritual retreat with the Franciscan friars. I met him at the altar of the tomb of the saint while we were both observing the long queue of pilgrims waiting to touch the marble of the tomb. When I asked him about how he felt about the relics, he told me, "It is a difficult issue. I am Catholic, but the veneration of the relics is not common in African Catholicism. In Africa, we do not venerate relics, or it is very rare. Dealing with body parts is a taboo in Africa." However, interestingly enough, the Catholic Church in Africa is increasingly encouraging the veneration of relics, slowly breaking the taboos attached to this peculiar devotional practice. An example of such is the travel of the relics of Saint Thérèse of Lisieux, known also as "The Little Flower" for the South African World Cup. On this occasion the diocese of Johannesburg released the following statement:

> The South African Bishops Conference announced today that the relics of St. Thérèse of Lisieux will be in South Africa during the upcoming FIFA Football World Cup. From June 27 to July 12, the relics of St.

Thérèse will travel around South Africa's capital Johannesburg, corresponding with the time frame of the international sports event. "The whole Church of South Africa is expressing the hope that the coming of the Relics of Saint Thérèse of Lisieux will inspire people, strengthen their faith, and challenge all of us to live our faith and follow our vocations/callings as St Thérèse did," the bishops said in a statement on Wednesday. . . . After residing in Johannesburg, the relics will travel "The Saint Thérèse Route," stopping in the South African provinces of Limpopo, Gauteng, Free State, Eastern Cape, and Western Cape.[26]

Other relics were traveling from Europe to Africa, including the relics of Saint Theresa D'Avila and the hand of Saint John Bosco, the founder of the Salesian order. The Kenyan newspaper *The Nation* reported the news of the arrival of the hand of Saint John Bosco with the following announcement:

After tens of thousands of kilometres and millions of dollars, the right hand of Saint John Bosco will finally land in Nairobi. It is expected that hundreds of thousands of faithful will turn out to pay homage to the relic during its seven-day stay in Nairobi from December 4, conjuring up images of the travelling world cup trophy in the run up to the games. Just like the trophy, the relic is transported in a private jet, has round-the-clock security and travels in a specially modified casket with a wax replica body lying in state. The casket in which the saint's replica travels weighs 820kg and is made of a steel base with a glass viewing window. The glass box that actually contains the hand is 253 cm long, 108 cm wide and 132 cm tall. The full urn is transported by two specially designed trucks.[27]

The newspaper reported the details of this festive arrival with an emphasis on the huge effort made by the Catholic Church to grant the relics due homage.

Certainly, the more frequent arrival of relics in Africa is not making Pentecostals comfortable. To Pentecostals, the veneration of the relics as well as ancestral veneration means worship of powers other than God, and as such, it is a practice against the Pentecostal universal project of salvation, according to which salvation can be achieved only through the victory of the one God over the other gods. Therefore, to Pentecostals searching for help, protection, success in life, healing, and salvation through the mediatory role of the ancestors, idols, deities, as well as witchcraft, use of medals, and amulets might bring initial results but will eventually end in death, destruction, and damnation.

Yet there are some similar understandings of ancestral veneration that Catholicism, Pentecostalism, and also African indigenous world views share. First and foremost, they all share the belief in the continuation of life after corporeal death and the communion between the living and the dead. But contrary to Catholics and ancestor worshippers, Pentecostals resist and strongly oppose this communion.

While conducting my research in Nigeria, I observed several prayers and practices against the spirits of the ancestors. At the deliverance programs I attended at the Mountain of Fire and Miracles Ministries in Lagos, I met several women and men who were participating in intensive and exhausting fasting and prayer programs in order to combat the spiritual attacks of the dead. A woman told me that her pastor had sent her to the deliverance program because she kept dreaming about her father, who had passed away a few months before. She told me, "I was seeing my father in my dreams very often. I told my pastor this, and he told me I was under spiritual attack. I told him that I was missing my father very much and that I was very close to him. But he strongly encouraged me to come to this church because dreaming about dead people is a bad sign."

To Pentecostals, physical and visual contact as well as any communication with the dead exposes people to evil forces and spiritual pollution. Contact with dead bodies or parts of bodies, like the relics, may open the door that separates the living from the dead. For this reason, dead bodies are not even allowed inside many Pentecostal churches. Visual or physical contact or contiguity with dead bodies allegedly unites the world of the living with that of the dead, and leads to spiritual pollution that is against the Pentecostal's desire for holiness and purity. The vulnerability of the body to desires and corruptibility makes it a hindrance to holiness and purity. A holy body resists evil forces or temptations and avoids contacts with other bodies, substances, objects, images, or evil polluting forces that can penetrate and threaten its social and spiritual integrity. According to Wariboko, Pentecostal spirituality demands to transcend the human body in order to experience spiritual power or divine love.[28] Such transcendence includes the rejection of any weakness of the flesh, like lust, but also corruptibility and fragmentation including bodily partitions, decay, and decomposition.

Pentecostals' anxiety related to the manipulation and partition of human bodies undergirds their condemnation of witchcraft and juju, a combination of traditional medicine and magic rituals including body parts such as hair, nails, or bodily fluids, along with animals, herbs, and other objects. Juju practitioners use human body parts to capture the souls of human beings and control their destiny, health, and wealth.[29] By virtue of the same doctrine of concomitance that is applied to relics, every tiniest part of the body of the person is believed to carry the fullness of the soul of the person. Pentecostals often express their anxieties about such use of body parts in their prayers, which make explicit references to bodily integrity and witchcraft practices. The following prayers I have heard in Pentecostal churches in Nigeria are examples of this:

> I recover my body parts deposited on evil altars, in the name of Jesus!
>   Any material taken from my body and now placed on a witchcraft altar be roasted by the fire of God in the Name of Jesus!
>   Any part of me shared out amongst village witches, I recover you in the name of Jesus!
>   Any organ of my body that has been exchanged for another through witchcraft operation be replaced now in the name of Jesus![30]

Both the rejections of the cult of the ancestors and the anxiety regarding body partitioning are linked to the Pentecostal understanding of spiritual and corporeal integrity and purity. As also discussed in Chapter 2, to Pentecostals the human body is both a threat to the stability of spiritual, social, and ethical boundaries, and a means to reach divine love and power. As such, the typical Pentecostal reaction to contact with anything that threatens the stability of the ethical order and precludes the experience of divine love reached through integrity, holiness, and purity is one of disgust. But in Italy, their disgust is not just a bodily reaction; it is also a political aesthetic response to the social and religious power of Catholicism, in the very land of Catholicism.

The Politics of Disgust and Desire

Disgust is a state of the body and the mind. Because of its profound and visceral force, scholars have even questioned the definition of disgust as an emotion.[31]

In his seminal work on disgust, William Ian Miller argued, "No other emotion, not even hatred, paints its object so unflatteringly, because no other emotions forces such concrete sensual descriptions of its object. This, I suspect, it what we really mean when we describe disgust as more visceral than most other emotions."[32] According to Miller, disgust functions in different ways according to social and cultural paradigms; systems of meaning; and hierarchies of objects, substances, and material forms that shape a community's emotional life. Such hierarchies rank people and things that are linked to ideas of pollution, but especially danger of desecration, destruction, and harm. Miller writes, "[Disgust] presents a nervous claim of [the] right to be free of the dangers imposed by the proximity of the inferior. It is thus an assertion of a claim to superiority that at the same time recognizes the vulnerability of that superiority to the defiling power of the low."[33]

To Miller, such vulnerability triggers a claim to be free from the polluting force, and for this reason disgust is also a political act that says no to the proximity to the disgusting, nevertheless powerful, matter that puts in danger the political, social, and moral order. As Miller nicely puts it, disgust is the subversion of "the minimal demands of tolerance."[34]

Despite the various nuanced theses on the roots of disgust, which are certainly historical, cultural, and contextual, disgust is an embodied and sensual response to something we do not want close to us. What are Pentecostals refusing to accept by their disgust? And following Miller's argument on the political role of disgust, what is the political statement expressed through the disgust for relics? In our interviews and during my ethnographic fieldwork, Pentecostals' disgust toward relics emerged as an embodied statement that responds to what they feel to be a polluting, evil power that separates them from God and brings them close to the danger of physical and moral decay. Wariboko describes the Pentecostals' disgust as follows:

> Desire for holiness creates disgust that in turn haunts it. The desire for God that comes after disgust of sin displaces the other without replacing it; they shadow each other. Such that each one of them can return to disrupt the other which disrupted it or appears to have replaced it. . . . Disgust and desire are interwoven as a complex tapestry in Nigerian Pentecostalism. Disgust to be properly understood must be connected with self-transcendence, which Pentecostal spirituality . . . fosters, and is associated with the goal of attaining spiritual power or purity.[35]

To Pentecostals, a relic is a disgusting and unholy power that unchains social and spiritual chaos by blurring the barriers between the world of the living and the dead, the past of their forefathers and their present. Their disgust is an aesthetic response to an in-between state of life and death, an ambiguous territory when both conditions are present in some form.[36]

Relics are an emblematic example of an in-between substance that blurs not only the boundaries of life and death but also of time and space, that materializes before a Pentecostal's eyes the specter of the cult of ancestral veneration, juju practices, and witchcraft. Their disgust stems from the fact that they are close to something that is beyond their control and that threatens their spiritual and bodily integrity.

By contrast, to Catholics a relic is an object of veneration and passion, something charged with charisma and power. It arouses devotion, excitement, loyalty, a sense of identity, memory, and national pride. Far from reminding the devout of the death of a saint or martyr, visual or physical contact with the relics reminds the devotee of the promises of eternal life and the victory of the body over nature, specifically death, decay, and decomposition. It intimately satisfies the profound desire for the resurrection of the body in its integrity and splendor.

When I was showing Ola the Marchetti funerary monument of the fathers of medicine in Saint Anthony's Basilica, I told him that the people and symbols depicted on the monument were part of the history and memory of the people of the territory. But the reality is far more profound. The figures and symbols, such as Aesculapius and his cockerel and the relics of Saint Anthony, are the metanarrative of the desire for immortality and resurrection that can be seen in several masterpieces preserved in the basilica. Through the iconography related to the diverse historical moments in which they were conceived, each monument and each carving reminds the devotees that their bodies also will overcome death and will rise again in integrity and magnificence, like the majestic and immortal phoenix, symbol of death and resurrection from the ashes, that takes flight in the Marchetti monument.

Catholics' and Pentecostals' visceral embodied responses to relics, although totally opposite to one another, disclose a shared sacramental principle through which both Catholics and Pentecostals invest these material forms with a real power. This power intrinsically reflects their desires and existential anxieties about death and life, salvation, bodily and social integrity, as well as holiness and divine love. This entanglement reveals a whole conundrum of individual and collective passions that arouse terror and joy, disgust and pleasure, dirtiness and holiness.

The result of this shared sacramental principle through which Catholics and Pentecostals invest the relics with divine versus evil presence triggers what Jacques Rancière called an aesthetic break, or dissensus. Rancière argues that what is at stake in politics, just as it is in the government of the senses, is the distribution of the sensible.[37] Politics, he says, involves not only the disruption of certain regimes and rules of the senses and feelings but also the eruption of distinct dissenting aesthetics. Therefore, by suspending the feeling rules, people intervene in consolidated regimes of sensation and create an aesthetic break, such as "the conflict between one who says white and another who also says white but does not understand the same thing by it."[38]

What Rancière describes fittingly frames Pentecostals' and Catholics' aesthetic encounter. They both attribute a strong power to the relics, but whereas to Catholics such power is divine, to Pentecostals it is evil. In this sense, Pentecostals break the aesthetic order established by the Catholic Church according to which to a certain substance—in this case the relics—there is a certain aesthetic response, awe and adoration. Through their disgust, Pentecostals suspend the role and possibilities assigned to the relics and alter the relation between bodies, objects, and the senses established by the Catholic aesthetic order.

As this chapter discloses, relics have an important role in the Catholic order. They create and consolidate the spiritual and social power of the Eternal City and of Roman Catholicism. The possession, control of, and trafficking in relics and their association with the selling of indulgences made it possible to build one of the biggest basilicas in the world—Saint Peter's Basilica—and to fill it with some of the most beautiful masterpieces of art in the world. Undoubtedly, the power and popularity of the veneration of relics has changed over the years. But even in contemporary Italian society, believers continue to ascribe to relics a form of power and authority that arouses honor and pride, as Alitalia's press release conveyed. Relics were able to bring the Italian State, the public authorities, the police, and the Vatican to a secret bargain with a local boss mafia and convince him to return the stolen tongue of Saint Anthony in exchange for the release of a criminal. This shows that the relics are not only intrinsic to Catholic aesthetics of presence. They were—and probably still are—constitutive of Catholic social and political power; of a religious, aesthetic, and social order; and of an articulated socioreligious governmental machine. To the Church of Rome, relics have two important theological and political functions: They mediate the divine presence and power of the saints and martyrs, and they form and support social and political power.

A Terrible Beauty

Saint Anthony's Basilica contains some of the most popular and venerated relics of a Catholic saint. Yet, I met several African Pentecostals there. I often saw a few Africans praying in the pews in the little chapel dedicated to the Blessed Sacrament in the basilica. The chapel is well known to have a certain atmosphere, a sort of ambience or aura that, as Gernot Bohme would say, "fill[s] the space with a certain tone of feeling like a haze."[39] The spectacular architecture, statues, images, and bright colors of the Chapel of the Blessed Sacrament certainly contribute to its atmosphere. The stained glass of the central rose window and of the two smaller rose windows on either side filters a gentle light. The pews are placed close to the altar, the first bench just one pace back from the two angels with their candlesticks. The high walls are decorated with bands of white, red, and blue marble, its soft shades accompanying the raised contours of the columns and inlays. On the side walls there are two funeral monuments dedicated to two famous persons in the history of the city and decorated with bronze statues of biblical characters. The altar is presided over by two life-size white marble angels, who are on their knees and hold two enormous candlesticks. Their clothes drape softly around the curves of their bodies, studded with tiny mirrors and colored stones. Their long hair frames their faces as they gaze toward the altar with a melancholy expression of adoration and reverence. But the wall behind the altar is undeniably what attracts the most attention, with its majestic illustration of a passage in the Apocalypse of Saint John the Apostle dominating the room.

From the tip of the equilateral arch that frames the image comes a beam of yellow light enriched with precious sparks that spreads from the center of a half-sun along with six lesser rays. The beam of light and the six rays around it together represent the seven spirits and the seven stars of God. The great beam of light that points downward illuminates the halos of an indistinct multitude of people gazing upward. The colors used to paint the sky change from pale blue to an intense emerald hue with hundreds of thousands of sparkling pieces of glitter. The scene painted on the wall is described in the biblical book of Revelation as follows:

> After this I looked, and, behold, a door was opened in heaven: and the first voice which I heard was as it were of a trumpet talking with me; which said, Come up hither, and I will shew thee things which must be hereafter. And immediately I was in the spirit: and, behold, a throne was set in heaven, and one sat on the throne. And he that sat was to look upon like a jasper and a sardine stone: and there was a rainbow round about the throne, in sight like unto an emerald. And round about the throne were four and twenty seats: and upon the seats I saw four and twenty elders sitting, clothed in white raiment; and they had on their heads crowns of gold. And out of the throne proceeded lightning and thunderings and voices: and there were seven lamps of fire.[40]

Sitting in the pews, one has the feeling of being part of the apocalyptic scene narrated in the Bible. Illuminated by the light from the rose windows, awestruck by the apocalyptic shades of the turquoise sky and the sparkling beam of light, people sit by the huge angel's side. The faraway burbling of the tourists, who flock in their thousands to visit this architectural masterpiece, fills the little room with a surreal background sound.

The regular presence of Africans aroused my curiosity, and I spent several months noting what went on in this evocative little chapel. Whenever possible, I exchanged a few words with these people and learned that many of them were Catholics, but many others were Pentecostals. I asked the latter why they came to pray in this particular chapel inside a Catholic church. Their answer was almost always the same, straightforward and surprising at the same time: "Because it's so beautiful here."

Once, one of the Africans who had been sitting among the benches stood up and went to kneel on one of the bottom steps below the altar. He raised his arms above his head in an imploring stance. He remained there for some time absorbed in his prayers, which attracted the attention of some of the tourists and other worshippers unused to such bodily gestures.

On another occasion, a man lay down at the foot of the altar and rolled to the right and to the left while reciting prayers in a tone that conveyed a sense of profound adoration. I had seen the same scene happen dozens of times in Nigeria at the Mountain of Fire and Miracles Ministries Pentecostal Church where I had conducted my fieldwork. There, the altar was considered a holy place filled with divine power. People envisaged the particular area where the altar stood as an open door to heaven and the land of miracles. Even the image used to decorate the church's altar suggested as much: It was a painting by Sade Olukoya, the wife of the church's founder, that depicted a huge staircase populated with angels that climbed from the foot of the altar up to the sky. Written in large letters was the phrase "Surely, the Lord is in this Place." Before the altar, people kneeled and prayed, lay down flat and rolled to the left and right, and took great care to ensure that every inch of their bodies touched the red carpet at the foot of the altar. A similar thing happened in Saint Anthony's Basilica in Padua. Sometimes, if this scene lasted for too long, the church guardians would intervene and ask these African worshippers to pray back in the pews.

Once, one of the guards told me that he had seen an African absorbed in prayer in front of a little side altar situated on the side opposite the altar dedicated to the much-venerated Byzantine Madonna. The guard explained that he had been surprised to see this man, a Nigerian, on his knees and praying while facing toward a painting that at the time was completely concealed by a protective screen because it was being restored; in other words, the man was praying in front of a white sheet. The guard was curious and asked him why, given all the other places in the great church, he was praying in front of this "nothing" instead of going to kneel before the altar to the Byzantine Madonna, for instance. The man simply answered, "I am a Pentecostal. I do not pray to the Madonna." On another occasion, while inside the church, I happened to meet some of the members of the Pentecostal churches that I visited on Sundays. When I stopped to greet them, I heard them say, "This church is magnificent!"

So, although Ola ran away when he saw the relics, other Pentecostals stop and stay where they find the right atmosphere. Drawn by the basilica's beauty, the Pentecostals seem to zigzag between holy and demonic images, and between statues and relics that dwell in the terrible beauty of the magnificent cathedral.[41] Carolyn Korsmeyer, a philosopher who devoted much of her study to contradictory and enigmatic aesthetics, defined *terrible beauty* as a positive aesthetic response in which we find beauty in something that is terrible: "With terrible beauty attention is arrested by elements that strain the heart—and yet they induce us to linger over them and savor them in all their heartache and woe."[42]

A terrible beauty is a difficult beauty intensified by disturbing subject matter and less-pleasurable emotions. It is a mix of appeal and rejection causing the arousal of discomforting emotions.[43] To the Pentecostals, the terrible beauty of the basilica juxtaposes the spectacular sacred art and the splendid paraphernalia with the horror of body fragments. This Basilica, as other churches in Italy, both fascinates Pentecostals and makes them shudder.

Despite the polluting force of the relics of Saint Anthony, Pentecostals go to the basilica and become part of a religious aesthetic order in which their embodied statement and prayers are also in open dissent with the dominant aesthetic. In the basilica, practices of praying and engagement with statues, images, and also the tomb of the saint and his relics, are strictly controlled and regulated. There is a high degree of real and implied surveillance of visitors—of their behavior, which includes appropriate dress, silence, restricted access to the chapels and altars; and above all, a regulated engagement with the body. Yet, Pentecostal aesthetics of disgust and prayer dissent and suspend such order of bodies and engagement with the spaces and its artistic treasures.

The basilica is a space of ambivalent and conflictual religious emotions and passions that go from the ecstasy of the Catholic pilgrims to the enchantment and anxiety Pentecostals experience before the terrible beauty of sacred art. In the basilica, Pentecostals navigate amid the disgusting relics, suspicious images, and statues, and they adopt a selective strategy by means of which to direct their sacred gaze, as David Morgan would put it, only on the images capable of elevating them toward the divine. Using what Brian Larkin called *techniques of inattention*, Pentecostals make visual contact only with selected images and architecture.[44] They certainly do not go close to the chapel where the relics are exhibited, but they go to and pray in the chapel of the Blessed Sacrament. Paradoxically a few steps away, the relics threaten them, arouse their fear and disgust, intensify their ambivalent passions, and capture in a breathtaking manner a visceral response that haunts Catholics' devotion and desire for divine presence.

4

Afro-Pentecostal Renaissance

Remediation and Mimesis of Raphael's
Transfigured Christ

*And Jesus came and touched them,
and said, "Arise, and be not afraid."*

—Matthew 17:7, NIV

T HE FIRST TIME I visited the New Life Pentecostal Ministries in Italy was
on a cold night in November 2013. Bishop John, a man of gracious
manners, had invited me to attend the celebration of his church's twenty
years of activity in Italy. New Life Pentecostal Ministries is one of the first
Ghanaian Pentecostal churches in Italy. Bishop John is an economic migrant who left Kumasi in Ghana to work in one of the then flourishing
factories of Northeast Italy. It was during the early years of his experience
as a migrant that he became a pastor. He brought together a small prayer
group in a room provided by a Catholic parish in the town of Vicenza.
Since then this prayer group has expanded to acquire seven sites in Italy,
one in England, and eleven in Kumasi, Ghana. That evening Bishop John
was celebrating the twentieth anniversary of his endeavor.

The headquarters of his church is located in San Vito di Leguzzano,
a small town with a population of approximately 3,600 in the lowlands
near Vicenza. Andrew Esiebo—the photographer with whom I directed
and produced the film *Enlarging the Kingdom: African Pentecostalism in Italy*—and I drove at a snail's pace for nearly an hour and a half through
a dense autumn fog in search of Bishop John's church.[1] After passing
through both tracts of countryside and industrial zones, we finally came

upon the industrial building occupied by the New Life Pentecostal Ministries. It was about seven o'clock in the evening, very dark and cold, with fog so dense you could see clearly no further than a few yards. There was not a thing in sight around the church apart from fields dotted with a few industrial sheds here and there.

By this point, we had already visited about twelve churches in Northeast Italy with a photographer and filmmaker, and we had become used to searching for them hidden away amid grey, half-abandoned suburban and industrial areas around Italy's cities. Many times we found ourselves wandering among industrial sheds and warehouses, trying to identify the churches by following the sounds of prayers and music and the vans shuttling members to and fro. Every time we visited such a church, we experienced the same sequence of sensations: first, malaise in the face of such squalor, then surprise and admiration when we stepped over the threshold to find spaces and altars exploding in colors blending beautifully with the bright African fabrics of the church's elegantly dressed members.

That evening, however, we had no idea of the particular surprise in store for us at the New Life Pentecostal Ministries. After driving through the fog and the flat countryside around Vicenza, we arrived at the shed occupied by the church. We wandered around the outside for at least fifteen minutes trying to find the door. We could hear prayers, so we knew we were in the right place. As we walked around the shed again, we finally came upon a little set of steps leading down into a cellar, with a glass and aluminum door at the end. This was the entrance to the church, and when we opened the door, we suddenly found ourselves to the left of the altar.

The sight before our eyes was astonishing. Here in this cellar, underneath an industrial shed immersed in fog and amid the desolation of an industrial zone, we saw an enormous reproduction of the upper portion of Raphael's *Transfiguration of Christ*, one of the great works of art of the Italian Renaissance, defined by Vasari (Raphael's biographer) as his most famous, the most beautiful and most divine.[2]

In this version, the enormous transfigured Christ, as in the original painting, is depicted ascending through the air with his arms raised. In the painting, the brightness of his robes and the beautiful transparency of the light reveal his divine nature. The figure of Christ shines from within a blindingly white cloud. To the right of Christ, Moses holds the Tablets of the Law, while on the left Elijah holds the Book of Prophecies. At their feet are Peter, James, and John, who appear to be stunned by what they see. They have fallen to the ground, blinded by this splendid vision.

The sight of that painting surprised and confused me. While conducting my research in Nigeria, Ghana, and Italy, I had heard several Pentecostal pastors expressing concern about Catholics' veneration of images and their use of material forms, objects, substances, embodied practices, and gestures. So why had the New Life Pentecostal Ministries chosen to reproduce this particular painting and make it such a focal point of their worship space? Aren't Pentecostals against worshipping images? And why would a reproduction of Raphael's *Transfiguration* so majestically dominate the altar of a Pentecostal African Church?

The painting is undeniably magnificent, but over the course of my research I have come to realize that the reproduction on show in the Vatican and in the New Life Pentecostal Ministries church is more than simply a work of beauty to believers. As I shall explain in more depth in this chapter, the reason is linked to an "obsession" that unites the vision of Raphael, as Christian Kleinbub puts it in his work on Raphael, and the Catholic and Pentecostal religious aesthetics.[3] Before returning to the transfigured Christ in that industrial shed cellar in San Vito di Leguzzano, let us take a step back in time to the studio in which Raphael conceived his masterpiece.

The painting portrays two different episodes of the Bible. The upper portion portrays the transfiguration of Christ. Moses and Elijah flank Jesus; Peter, James, and John are further witnesses. Mark's Gospel depicts the vision transpiring on Mount Tabor, ten miles southeast of Nazareth:

> After six days Jesus took Peter, James and John with him and led them up a high mountain, where they were all alone. There he was transfigured before them. His clothes became dazzling white, whiter than anyone in the world could bleach them. And there appeared before them Elijah and Moses, who were talking with Jesus. Peter said to Jesus, "Rabbi, it is good for us to be here. Let us put up three shelters—one for you, one for Moses and one for Elijah." (He did not know what to say, they were so frightened.) Then a cloud appeared and covered them, and a voice came from the cloud: "This is my Son, whom I love. Listen to him!" Suddenly, when they looked around, they no longer saw anyone with them except Jesus. As they were coming down the mountain, Jesus gave them orders not to tell anyone what they had seen until the Son of Man had risen from the dead. They kept the matter to themselves, discussing what "rising from the dead" meant.[4]

Figure 1. Raphael Transfiguration, ca. 1518–20, oil on panel, about 13 ft. x 9 ft. (4.05 X 2.78 m). Pinacoteca, Vatican Museum (artwork in the public domain). Photograph provided by Scala, Firenze.

The lower part of the painting illustrates the miracle that follows immediately after the transfiguration, in which Jesus heals a boy to demonstrate the power of faith and prayer:

When they came to the other disciples, they saw a large crowd around them and the teachers of the law arguing with them. As soon as all the people saw Jesus, they were overwhelmed with wonder and ran to greet him. "What are you arguing with them about?" he asked. A man in the crowd answered, "Teacher, I brought you my son, who is possessed by a spirit that has robbed him of speech. Whenever it seizes him, it throws him to the ground. He foams at the mouth, gnashes his teeth and becomes rigid. I asked your disciples to drive out the spirit, but they could not." "You unbelieving generation," Jesus replied, "how long shall I stay with you? How long shall I put up with you? Bring the boy to me." So they brought him. When the spirit saw Jesus, it immediately threw the boy into a convulsion. He fell to the ground and rolled around, foaming at the mouth. Jesus asked the boy's father, "How long has he been like this?" "From childhood," he answered. "It has often thrown him into fire or water to kill him. But if you can do anything, take pity on us and help us." "'If you can'?" said Jesus. "Everything is possible for one who believes." Immediately the boy's father exclaimed, "I do believe; help me overcome my unbelief!" When Jesus saw that a crowd was running to the scene, he rebuked the impure spirit. "You deaf and mute spirit," he said, "I command you, come out of him and never enter him again." The spirit shrieked, convulsed him violently and came out. The boy looked so much like a corpse that many said, "He's dead." But Jesus took him by the hand and lifted him to his feet, and he stood up. After Jesus had gone indoors, his disciples asked him privately, "Why couldn't we drive it out?" He replied, "This kind can come out only by prayer and fasting."[5]

Raphael unites both biblical episodes into a single work of art. In the upper portion, the depiction of the transfiguration, the radiant Christ floats in the clouds above the hill, flanked by Moses and Elijah. Below them, lying dazzled and sprawled on the ground, are his disciples and a crowd trying vainly to understand the nature of evil that is tormenting a young boy.[6]

Cardinal Giulio de Medici (1478–1534), who became Pope Clement VII (1523–34), commissioned Raphael to create an altarpiece for the French Cathedral of Narbonne, but the masterpiece never reached the cathedral. When the cardinal saw the painting, he kept it in Rome, and on his accession to the papacy in 1523 gifted it to the Church of San Pietro in Montorio, Rome.[7] In 1774, the new pope, Pius VI (1775–99), had a mosaic copy of it made and installed in Saint Peter's Basilica. Today, the original painting is on display at the Vatican Museums, and a mosaic copy of it is still in Saint Peter's Basilica in the Vatican at one of the altars in the left nave.

Raphael envisaged the *Transfiguration of Christ* at a time of great artistic and religious ferment. The threatening winds of the Reformation that were blowing in Rome were shocking even the creative minds of artists. Artists' studios became places for the elaboration of controversial theological issues that were irremediably dividing Catholics and Reformers. The immanence and transcendence of God was one of the controversial issues that marked this crucial time in the history of religion as well as the artistic, social, and political history of Europe. Reformers were emphasizing the transcendence of God over his immanence, his infinitude over finite forms, and his otherness over his sameness, while the Catholic Church, with its incarnational and sacramental thinking, was emphasizing the immanence of God, and his divine presence and power in images, sacramental objects, and substances.[8] While Reformers condemned and denied any role of these material forms in mediating divine presence (although their attitude was never radically iconoclastic[9]) Catholics openly embraced what Bette Talvacchia has called "the sensuality and the efficacy of carnality" and images, statues, relics, sophisticated liturgy, music, and processions, to access divine presence and power.[10]

In this tumultuous time of theological debates, images played an important role. Protestants either destroyed or kept the use of images under careful doctrinal control while Catholics reaffirmed their religious role in the Council of Trent's 1563 decree "Invocation, Veneration and Relics of Saints and on Sacred Images." The role of art became deeply entangled with the aspirations of artists and the desires of believers to make the divine knowable, visible, tangible, and present.

In his magisterial work *Likeness and Presence*, Hans Belting describes the Renaissance as an epochal time of passage from the cult of images to the cult of art. Images and objects emerged as both visible presence of the sacred and expression of beauty and perfection of art, serving as links between heaven and heart and as the manifestation of artists' ideas and fantasy.[11]

The doctrine of immanence, and especially the incarnational thinking and sacramentality of the Catholic Church, were intersecting theories of art and visuality, religious perceptions and sensation.[12] As Brigitte Miriam Bedos-Rezak writes:

> [The doctrine of the Eucharist] in producing a conflation of sign and thing, disabled the dynamics of reference, and undermined the semiotics of representation. Thus, although strictly speaking this mode of signification pertained only to the Eucharist, the argument for real presence and its principle of immanence ultimately realigned theories of representation with consequences for society as a whole.[13]

Alexander Nagel argued that within these particular theological debates and new artistic scenarios, altarpieces drew believers' eyes, minds, and spirits to the Eucharist, the mystery that inspired in artists, intellectuals, and theologians some of the deepest reflections and artistic production on the immanence of God.

The *Transfiguration of Christ* of Raphael is an extraordinary example of such. In this altarpiece, Raphael articulated his lifelong concern about the relationship between the terrestrial and the celestial, the earthly and the divine, between images and spiritual experience, and as Christian Kleinbub wrote, "the ever pressing problem of how to make the invisible visible in painting."[14]

But the popularity of this painting exceeds its authority in the field of art and theory of vision of the Renaissance. Raphael's *Transfiguration* has for centuries enjoyed incredible attention and admiration.

The painting left Rome only once—and that in the hands of Napoleon. Through the 1797 Treaty of Tolentino, Napoleon imposed on Pope Pius VI huge war fees in the form of money and lands, and forced the Pope to surrender to him several works of art including statues, paintings, and bronzes. Masterpieces of unparalleled value left Italy to go to Paris. From almost each city, Napoleon took the most precious and symbolic masterpieces, and from Rome, among other oeuvres, he wanted the *Transfiguration*. As Martin Rosenberg observed, this special painting became a political instrument to Napoleon, who saw in the masterpiece a power that transcended its beauty.[15] Such power was related to the beauty of the masterpiece but also to the creative power and genius of its creator, Raphael, who Napoleon believed was Italy's greatest artist ever. He was the incarnation of the artistic ideal that Napoleon desired: excellence and superiority. The emperor was not an art critic or expert, but to him, owning such an unparalleled artistic treasure was a means to further enhance his political power. According to Napoleon, the

Transfiguration was the glory of Rome, as the famous sculptor Antonio Canova also commented on the departure of the painting from Rome, and Napoleon wanted desperately to transfer that glory from Rome to Paris. Napoleon planned the arrival of the *Transfiguration* in the most pompous way with a triumphal parade, imitating the practices of the Roman Empire. In this parade, the *Transfiguration* was the first painting in the forty wagons of works of art that Napoleon brought from Rome to Paris, and the only painting that was paraded unveiled and in plain sight. Napoleon deliberately scheduled the arrival of the works on July 27, 1798, to coincide with the anniversary of the fall of Robespierre. Troops, a military band, and wagons with caged bears, lions, and camels accompanied the parade of art treasures.

Napoleon did not intend to use the painting for its spiritual value but to enhance and exhibit his political power through it. Having that painting was a reminder to the world that the Pope had submitted to him and had given Napoleon one of his most precious art pieces, a source of spiritual and political power. To ensure that this message was widely received, Napoleon celebrated the most important rituals of state, including his wedding, beneath the *Transfiguration of Christ* in the Napoleonic museum.[16]

Napoleon saw in the image not only a symbol of the glory of Rome but also a part of Rome's "machine" of governance. While devising his strategy to defeat the Pope and impose his Tolentino Treaty, he wrote: "My opinion is that Rome, once deprived of Bologna, Ferrara, the Romagna, and the thirty millions we are taking from her, can no longer exist. The old machine will go to pieces of itself."[17] To him, the machine was made up of economic power and lands, but also of the ownership and possession of eternal masterpieces. And he wanted to appropriate part of this machine, or as Christopher Johns puts it in his work on the intimate relationship between art and politics in papal Rome, he wanted the "papal arsenal," such as his unparalleled masterpieces.[18]

Remediation, Immediacy, and Mimesis

The person who reproduced the upper portion of the *Transfiguration of Christ* that now hangs in the New Life Pentecostal Ministries church is Isaac, a member of the church, a Ghanaian man in his forties from Kumasi. Isaac arrived in Italy in 1999. When he left Ghana, he was a student of science and technology at the University of Kumasi. He had always been passionate about art and had a flair for drawing and painting. After spending several years in art studies in his primary and secondary education, Isaac understood that art was not going to pay his bills, and so he decided to put his passion aside and focus on a field of study that was more likely to lead to a decently paying job. Although he was Anglican, he attended a Catholic secondary school, considered to be the best in the city.

When he started his first year at the university, he realized that his family was struggling to support him, so he decided to continue his study in Europe, where he thought he could support his studies on his own. He told me he had intended to go to an English-speaking country, but when the first visa granted to him came from the Italian embassy, he decided not to delay and left:

> When I arrived in Italy, I realized that I could not continue my study. Language barriers and lack of information about migration law affected my plan, and I decided to start looking for a job, as most of us do in these cases. I wanted to do something related to my love for art and images, and I was lucky enough to find a job in the graphic and printing industry. However, because of the economic crisis, the printing company, which was a hundred years old, had to close down. I worked there for eight years. I then found another job in another printing images company and I stayed there until also this company closed down.

It was when he moved to the city of Vicenza for a job at the second printing company that he began attending the New Life Pentecostal Ministries. The church, and especially its founder, Bishop John, welcomed his artful membership and invited him to decorate the altar of the headquarters in San Vito di Leguzzano.

But the *Transfiguration* was not the first image he made to decorate the altar. His first work was a huge dove. However, after a while he realized that something was missing from that image:

> I was trying to get some images that could be more powerful and poignant, that would speak to people's spirit. The Holy Spirit is powerful, but our salvation doesn't come from the Holy Spirit. Our salvation comes from Christ, so our focus should be on Jesus Christ. I was also thinking that I have seen many images of Christ on the cross but I did not want to give a message on the suffering of Christ. Of course, Christ died for us and suffered for us to redeem us, but he also brought us to a new level.

This level is glory. Jesus says, "I go to the Father to prepare a place for you so that where I come you also come" (John 14:3). I did not have images from this place, heaven, because I have not been there. But we know that the moment when Christ is transformed is the highest image close to heaven. The transfiguration was the point at which Jesus showed us his nature.

In describing his project for the altar, Isaac added:

I wanted an image of the transfiguration and was looking for the most beautiful image, and when I saw this one, I felt that it was speaking to me. I wanted to create the perception that Jesus is here, that people could touch him and experience His glory.

Interestingly, both Raphael and Isaac had a similar vision concerning their altarpieces. Raphael wanted an image that could invoke a beatific vision. He wanted to make the invisible visible. Isaac, the Ghanaian contemporary artist, wanted more than this. He wanted to make the invisible Jesus not only visible but also tangible and, as we shall see, also audible. To realize his kinesthetic and multisensuous presence, he remediated the original painting of Raphael.

Let me unpack what a remediation is by first recalling the meaning of *mediation*. As discussed in the introductory chapter, mediation is the process through which people create and perceive the divine and the supernatural through the body, the senses, and material forms such as objects, images, and substances. A mediation generates a sense of immediacy and the conflation of spirit and matter, and the breaking down of distance between signifier and signified.[19] A remediation is the refashioning or re-purposing of a medium. In other words, it means to take a property from one medium and reuse it in another.[20] According to David Bolter and Richard Grusin, authors of the book *Remediation: Understanding New Media*, remediations occur when media are faced with new challenges and desire of immediacy as they manifest in diverse times and societies:

Each new medium is justified because it fills a lack or repairs a fault in its predecessor, because it fulfills the unkept promise of an older medium. . . . In each case that inadequacy is represented as a lack of immediacy, and this seems to be generally true in the history of remediation. Photography was supposedly more immediate than painting, film than photography, television than film, and now virtual reality fulfills the promise of immediacy and supposedly ends the progression.[21]

In this passage of their book, Bolter and Grusin traced the historicity of remediations starting from painting and ending (for now, at least) in virtual reality. In another passage of their book, they take a further step back and locate the first historical stage of remediation as words remediated by images.[22] By following Bolter and Grusin, one can therefore look at the painting of the transfigured Christ at the New Life Pentecostal Ministries as a remediation of a remediation because Raphael himself remediated the events narrated in the Bible into an image, thus fulfilling the failed promise that words could convey the magnitude of the glory of the transfiguration.

Isaac's remediation is surprising and intriguing for several reasons. To remediate the original painting, the artist of the New Life Pentecostal Ministries did something more than just reproduce the upper portion of the painting on a larger scale. To generate the perception of Jesus's multisensuous presence, he placed a special lighting system behind the image of Jesus. He described his project as follows:

> I saw that with this one I could play with color and light. For special events and prayer, we put on the light and we create the right environment to feel the presence of God. The light and the image help to create the perception of his presence. Whenever we put on that light you see people, sort of, they get to the understanding, the impression . . . of Christ's presence. That light creates the atmosphere to perceive the presence of Christ here. We do not do this all the time. Only at special events and when it is dark outside.

Isaac repurposed Raphael's painting in a refashioned way. He appropriated and manipulated part of it by enlarging it, and included another medium in it. To Isaac, the light is meant to enhance the splendor of the white garments of Jesus and to create the optical effect of Jesus stepping out of the painting and moving toward the people to encounter and touch them.

Having been part of one of those special events, I know that the light behind the image of Jesus creates a very strong effect. But, as I could observe during my fieldwork at the New Life Pentecostal Ministries, the power of the image lies in more than the genius of Raphael and the creativity of Isaac; the space, the people, the sounds, and the gestures of prayer are also an integral part of this intriguing remediation of Jesus's real presence.

On the evening I attended a service, Bishop John was standing at the altar with two other pastors—the Nigerian Reverend Michel and Pastor Frank. Bishop John and Pastor Frank were dressed in their church's blue and white garments of praise, made of African fabric and printed with the emblem and the name of the church. From where I sat, I watched Bishop John and the other two pastors praying ardently, urging the audience to express their heartfelt prayers with their words and bodies. The three pastors, their arms raised skyward, invoked the power of the Holy Spirit while the congregation, as their bodies leaned forward and arms extended toward the altar, opened their hands as if to receive divine power. The most intense moment was the collective prayer at the end of the sermon. Those praying called upon the power of the Holy Spirit to heal the faithful of their physical, spiritual, and social afflictions. The sound of their voices was deafening. Reverend Michael, standing at the left of Bishop John, was praying with great vehemence and passion, the sound of his voice amplified by a microphone on at full volume. Amid all the noise, I caught the odd word in English—such as *Ghana*, *Nigeria*, *work*, *family*, *visa*, *hospital*, *passport*, *residence permit*, *wedding*, *money*—as if the life story of this community in prayer was bubbling to the surface on that powerful sound wave.

Their shouting and the emotions triggered by their prayers contorted the faces of the faithful. Their bodies seem to be alive with a supernatural energy as they trembled, twisted, and turned, some of them dropping to the floor. Their body movements brought the colors of their clothes to life, and the patterns on the African fabrics seemed to dissolve and form an indistinct aura of color at the foot of the altar. As the temperature rose in the room and the sweaty smell of so many bodies intensified, one person hurled himself to the floor, displacing whole rows of people like dominoes falling.

All this intense physical, emotional, and vocal participation of the community of the faithful was happening surrounded by the squalor of the industrial suburbs of a provincial town in northeast Italy, at the foot of Raphael's remediated *Transfiguration*. In the intensity of that moment, I looked toward the altar and noticed the remarkable alignment between Bishop John, standing in the middle of the altar and praying with his arms outstretched and raised to the sky, and Raphael's Christ transfigured. Bishop John's tunic was of the same blue-white hue as Christ's robes, and a spotlight lit up Bishop John's face from left to right, exactly in the same way as the light falling on Raphael's painting of Christ. Alongside Bishop John, Reverend Michael gripped the microphone while the other pastor lead the prayers accompanied with arm gestures.

Figure 2. New Life Pentecostal Ministries, Italy. Photograph by
Andrew Esiebo.

The three pastors presided over the altar just as Christ, Elijah, and Moses presided over the scene painted by Raphael. I was not the only one who noticed this extraordinary moment. Andrew Esiebo, the photographer and filmmaker who was with me that evening, saw the same thing and captured the moment with his camera.[23]

The picture shows Bishop John with his lifted hands miming the gestures and the gaze of the dazzling Renaissance Jesus. The scenario conveyed by this mimesis is extraordinarily creative. The bishop, perfectly overlapping Jesus, seems to replace him in the painting, creating a stunning living Afro-Pentecostal Renaissance art piece in which the transfigured Christ on Mount Tabor is turned into an ecstatic Ghanaian pastor dressed in bright African textiles.

The overlapping figures of Bishop John and the transfigured Christ can be understood as an emblematic example of what Michael Taussig called *mimesis*.[24] According to Taussig, mimesis is the ability "to copy, to imitate, to yield into and to become Other" in such a way that the copy draws power from and influences the original.[25] He added, "The wonder of mimesis lies in the copy drawing on the character and power of the original, to the point whereby the representation may even assume that character and that power."[26] But mimes can be even more than this. As Paul Stoller argued, mimesis is also an act of political creation, or an "embodied opposition," through which the power of "the other" becomes tangible, accessible, and consequently available to appropriation and manipulations.[27]

At the New Life Pentecostal Ministries, Bishop John's mimesis of the transfigured Christ makes present, visible, tangible, and especially, appropriable the saving and healing power of Jesus. By miming the physical and kinesthetic features of Raphael's Jesus, the Bishop appropriates his power to deliver from evil and glorify those who stand in his presence. Through this mimesis, Bishop John temporarily suspends the boundaries between his human condition and divine power, becoming himself a living presence of the healing, saving, and glorified and glorifying Jesus.

But this is not the only mimesis that took place. At the foot of the altar, the congregation seemed to give form and presence to the crowd at the foot of Mount Tabor that Isaac did not reproduce in his remediation of the *Transfiguration* of Raphael. Maybe he knew that that crowd was going to appear anyway via the praying bodies of the congregation.

To Raphael, the crowd expressed the contrasting views on spiritual visions of the Renaissance: The young boy suffers under the grip of a mysterious force that only a few people recognize. How and where to search for his deliverance and salvation? Who will be able to see the beatific and salvific vision of Christ?

As Kleinbub explains, the painting represents "the battle between two worldviews: a confrontation between the empirically minded, who are bent on external explanations, and those of higher spiritual wisdom."[28] In this way, the painting creates a unique narrative of rationality and spiritual passion, suffering and joy, vision and blindness, damnation and salvation.[29] It depicts a continuum of two opposite poles in constant interaction: the search for salvation of those who have imperfect faith and earthly wisdom and vainly seek salvation in doctrine, and those who are able to see with their spiritual eyes and experience the beatific visions of Jesus.

The crowd depicted by Raphael at the foot of Mount Tabor is in search of deliverance from evil, much as the people gathered at the foot of the altar in the Pentecostal church seek deliverance from spiritual and social afflictions. With their bodies, their raised hands, their emotions and passions, the members of the church mime the movements of the agitated crowd depicted by Raphael that with their gestures, faces, and gazes express their contemplation of spiritual things, wonderment, and visionary ecstasy. This is what I was able to observe in the praying congregation.

Raphael's altarpiece and message seems to take on life at the New Life Pentecostal Ministries, and it becomes inextricable from the religious aesthetics and everyday spiritual and social needs of the congregation.

At the church, a series of media open up various windows to divine power. Bodies, gestures, sounds, touch, and colors together create multisensorial perceptions and experiences of the divine that seems to move from the painting throughout the space, to reach out and touch the bodies of the people, to shock them even to the point of making them fall to the floor. In those moments, bodies are both recipients and channels of divine power. They receive this power, speak in tongues, tremble, and shake, and consequently themselves become media and manifestations of such power. The remediation therefore reaches its full cycle in a hypermediated sensuous mimesis.

The Unstable Image and the Danger of Likeness

Both Pentecostals and Catholics used the *Transfiguration of Christ* to mediate or evoke the divine presence of Jesus, but despite this, Isaac and Bishop John were very rigorous in distancing themselves from Catholic devotional practices.

Isaac's comment on Catholic worship of images is particularly interesting. He is very familiar with Catholic religious iconography. He was a student at a Catholic school and regularly attended Catholic Mass, prayer, and celebrations there. Over the course of time, he became very used to Catholic religious paraphernalia and devotional practices, but he never identified himself as Catholic. When I interviewed him, he was very firm in stating that Catholics "go [a] little bit far" when it comes to devotional practices. But then, what is the boundary between admiration or contemplation of an image and idol worshiping? When does the relationship with images go too far? According to Isaac, the transfigured Jesus is an image able to successfully mediate divine presence only in certain circumstances:

> The true worshipper of God worships in truth and spirit. Wherever you are, if you have God in your spirit, you close your eyes and say, God, I am with you. You don't need altars or other images to do it. When you begin to think that you can see God only when you come here, it means you are making [the painting] an idol.

Isaac's statement reveals an intriguing aspect of Pentecostal iconography, such as the unsteady status of the images, which can both mediate good and evil power and therefore become idols.

In her study on the image of Jesus in Ghana, Birgit Meyer showed how the unstable epistemic nature of images, including images of Jesus, is embedded in a dualistic structure of good and evil whereby images of Jesus can "accommodate," or mediate, evil and can function to mask evil forces and idols.[30] But as Meyer argued, what turns a sacred painting into an idol is not intrinsic to the image but depends on the aesthetic formations that include a certain beholder's gaze, and authorized and unauthorized form of mediality, which are part of historicized and contextualized cultural and social practices.

As Hans Belting argued in his work, every aesthetic that serves an institution has its own mediality that establishes the rules concerning the status, power, and possibility of various media or material forms (be they images, statues, substances such as oil and water, or relics), and the hierarchy of the senses through which to engage such forms.[31] Each mediation of divine power and presence is accomplished through practices in which material forms, sensations, feelings, time, space, and bodies have their precise roles and possibilities enshrined in conventions, institutions, and traditions. Violations or modifications of such rules can result in an altered mediation that invokes evil forces rather than divine power.

At the New Life Pentecostal Ministries, there are rules that fix the status of the image of the transfiguration. Isaac says, "When we study the Bible, in the Old Testament, God was specific about worship of images. We don't have to worship images. One of the things that God does not approve is the worshiping of idols instead of him. Here we don't allow people to worship this image. You don't see people going to the altar and bowing down." According to Isaac, there is a sort of control over the engagement of bodies and gestures that might destabilize the status of the image. Going to the altar and bowing down is one of them.

When describing body gestures that are not authorized or acceptable, Pentecostals often make reference to Catholic devotional practices. When I asked both Isaac and Bishop John about the presence of the image of Jesus at the altar, they felt the urge immediately to clarify that what they do is not like what the Catholics do.

Isaac noted, "Here in Italy, there are times that you enter in the Catholic churches and you see people worshiping statues and kissing their feet. I think that is going a little bit . . . far! It means they are paying homage to those statues. God doesn't want this."

The statues of Catholic saints, Madonnas, and Jesus seem to make these Pentecostals extremely uncomfortable. Yet in Italy they have found themselves totally immersed in a religious material culture and aesthetic regime in which images, and especially statues, are intrinsic to religious practices. Catholics display statues of saints, Jesus, and Madonnas in churches, public squares and buildings, hospitals, schools, and home altars, and they proudly take these statues with them on processions, as I also described in the previous chapter. To Pentecostals, such paying homage, bowing down, kissing, and touching images or statues is very similar to the way people pay homage to idols of African traditional religions. Although Pentecostals reject the authority of these idols, they nonetheless also acknowledge their evil power as well as the power of a certain aesthetic engagement with the material forms mediating the idols. In fact, the power of these statues is not inherent to their material forms and shapes but needs a certain human agency to become active and effective.[32] After the statue of an idol has been crafted, it depends on the body gestures and rituals (such as the offerings of food, smoke, drinks, dancing, music) to give it power—the same power that will eventually act upon those people who create it.

To defeat the power of the idols, Pentecostals reject both the material forms that give shape to the idols (they burned and destroyed wood and clay statues) and also reject and condemn the aesthetics and sensual engagement with such material form.[33] Their battle was—and still is—with the material forms and the aesthetic regime.

For example, engaging the picture with the wrong body gestures—as Isaac also noted concerning the image of the transfiguration in his church—can destabilize the nature of the picture and turn it into an idol. But if the picture is in the right space, such as the church, the service or the event is happening, and the pastor is there as the authority, then it is very unlikely that the picture will turn into an idol. This means that bodily engagement, space, time, and authority are crucial to control the epistemic nature of the picture.

Interestingly, Catholicism also includes aesthetic regimes that control the epistemic nature of pictures. According to the contemporary art critic Marco Agostini, the original image of the *Transfiguration of Christ* changed its "ability to speak" when it was moved from the altar of the church to the museum:

> A work of sacred art placed in a museum, even with the best of intentions and perhaps better protected, loses three quarters of its ability to speak only for the fact that is located outside of the context for which it was created. Today, in the Art Gallery, the Transfiguration is only an object, although among the most excellent, aligned between many, but without the power that comes from being part of the liturgical mystery in the space of the prayer.[34]

This indicates not only that Pentecostals and Catholics share a similar *sacred gaze*, as David Morgan would put it, but that, in the particular case I explored, they also share the same image to mediate divine presence.[35] Despite Pentecostals' critique of the Catholic use of images, the case of the remediation of the *Transfiguration of Christ* shows that in Pentecostalism, images certainly are intrinsic to their religious practices, albeit in distinct ways.

The Catholic and Pentecostal sacred gaze is part of two religious aesthetics of presence that involve images, spaces, organized liturgies or prayers, and religious authorities aimed at policing conformity within the aesthetic order. The case of the *Transfiguration* is an example of this. Both Catholics and Pentecostals similarly use the painting as an altarpiece to mediate the real presence of Jesus.

When the original painting was over the altar of the church of Saint Pietro in Montorio and in the basilica at the Vatican, it was part of the mystery of the Eucharist. According to Agostini, the host lifted by the priest perfectly overlapped the white garments of Jesus, allowing both priest and devotee to experience the beatific vision of the host fading into the brightness of Jesus's vestment.[36] The same host was thereafter ingested, allowing the transfigured Jesus to eventually be in communion with the bodies of the faithful in a sublimated state of silence and meditation, permeated by the perfumes of incense and old wood.

The New Life Pentecostal Ministries remediated the transfigured Jesus in such a way that Jesus seems to step out of the painting and walk toward the faithful, to fade into the praying bodies of the pastors and make them shake, vibrate, and fall to the floor.

There are certainly differences between the Catholic and Pentecostal aesthetic styles and engagement with the pictures. When the original picture was at San Pietro in Montorio, the sight and hearing of the faithful were immersed in the artworks of prominent sixteenth- and seventeenth-century masters, such as Sebastiano del Piombo, Michelangelo, Niccolò Circignani, as well as Renaissance frescoes of Giulio Mazzoni and Pinturicchio. The silence was revered while the priest raised the host, which looked as if it were fading into the white garments of Jesus. The smell of incense, old wood, and the burning wax of the candles wafted through the air while the mouths of the faithful anticipated the sweet taste of the wafer host.

At the New Life Pentecostal Ministries, the remediated image is immersed in a vibrant soundscape made of ardent prayers; speaking in tongues; amplified voices of the pastors; the music and songs of the choir; the energy and touch of the congregation, its movements, colorful African textiles, and murmurings of adoration and supplication.

Catholic and Pentecostal aesthetics seem to be governed by a diverse intensity and hierarchy of the senses. In the Catholic Church the gaze on the image and on the overwhelming works of art follows the taste of the host while the smell of the incense and the "sound of silence" waft in the air. There is no touch apart from the one of the ingestion of the host.

At the event I attended at the New Life Pentecostal Ministries, what predominated was the gaze on the image, the overpowering sound of prayer, and the inevitable touch of the moving congregation. The congregation didn't ingest any substance and the pastors did not use any incense or perfume to engage the sense of smell, although the air was certainly filled with the scent of the praying bodies.

But the image was for both groups the focus and locus of the hypermediated sensuous mimesis. However, in the Pentecostal Church, the transfigured Christ has a specific eschatological and political meaning.

The Theological and the Artful Political

Although it was conceived in a tiny studio in Rome more than five hundred years ago, the *Transfiguration of Christ* has crossed the boundaries of time and space. In his comments about the big transfigured Christ by his altar, Bishop John told me: "This image ensures the presence of Christ and reminds us about his glorified body, his resurrection, and also our resurrection. When this will happen, we will not have this body, my black skin, your white skin. We will have the same color. No more black and white, no more discrimination and racism, no more Italians and Ghanaians."

As he said "black skin and white skin." Bishop John showed me the color of his hands and put them close to my small white hands. He describes a time to come when neither there will be Italians nor Ghanaians, but freedom from the burden of citizenship and nationalities, freedom from imposed social suffering and from what Jacques Derrida called the "violent hierarchy" of binary oppositions (black/white, Ghanaians/Italians), in other words, a move beyond their bodies while remaining within them.[37] Through the remediated transfiguration of Christ, Pentecostals envision a new humanity to come: a humanity with no race and nationality that dwells in the space described by Mark Lewis Taylor as *transimmanence*, a time of

> existence refusing to be locked in a place, locked down in systems that resist continual opening and reopening. It is a kind of passing, a traversing of manifolds and relations of immanence, which can be discerned especially along the boundaries making agonistic strife between the powers that seek to dispose of weaker peoples and those peoples who resist being so disposed.[38]

After so many centuries, the image in the *Transfiguration* still reveals Raphael's visionary project to people who are attuned to experience a spiritual and beatific vision. Today, African Pentecostals in Italy are turning this Renaissance image of Jesus into a transcultural, transnational, and transracial image that collides with and dissolves social boundaries, that critiques and suspends nationalities and hierarchies, divisions, and conventions, creating the possibility of imagining a new social and spiritual order.

As I discussed in the previous chapter, African Pentecostals in Italy carry the imposed weight of blackness and nationality. They are weighted with agonistic tension. The agonistic, according to Taylor, is the condition of human pain and suffering, the agony and the struggle of the dispossessed, the spectral existence of those who are "the part that has no part," as he writes, quoting Rancière.[39]

Although Pentecostals use the image of the *Transfiguration* as an altarpiece as Catholics did in the past to mediate a divine presence, there is a difference between the Catholic and Pentecostal socioeschatological meaning of the transfigured Christ. As Kleinbub argued, the original *Transfiguration of Christ* was conceived as the end of a "devotional program," or a spiritual journey that culminates in the beatific vision of God experienced by the blessed in paradise. Raphael wanted to anticipate this vision to the extent that he himself experienced it in his final creative effort. Kleinbub writes:

> It was thus natural for Vasari [the painter, art historian, and biographer] to imagine Raphael taking part in a spiritual exercise that moved the artist so close to the actual beatific vision that he, in fact, completed it by dying. Like Dante, Vasari's Raphael had attained the lofty vision for himself, but having revealed it to his fellow men in his greatest painting, he passed back over to the beyond.[40]

In short, the transfigured Christ was conceived as an anticipation of the glory and beatitude that humankind will enjoy after death.

But to Pentecostals, the glory of Jesus, visible and tangible through the remediated image, creates a transimmanence, a here-and-now liberation from the bondages of race and nationality, a new dimension of social existence, a suspended space between the transcendence and the immanence that is, as Wariboko argued, the very ethos of Pentecostalism.[41] The transfigured Christ invokes an immediate experience of deliverance from social and spiritual affliction, of glory despite suffering, freedom despite bondage, honor despite shame, and prosperity despite poverty and lack.

Their transfigured Jesus is an artful theological and political statement. But here theology is not about doctrine and dogmas; it is the theological with a small *t* elaborated by Lewis Taylor in his work *The Theological and the Political*: "[The theological] traces and theorizes the ways that persons and groups rendered subordinate and vulnerable by agonistic politics and its systemic imposed social suffering, nevertheless haunt, unsettle and perhaps dissolve the structures of those systems."[42] The theological is the creative way people dwell in the transimmanence, the fluid space and moment of sense making in which the divine and the diverse conditions of human existence coexist and interpenetrate, like in a sacred mimesis.

The Pentecostals' remediation and mimesis of the *Transfiguration of Christ* in Italy become an embodied political statement. Their oppositional statement doesn't take place in the realms of government, party politics, or the conventional arenas of political debates. Neither is their opposition consciously articulated or explicitly declared. However, the fact that their dissent is not open and addressed directly to the authorities that police the hegemonic social order they inhabit doesn't make it less relevant.

In this regard, Jean Comaroff elaborated one of the most poignant analyses of conscious and unconscious political practices of opposition to hegemonic orders. In the concluding remarks of her book on the Thsidi religious practices of appropriations and bricolage of the European socioreligious system, she wrote:

> The failure to recognize that there exist mechanisms capable of reproducing the political order independently of direct intervention has condemned us to ignore a whole range of conduct concerned with power, defining the political only in terms of a "preconstructed object" foisted on our science by our own ideological categories. As it is with politics, so with resistance. We cannot confine our assessment of historical practice to the utilitarian operations of tangible domination or explicit opposition.[43]

In the same way, Pentecostals' remediation and mimesis is not an explicit political opposition to their subordinated position in the hierarchical order of the Italian society but a prodigious art form that turns the painting into a contact zone, a transcultural space, in which the powerless suspend social hierarchies and break the boundaries of time and space.

Interestingly, Pentecostals do it using an image that is particularly important for the Italian artistic heritage and Catholic religious history.

Raphael's *Transfiguration* has long been part of the Catholic Church's conspicuous artistic capital and a powerful and spectacular medium of the mystery of the Eucharist. When I asked Isaac whether he knew the story of Raphael's painting and its contemporary location, he seemed to know very little. He only knew that a similar masterpiece was probably at the Vatican:

> I never saw the original, but considering that it is a Raphael painting, that this is a very important art work, and has a very powerful spiritual messages . . . I guess [it] is in the Vatican. I know that they keep all the important pieces in the Vatican. [The] Vatican is spiritual and artistic. The things you see in the Vatican, you cannot see them anywhere. I did not study Italian art, but I knew that great artists come from Italy, especially sacred art.

Isaac did not know that another copy of Raphael's *Transfiguration* is in Saint Peter's Basilica. He did not know the whole story of the painting, of Pope Clement who, after seeing the masterpiece, did not send it to France; of Napoleon who took it from the Pope, unperturbed and indeed thrilled to take away the glory of a religious empire and the genius of Renaissance Italy. And yet Isaac guessed that this spiritual and artistically powerful image could only be in the hands of the Catholic Church.

Pentecostals' prodigious art recalls the everyday practices observed by Michel de Certeau. Those are the practices of the weak, of the apparently passive marginal and subjugated subjects that creatively use space, time, and material worlds of the order that is oppressing them, and turn them into opportunity. De Certeau looked at these practices over a long historical period ranging from colonial history to contemporary everyday activities. Concerning the colonial era, he described the tactic of the colonized under Spanish colonization:

> Submissive, and even consenting to their subjection, the Indians nevertheless often made of the rituals, representations, and laws imposed on them something quite different from what their conquerors had in mind; they subverted them not by rejecting or altering them, but by using them with respect to ends and references foreign to the system they had no choice but to accept.[44]

The condition experienced by African Pentecostals in Italy is certainly different from the colonized described by de Certeau, but what is similar are the procedures of consumption. As de Certeau argues, these are ways of doing things, little victories of the "weak" over the "strong," to get away with things through joyful discoveries, that are "poetic as well as warlike."[45]

Conclusion

*Jesus saith unto her, Touch me not; for I am not yet ascended
to my Father.*

—John 20:17, KJV

W HEN AS PART of my fieldwork in Rome I attended evening services at the Mountain of Fire and Miracles Ministries, I experienced very intense moments of prayer. The church, famous for its aggressive and even violent prayer, teaches its members to pray as if they
had to convince the Holy Spirit as well as evil powers to surrender to
their fury—"by fire or by force," as the church states. After attending
Sunday services, evening prayer meetings, and special events, I learned
that when the pastor says, "Open your mouth and pray!" I had to be
particularly aware of who was standing beside, behind, and before me.
Anything could happen at those times, including being knocked down
by believers manifesting the presence and power of the Holy Spirit or
fighting against evil forces that seemed to materialize before their eyes.

One time, one of the pastors of the church asked me, "*Oyinbo*,[1] what
do you think about our prayer? Do you think we are crazy?" I candidly
answered him, "No. I grew up with people who sometimes prayed like
this." "Ah! You grew up Pentecostal then!" he said with surprise. "No,
Catholic," I replied. My answer made his sweet smile fade. Another
time, something similar happened with another pastor, but his response
was, "*Oyinbo*, you need deliverance!"

Through my research I learned that suggesting to a Pentecostal that
Pentecostalism has much in common with Catholicism tends to rile him
or her. Indeed, this affirmation questions the fundamental conviction
that Pentecostalism is protestant and therefore has little in common
with Catholicism.

In this book I have highlighted what Roman Catholicism and African Pentecostalism have in common. I have also shed light on the paradox of Pentecostal anti-Catholicism and Catholic anti-Pentecostalism, and I focused on the catholicity, or sacramentality, that manifest in both Catholics and Pentecostals aesthetics of presence.

More than twenty years ago, Harvey Cox talked about the commonality between Catholicism and Pentecostalism. In his magisterial work *Fire from Heaven*, referring to the work of Francisco Rolim,[2] Cox wrote: "Pentecostalism is not Protestantism. It is what another writer calls 'Catholicism without priests,' a radical religious symbolic movement that could eventually bring a thorough-going, even revolutionary change to the South American continent."[3]

Rolim also said that folk Catholicism in Latin America was a kind of staging ground, a personal and cultural preparation for Pentecostalism. In a similar way, despite Pentecostals harsh rejection of African tradition religions, I argue that African traditional religions prepared the ground for Pentecostalism in Africa. As in Latin America, also on the African Continent, Pentecostalism brought a massive cultural and religious revolution, as several scholars have shown.[4] Pentecostalism did emerge as a new form of Christianity and as a new political and ethical project, but its gritty materiality and enchanted expectations blossomed from the seeds of sacramentality of African traditional religions. For this reason, African traditional religions keep haunting African Pentecostalism in a way similar to how pagan religions keep haunting Roman Catholicism in Italy. Both Roman Catholicism and African Pentecostalism have in them the sacramental seed of traditional and pagan religions, and the more they reject this embryonic presence, the more they feel its power. Intriguingly, African Pentecostals see this presence and power in the idolatrous practices of the Catholics, and the suspicious Catholics see it in Pentecostalism. So if Pastor Sola in talking about Catholicism said, "We know what all that is because we have seen it in African traditional religions" a suspicious Catholic priest refered to Pentecostalism as "a mix of Christianity and African traditional religion."

In Italy the sacramentality of African Pentecostalism, African traditional religions, popular piety, and Roman Catholicism pulls these diverse religious expressions into perpetual confrontations. In this European contact zone, these religious expressions are like wires that convey a current that, when they inadvertently come into contact with one another, produce religious short circuits. The current is their common sacramentality and their deep longing for real presences that they can see, touch, hear, smell, and taste. Sparks appear in the form of conflicts, and smoke arises in the form of paradoxes, ambiguities, and contradictions, such as Catholic priests being skeptical about Pentecostal practices of deliverance from evil spirit but also afraid of being touched by the pastors' "powerful" hands. Ambiguities also emerge from the Pentecostal side, such as when Pentecostals make use of images, at times the same images that are displayed in Catholic churches, but say that they are not like the idolatrous Catholics that worship images. As I show in this book, the locus of these ambiguities and contradictions rests in the impossible immateriality of their aesthetics of presence and in the different way through which Catholics and Pentecostals authorize a certain use of images, body gestures, and sensations to mediate real presences.

Intriguingly, in Italy several Pentecostal aesthetics of presence incorporate Catholics spaces, including the empty parish halls, as well as the basilica of the Saint Anthony where Pentecostals go to pray, cautiously avoiding visual contact with the relics of the saint and other images and statues that, according to them, might conceal the real presence of evil forces. These aesthetics also incorporate a wide range of objects, images, and substance that are also used as sacramental objects in Catholicism. In a way that seems to be much more Catholic than Protestant, Pentecostals load images and objects with great power, both good and evil, but power nonetheless. The real presences that African Pentecostals generate or perceive are various forms of divine power as well as evil powers. It can be the Holy Spirit, or divine *potencia*, that flows through the olive oil, holy water, the host for the healing communion, or evil forces that can possess human bodies or dwell in various material forms, including relics and the statues of Catholic saints.Through their poietic and, at times, poetic religious aesthetics, Pentecostals give a material and finite form to the indefinite beyond, and they sublimate their intimate and visceral desire to spell the invisible.

The Sensuous Anarchic Presence

My ultimate question is: What is at stake with the materialization of the beyond and with the aesthetics of presence? Orsi argued, "Once made material, the invisible can be negotiated and bargained with, touched and kissed, made to bear human anger and disappointment, as we have seen in men and women's relationships with the saints."[5]

To be able to negotiate and bargain with these real presences, both Catholics and Pentecostals give them material forms that respond to the vibrations of human sensations, desires, and passions. Catholics and Pentecostals not only want to touch the untouchable; they want to be touched back. Pentecostals and Catholics bring to these material and embodied presences, not only human joy and pain, but also the very aesthetics of a human sensorium. Catholics talk to the saints, offer them flowers and candles, and on special occasions make them presents such as jewelry, money, and dresses. To Catholics, the saints can become happy, sad, and even terribly mad at them. And the more their statues and images look real, the more intense and sensuous seems to be Catholics' relationship to them.[6]

The anthropologists Taussig and Stoller call this process *sensuous mimesis*, a faculty of imitation and deployment of that faculty in sensuous knowing, or sensuous othering, that turns the otherness into sameness.[7]

In his provocative work, Slavoj Žižek also talks about the power of sameness. He argued that the incarnation of Christ was an epochal achievement of Christianity. This was a crucial moment in which humanity reduced otherness into sameness and generated an extraordinary and exceptional political event of disruption of the old cosmology. In the new beginning, the "Big Other" (such as God) became "just another human being, as miserable and indiscernible from other humans with regard to his intrinsic properties."[8] To Žižek, the end of the transcendence of the "Big Other," the incarnation of Christ, is the very perverse core of Christianity: to turn God into a mortal human, a man among other men. In this context, Žižek tells the story of three men who find themselves together and brag to each other: "I was thrown to the lions in the arena for believing in Christ," and "I was burned at the stake for ridiculing Christ," and "I died on the Cross, and I *am* Christ!"[9]

In this sense, the making of the real presence of the divine and the supernatural marks the ultimate liberation of humankind from the unreachable and untouchable. This is indeed also the perverse core of the aesthetics of presence: the liberation from "the Big Other."

The aesthetics of presence that I describe in this book are ephemeral events that disrupt and invert the relations of power between human beings and the divine and the supernatural through which humanity experiences new and infinite possibilities of radical freedom and play with the Big Other.[10]

There are intense excesses of life in these aesthetics, and they are part of what Harvey Cox has called *primal spirituality*,[11] a dimension that passes through religions and times and across Catholicism, Pentecostalism, and African traditional religions.[12] It is not a form of regression to what might be considered primitive spirituality according to a Western and Weberian hierarchical evolutionary approach to religion, as Orsi and Meyer argued in their work. *Primal* refers to a deep, visceral, fetal dimension of human's desire to overcome the limits of human existence. As Žižek pointed out, the too-much life is what Kant refers to as *uncanny unruliness*; it is the indiscipline against the law of culture, organizations, institutions, and hierarchies that seeks to give transcendence a suprasensible dimension.[13]

The often paradoxical, contradictory, fragmentary aesthetics of presence that I present in this book are indeed sensuously undisciplined and often lyrically anarchic. They dwell in the irreducible tension that withstands authorities, doctrines, and dogmas, and that defines the relationship between human beings and the invisible, indefinite, and infinite beyond. Aesthetics of presence are poetically disruptive of the spiritual order and provide audacious forms of freedom from the limit of possibility of humanity to act on divinity.

This freedom and power is intrinsic to Pentecostalism, Catholicism, and also African traditional religion, as Wariboko nicely showed in the story of the dismissal of the Owu Akpana cult (the shark cult) by the Kalabari people, the inhabitants of New Calabar (Elem Kalabari) in present day Rivers State. The story goes as follows:

> Monday, 18th September 1857, [I] went up to [New] Calabar town this morning and while there heard that the chief had a meeting in their palaver house yesterday, in consequence of several of the natives having been lately attacked by their big Jew Jew (juju=god), the Sharks, they came to the conclusion that it no be use for have wowo jew hew (useless god) all same shark no more and it is therefore no longer held as such, but the natives are catching them as fast as possible as now allow "white men" to do the same if they like which of course we shall do whenever we have a chance as the shark is the sailor's greatest enemy.[14]

Commenting on the story, Wariboko writes: "If the god becomes too furious or demanding, the withdrawal of worship from or worshipful dependence of the god deprives the god of its power and authority to act on humans or control human activities."[15] By firing the shark, the chief manifested the quintessential dimension of his power, a form of radical equality that springs forth from an insurrection against the sacred. These acts of insurrection manifest in every aesthetic of presence, in which human beings artfully and passionately act on the "real presence" they have generated, and hold its ephemeral material and corporal absent presence and present absence. By doing so, they also dwell in the very paradox of Christianity.

The insurrection against the sacred is not coercive, as Max Weber argued in his harsh critique of Catholicism. As Werner Stark wrote, Weber considered Catholicism a coercive religion, whose Mass represents a "sorcerer's shibboleth which *forces* God, whether he likes it or not, to descend onto the altar and to incorporate Himself in the bread. In other words, he charged Catholics with the belief that their priests are stronger than God Himself."[16] To Weber, the Eucharist is a coercion of God. I would rather see in it a form of sublime persuasion.

Aesthetics of presence capture the ephemeral beyond through touch, smell, taste, sound, and sight. They also make the sacred and the supernatural sensuously permeate material forms, images, substances, and bodies. Through the audacious power of the senses, as Jean-Luc Nancy has argued, human beings generate beings and presences.[17] A mysterious scene narrated in the Bible reveals the sublime insurrection intrinsic in sensing, seizing, and touching the divine. The scene is the encounter between Jesus and Magdalene after Jesus's resurrection. *Noli me tangere!* meaning, "Don't touch me" or "Touch me not," Jesus says to Mary Magdalene.[18] The Gospel of John narrates the exchange as follows:

> Jesus saith unto her, Mary. She turned herself, and saith unto him, Rabboni; which is to say, Master. Jesus saith unto her, Touch me not; for I am not yet ascended to my Father: but go to my brethren, and say unto them, I ascend unto my Father, and your Father; and to my God, and your God.[19]

Magdalene's attempt to touch Jesus and Jesus's withdrawal is an oxymoron of the absence-presence of the divine and the very power of physical closeness and tangibility of the divine. Touch is inseparable from the experience of the sacred, and for Magdalene to touch Jesus would have been to experience "sensing the insensible and being seized by it"; it would have been "to touch his eternity" and, as a consequence, to hold Jesus in his immanent material existence.[20]

I contend that this is what aesthetics of presence do: They seductively hold the beyond in immanent material existence in which the divine and humanity stand together in a state of radical equality, a state in which they can sense, taste, and touch each other.

In those intense aesthetic moments in which human beings suspend the limits of human existence, these aesthetics redefine what a human body can feel and perceive; they reshape the relationship between the human bodies, the world, and its material forms and objects, and open up multidirectional flows of perceptions. Borrowing a term from modern media studies, I refer to this multidirectionality of perceptions as hypermediacy, like the opening up of multiple windows on the world, the self, the divine, and the supernatural.

Conflictual Consensus Aesthetics

In Italy, these aesthetics of presence suspend both the spiritual and sociopolitical order. Through these aesthetics, African Pentecostals also suspend the imposed role and place that they have in the Italian Catholic aesthetic order and instead contest the Catholic hegemonic power to generate and control real presences.

In Italy, on the one side, there is Catholicism that tries to preserve and restate its hegemony over the aesthetics of presence. On the other side is Pentecostalism, the Christian expression of a marginal and peripheral population—economic immigrants from Ghana and Nigeria—that creatively tries to dissent from the hegemonic aesthetics and claim its right and power to mediate real presence.

As this book shows, African Pentecostals' aesthetics of presence of nomadic subjects and objects are artful political devices of dissent that emerged from between the faults and cracks in the institutional forms of belief that temporarily dissolve the limits of the peripheral existence imposed on African Pentecostals in Italy. The spaces between these faults and cracks are occupied by a radical imagination and a creative spirit manifest in objects, images, material forms, bodies, feelings, and practices that criticize and redesign regimes of absolute truth and social hierarchies. In these spaces, Pentecostals who live on the margins of society craft their social, material, and religious worlds.

Their dissent takes place within the Catholic aesthetic order, through aesthetics of presence made of a rich material culture, sensations, sounds, and gestures that fills Catholic spaces and society with a Pentecostal sensorium. Through these transcultural aesthetics of presence, Pentecostals also contest their assigned political, social, and economic marginality. Officially denied their religious authority by Italian law and recognized in the Italian territory only as cultural operators, these Nigerian and Ghanaian pastors deploy their spiritual power in the very spaces in which spiritual power and authority is defined by the Catholic order. Among these pastors there are also women who irrupt into Catholic society, making visible their presence and insinuating within the Catholic patriarchal order the possibility to visualize the unthinkable, such as to see African women migrants as religious leaders in Italy. Navigating the ambivalent relations of power that they experience within and outside their religious communities, these women make their statement of emancipation and equality, and tell their counternarrative about the contemporary history of African female migration in Italy. This is the politics of aesthetics: They give a voice to the voiceless; they allow one to speak in a time and place where one is not supposed to, where one is meant to keep to one's assigned role and place.

However, despite the clashes and tensions, despite the sparks and smoke that arise when Pentecostals and Catholics meet, I argue that they are not enemies but adversaries. According to the political theorist Chantal Mouffe, contrary to what happens with the enemy to be destroyed, an adversary is somebody with whom there is common ground and shared understanding about what is at stake in the confrontation.[21] Adversaries share the same ethicopolitical principles but disagree on the implementation of those principles. In antagonism between enemies, conflicts do not find any rational solution, whereas adversaries in agonism will eventually end in what Mouffe calls *conflictual consensus*, such as the disagreement about the diverse ways in which one can interpret the ethicopolitical order.

Drawing from Mouffe's thesis, I argue that the disputes between Roman Catholicism and African Pentecostalism in Italy are not an antagonism but an agonism. They are not enemies disputing over the possibility of generating real presences, like the Catholics and the Reformers did, but adversaries in conflictual consensus who claim their own legitimacy and power to mediate real presences and interpret for themselves the politicotheological order.

Their dispute takes the form of somatic and iconographic clashes as these two adversaries disagree over the hierarchies and intensity of the senses, over the forms and shapes of the real presences, as well as on the authority and legitimacy to act on them.

In agonistic pluralism, it is impossible to establish consensus without exclusion. The perfect religious democracy, in Italy as in other countries, is and will always remain an illusion. The only vital force left to any democracy is contestation and dissent.

In Italy, Pentecostals have no illusions. They are perfectly aware of the multiple and multilayered forms of exclusions they experience and of the limited space of power they have. They also know they cannot overthrow the Catholic aesthetic order and hegemony. In fact, this is not what happens through their aesthetics of presences.

These aesthetics produce breaks and cracks that temporarily suspend the order of things determined by the Italian ethnoreligious aesthetics. These are moments in which Pentecostals go from relegation to emancipation, through which they claim and experience an equal share in the possibility of reconfiguring the spiritual and social order. As any form of politics, these aesthetics question the supposed naturalness of orders and, as Rancière would put it, replace order with controversial matters of division.[22]

The Subaltern Presence

In this book I have tried to position African Pentecostalism in the long sweep of Catholic hegemony in Italy. By doing so, I repropose the Gramscian analysis of Catholic hegemony in Italy and the role and place of folk Catholicism. For Antonio Gramsci, the struggle of folk Catholicism against the hegemony of official Catholicism was a subterranean, not fully conscious subjective terrain in which people at the margin of the social and religious order were redefining the rules of feelings and the order of sacred things.[23] Gramsci saw the subaltern cultures (including popular Catholicism) as the product of pure sentiments and crude sensations. In this book, I recognize in the African Pentecostals' practices some of the passions of the crude sensations of folk Catholicism described by Gramsci, of the dissenting and disruptive aesthetics of those peasants who challenged the Catholicism of the elites and its hegemony by adopting, manipulating, and retuning Catholic material and visual culture.

While conducting my ethnography in the African Pentecostal church-es, I saw many of those same crude sensations that I myself experienced as a child when I went with my grandparents to visit sanctuaries deep in the mountain regions of central Italy. With a mixture of curiosity, surprise, and the awe of a child, I witnessed an intimate, almost carnal emotional relationship with the sacred and the supernatural that took shape in the believers' bodies and in the spaces, images, objects and material things around them. In those places, prayers were embodied and wildly felt. Peo-ple dropped to their knees in front of altars to beg for miracles, elbowed each other to get close enough to touch or kiss the feet of statues of saints and reliquaries, or struggled up the steps of churches on their knees, just as I too was obliged by my grandmother to do several times. This is what Orsi would call the *corporalization of the sacred*. The faces I saw in sanctuaries and on pilgrimages were the faces of three generations of working-class Southern Italians: people who had fought in World War II and had suf-fered extreme poverty, those of the postwar years who had seen the first signs of the economic boom taking place around them, and my own gen-eration, born in the 1970s. There were no middle- or upper-class people at the sanctuaries, none of the wealthier types who still commanded great respect and often treated the poorer classes with a proud air of superiority.

Many of the feelings and sentiments I experienced as a child resur-faced in my mind like ghosts of a past that I had tried, clearly in vain, to deny when I moved to Northern Italy as a young leftist feminist and graduated from the university of the so-called bad teachers.[24] To be-come fully emancipated from the patriarchal community in which I had grown up, I also needed to rid myself of their God and saints. Condemn them to condemn everything: That was what Ludwig Feuerbach and Karl Marx said we should do. But it did not work. It only took a few months of my ethnographic journey around the African churches in Italy for those same deep, visceral, raw emotions that I had experienced on the margins of official Catholicism, in the gaps in the doctrine taught by the priest, to give me goose bumps again.

Those were not the only feelings that reminded me of the wild sacra-mentality of popular Catholicism, however. There was another element that brought my memories of popular Catholicism back to mind: It was the sense of separateness, of being far removed from the people who counted and influenced society. I perceived much the same separation and marginality in the African churches. Both were peripheral realities.

I do not mean to suggest that the relations of power and oppression experienced by the people on the margins that Gramsci described and by the African Pentecostals in Italy today are in any way equivalent. I am fully aware that these African Pentecostals experience social conditions imposed by neoliberal regimes of economic exploitation, racial discrimination, and ethnoreligious policies that derive from a local and global historical context dominated by national, economic, racial, and religious hierarchies. I would nonetheless like to juxtapose Gramsci's marginalized people with today's African Pentecostals to show that, although their similar peripheral, marginal social positions belong to different times and social settings, the latter have more or less consciously embraced a similar political project of dissent, using analogous aesthetic strategies and being cast in the same part—the part that has no part.

African Pentecostalism, in a similar way, survives and even thrives in Italy as a dissenting form of Christianity. Despite its contradictions and paradoxes, African Pentecostalism suspends the Catholic order by irrupting within it with its religious aesthetics and transcultural, transtemporal, and transreligious material world. These aesthetics are ways of knowing, of making sense of the beyond and of daily lives. They appear as acritical, and at times paradoxical, but they have an intrinsic and coherent political and ethical aim. Through their aesthetics, African Pentecostals are claiming their role and power to participate in the mediation of real presences by paradoxically adopting the same materiality that they apparently reject.

How do Pentecostal aesthetics and mediation of real presence function in the daily struggle of African Pentecostalism in Italy? For some skeptics, particularly Marxist scholars, Pentecostal aesthetics and their embodied religious worlds might look like emblematic examples of how religion is a futile happiness, a distraction, or at worst a narcotic that keeps Africans away from the real battleground of struggle for economic and racial justice, dignity, and freedom of movement.

Several scholars have tried to respond to these assumptions, and for some of them, the challenge has been to question the rigidity of concepts and ideas about what politics is and show how the political takes place also in nonconventional political arenas.[25] About thirty years ago in her book *Bodies of Power*, Jean Comaroff magisterially addressed this thorny issue. She explored the seemingly apolitical everyday discourses and practices of the Thsidi churches in South Africa: "While awareness of oppression obviously runs deep, reaction may appear erratic, diffuse and difficult to characterize. It is here that we must look beyond the conventionally explicit domains of 'political action' and 'consciousness.'"[26]

In the same way, the religious aesthetics of African Pentecostals in Italy, the part that has no part, are the politics of dissent of the "floating subjects" that demand to be included in Italian society as legitimate religious authorities and to have an equal share along with Catholicism in the given mediations of real presence. Certainly, they are not the only religious community that makes such a claim in Italy. Other religious minorities, including Italian Pentecostals, are still navigating their complex relations of power with the Catholic Church, along with other Protestant and Christian churches and other religions such as Islam, Hinduism, and Sikhism.

Yet African Pentecostals make their claim from the peculiar position assigned to them in the Catholic aesthetic order and in Italian society. Their politics of dissent, as African pastors told me, are born from their racialized positions, imposed marginality, and second-class Christianity. It is from such a position, tossed about by ambiguities and contradictions, that they articulate their spiritual and political subjectivities. African Pentecostals' aesthetics of presence respond to the spectral existence of African Pentecostals in Italy and, through exhilarating states of presence, open up a radical realm of equality where there are no barriers of gender, race, and class. By doing so, they claim their being, their own way of doing, their possibility to intensively express awe and disgust, even for those real presences like the relics that are intrinsic to the spiritual and political power of Roman Catholicism.

These politics do not appear in conventional arenas of government, political parties, public politics, and social activism in which Africans in Italy also participate. They appear in the Pentecostal churches that populate the suburbs of the Italian cities or in the Catholic parishes. Their politics of aesthetics of presence appear sporadically via disturbances in the established system of social inequalities. This is the politics of dissent, and this is also the paradigm of presence. It is a temporary moment of being and feeling, fully, deeply, and in a state of radical freedom.

These domains of political action are often dismissed as irrelevant, invisible, with zero impact on the social hierarchies and the established order. In fact, Pentecostals' aesthetics of presence are not shaking the consciousness of those who impose on them a certain role and place in the Italian aesthetic order. However, these religious aesthetics are not separated from politics. The separation between religion and politics is a Western vision that is not universally shared. As the political scientist Ruth Marshall argued in her work on Pentecostalism in Nigeria, "religion is a mode of historical and political transformation . . . as a specific regime of practice, in and through which particular moral and political subjects are produced."[27]

The political subjectivities produced in the African Pentecostal churches in Italy are wildly creative. They are the fruit of aesthetics of presence that do what art does: They trigger emotions and passions. As this book discloses, such religious aesthetics are charged with ambiguities and contradictions. I did not sidestep them, but have identified them and turned the spotlight on them, and made them an integral part of the sensuous spirituality and gritty materiality of African Pentecostalism. I did what Johannes Fabian suggests in his book *Moments of Freedom*: I let the contradictions and ambiguities stand[28] in order to grasp their role as repositories of tensions and as a way to overcome the limit of meaning in the study of religion and within humanities.[29] In this book, I dwell in the unconformable cradle of paradoxes and ambiguities of moments of real presence that might not produce meaning, but bring forth tangible worlds, bodies, sensations, and objects, and generate a space of infinite possibilities that overthrow the consolidated order of things.

The ambiguities that I let stand haunt the study of Roman Catholics and African Pentecostals' aesthetics of presence with further questions that open up new spaces of inquiry swamped with taboos and mysterious silences. But this is the terrible beauty of engaging real presences; doing so means getting our hands dirty in the risk and the bliss of the indefinite real.

Notes

Introduction

1. See, among others Grace Davie, *Religion in Britain Since 1945: Believing without Belonging* (Oxford, England; Cambridge, MA: John Wiley & Sons, 1994); Michael Warner, Jonathan VanAntwerpen, and Craig J. Calhoun, *Varieties of Secularism in a Secular Age* (Cambridge, MA: Harvard University Press, 2010).
2. Certainly, there are Catholic churches where Sunday Mass is attended by a more lively and numerous congregation. A few kilometers away, for instance, Saint Anthony's Basilica attracts several hundred people. Different generations of parish priests, each with their own personalities and styles, also give rise to very different liturgical scenarios, some more spirited than others.
3. S. Brent Plate, "The Skin of Religion: Aesthetic Mediations of the Sacred," *CrossCurrents* 62, no. 2 (June 1, 2012): 162–80.
4. Nimi Wariboko, *Nigerian Pentecostalism* (Rochester, NY: University of Rochester Press, 2014), 46. In his work, Wariboko discusses enspirited matter as matter that is spiritual corporeality and the spirit as corporeal spirituality.
5. On Orsi's discussion on real presences, see Robert A. Orsi, *Thank You, St. Jude: Women's Devotion to the Patron Saint of Hopeless Causes* (New Haven, CT: Yale University Press, 1998); Robert Orsi's new preface of the third edition of his book *The Madonna of 115th Street: Faith and Community in Italian Harlem, 1880–1950* (New Haven, CT: Yale University, 2010); Robert Orsi, "Material Children: Making God's Presence Real through Catholic Boys and Girls," in *Religion, Media and Culture: A Reader*, ed. Gordon Lynch, Jolyon P. Mitchell, and Anna Strahan (London, UK: Routledge, 2012), 147–58; and his research page "Real Presences: A Curatorial Introduction," in the blog *Reverberations*,

March 18, 2013, available at http://forums.ssrc.org/ndsp/2013/03/18/real-presences-catholic-prayer-as-intersubjectivity/.

6. In this book, *real presence* is the perceived, tangible, and material presence of the divine and the supernatural that manifests through different forms, shapes, and possibilities. Certainly, the words *real presence* strongly resonate with the Catholic doctrine of transubstantiation that has proclaimed since the 1551 Council of Trent that the body and blood of Jesus Christ are truly, really, and substantially present in the sacrament. However, here I do not intend to juxtapose the Catholic real presence of Jesus in the host with the real presence of the divine and the supernatural that are made "real" and "present" in material forms, substances, and bodies by Pentecostal asthetics of presence. What the real presences I refer to in this book and the real presence of the transubstantiation have in common is not the substance but the process through which the Spirit conflates with matter and generates enspirited matter. Because this process generates diverse forms of real presence, I will use both the singular and plural terms *real presence* and *real presences*. As this book unfolds, this "real" can be the real presence of Jesus in an image or the power of a saint in the relics, the power of the Holy Spirit in annointed olive oil or the real presence of evil spirits possessing human bodies and various material forms. I am particularly grateful to my colleague Peter Ben Smith of Utrecht University who urged me to clarify the difference between the theological and anthropological understanding of real presence and its relationship with the Catholic doctrine of transubstantiation.

7. Major doctrinal differences between Roman Catholicism and Pentecostalism mainly reflect differences between Catholicism and Protestantism. Pentecostals and Protestants share several doctrinal disagreements with Catholicism including, among others, ecclesiological issues; the question of the authority and infallibility of the pope; the role of faith, grace, and human deeds in salvation; the devotion to Mary and the saints; the role and power of scripture versus tradition; worship style; the doctrine of purgatory; and the celibacy of priests. For a more comprehensive critical reflection on these and other doctrinal differences and ecumenical initiatives, see Thomas Rausch, "Catholics and Pentecostals: Troubled History, New Initiatives," *Theological Studies* 71, no. 4 (2010): 926–50; Kilian Mc Donnell "Improbable Conversations: International Classical Pentecostal-Roman Catholic Dialogue," *Pneuma: The Journal of the Society for Pentecostal Studies* 17, no. 2 (1995):163–74; Cecil Robeck Jr., "The Achievement of Pentecostal-Catholic International Dialogue," in *Celebrating a Century of Ecumenism: Exploring the Achievement of Ecumenism*, ed. John Radano and Walter Kasper (Grand Rapids, MI: Wm. B. Eerdmans, 1992),163–94; Juan Usma Gómez, "Dialogue with Pentecostals," *L'Osservatore Romano: Weekly Edition in English*, March 28, 2001, http://www.ewtn.com/library/curia/pccupent.htm; Jerry Sandidge, *Roman Catholic/Pentecostal Dialogue (1977–1982): A Study in Developing Eucumenism* (Bern, Switzerland: Peter Lang, 1987); Veli-Matti Kärkkäinen, *Ad Ultimum Terrae:*

Evangelization, Proselytism and Common Witness in the Roman Catholic-Pentecostal Dialogue (1990–97) (Frankfurt am Main: Peter Lang, 1999). The Fourth Session of the Sixth Phase of the international Catholic-Pentecostal Dialogue took place in Sierra Madre, California, United States, in July 2014. The general theme of the session was "Charisms in the Church: Their Spiritual Significance, Discernment, and Pastoral Implications." The theme of the 2013 session was "Healing," and it followed the 2012 session "Discernment" and the 2011 session "Common Ground."

8. Joseph Ratzinger, "'Declaration Dominus Iesus': On the Unicity and Salvific Universality of Jesus Christ and the Church," 2000,http://www.vatican.va/roman_curia/congregations/cfaith/documents/rc_con_cfaith_doc_20000806_dominus-iesus_en.html.

9. On Pentecostalism and Catholicism in Brazil, compare Ari Pedro Oro, *Avanço Pentecostal e reação Católica* (Petrópolis, Rio de Janeiro: Voces, 1996); Paul Freston, *Evangelicals and Politics in Asia, Africa and Latin America* (Cambridge, UK: Cambridge University Press, 2001); Andrew Chesnut, *Born Again in Brazil: The Pentecostal Boom and the Pathogens of Poverty* (New Brunswick, NJ: Rutgers University Press, 1997). On the Catholic Church in Brazil, see also Manuel Vazquez, *The Brazilian Popular Church and the Crisis of Modernity* (New York, NY: Cambridge University Press, 1998).

10. Martin Luther, *The Babylonian Captivity of the Church*, trans. A. T. W. Steinhäuser, 1520, http://www.onthewing.org/user/Luther%20-%20Babylonian%20Captivity.pdf.

11. As several scholars have noted, the attitude of the Reformers toward images and sacramental objects was very ambiguous. In fact, despite Reformers' condemnation and apparently iconoclastic attitudes, images and objects never fully disappeared during the Reformation. In this regard, compare (among others) Joseph Leo Koerner, *The Reformation of the Images* (Chicago, IL: University of Chicago Press, 2008); Willem van Asselt, Paul van Geest, Daniela Müller, and Theo Salemink, eds., *Iconoclasm and Iconoclash: Struggle for Religious Identity* (Leiden, Netherlands: Brill, 2007); Sergiusz Michalski, *Reformation and the Visual Arts: The Protestant Image Question in Western and Eastern Europe* (London, UK: Routledge, 2013).

12. Daniel Olukoya, *Prayer Rain* (Mountain of Fire and Miracles Ministries, 2013), 380–84.

13. The world data banks, such as PEW and Global Christian Encyclopedia, include Pentecostals under the Protestant umbrella. Moreover, the expression "the protestantization" of Latin America and Africa often appears in the flourishing literature on global Pentecostalism. See David Stoll, *Is Latin America Turning Protestant?* (Los Angeles: University of California Press, 1991); David Martin, *Tongues of Fire: The Explosion of Protestantism in Latin America* (Hoboken, NJ: Wiley-Blackwell, 1993).

14. On the Pentecostal sacramental principle, see Frank Macchia, "Tongues as a Sign: Towards a Sacramental Understanding of Pentecostal Experience,"

Pneuma 15, no. 1 (1993): 61–76; Amos Yong, *Discerning the Spirit(s): A Pente-costal-Charismatic Contribution to Christian Theology of Religions* (London, UK: A & C Black, 2000); James K. A. Smith, *Thinking in Tongues: Pentecostal Contribu-tions to Christian Philosophy* (Grand Rapids, MI: Wm. B. Eerdmans, 2010); Nimi Wariboko, *The Pentecostal Principle: Ethical Methodology in New Spirit* (Grand Rapids, MI: Wm. B. Eerdmans, 2011). Frank Macchia wrote about Pentecostal sacramentality looking at glossolalia as the manifestation of the real presence of the Holy Spirit dwelling in people's bodies. He talked about the real presence and evidences of the Holy Spirit, tracing some of the simi-larities between this and Catholic sacramentality and the real presence in the Eucharist. For another view on the theological affinities between Catholi-cism and Pentecostalism related to the Catholic substance that Paul Tillich reclaimed as a necessary complement of Christianity, see Paul Tillich, *The Protestant Era,* trans. James Luther Adams (Chicago, IL: Chicago University Press, 1948). In this work, Tillich highlighted how the Protestant principle, or pronounced prophetic iconoclasm, the rejection of all forms of social and symbolic mediation existing in the Catholic sacraments and the denial of grace in tangible things, nurtured an extreme form of rationalization of the faith. According to Tillich, the Protestant principle tended to radicalize the transcendence of God, and that was why Protestantism needs the sacramen-tality of Catholic substance. As a result, the challenge for the new church would be to balance Protestant principle with Catholic substance. Protes-tantism therefore needed to take a step back, not to convert back to Catholi-cism, but to retrieve the sacramentality and the presence of the sacred im-plicit in Catholic substance, in Catholic piety, aesthetics, and material culture. While continuing to judge as unacceptable what he called "the magical ele-ments in Catholic sacramentalism," such as transubstantiation, Tillich saw Catholic substance as a necessary complement to the Protestant principle, although any tendency toward idolatry (typical of Catholicism) had to be kept under control. In response to Tillich, various Catholic theologians pointed out the traps inherent in the radicalization of the Protestant princi-ple and the need for a principle that could balance the Protestant one.

15. On the meaning and understanding of catholicity, see Avery Dulles, *The Catho-licity of the Church* (New York, NY: Oxford University Press, 1987); Wolfgang Beinert, "Catholicity as Property of the Church," *Jurist* 52 (1992): 455–83; Paul Murray, "Redeeming Catholicity for a Globalising Age: The Sacramental-ity of the Church," in *Exchanges of Grace: Essays in Honour of Ann Loades,* ed. Natalie Watson and Stephen London (Norwich, UK: Hymns Ancient and Modern, 2008), 149–69; Richard Lennan, "Catholicity: Its Challenge for the Church," *New Theology Review* 24, no. 4 (2011): 36–48; Karl Rahner, "The The-ology of the Symbol," in *Theological Investigations,* vol. 4 (New York, NY: Cross-road, 1982), 221–52. This catholicity is also intrinsic to what David Tracy and Andrew Greely, respectively, called the analogical and the enchanted imagina-tion, which they also see as one of the elements that differentiates Catholicism

from Protestantism. According to David Tracy, analogial imagination sees God as immanent, familiar, and analogous to the human experience of the body and the senses. To Tracy, this is in contrast to the Protestants' dialectical imagination that stresses the alterity, otherness, and transcendence of God. The analogical imagination undergirds a sacramental view that acknowledges that certain practices and material forms are means by which to mediate divine presence. Greeley built on Tracy's notion of the analogical imagination to describe what he called catholic enchantment. Compare David Tracy, *The Analogical Imagination: Christian Theology and the Culture of Pluralism* (New York, NY: Crossroad, 1998); and Andrew Greely, *The Catholic Imagination* (Berkley and Los Angeles: University of California Press, 2001).

16. Birgit Meyer and Dick Houtman, eds., *Things: Religion and the Question of Materiality* (New York, NY: Fordham University Press, 2012).

17. The complicated attitude toward real presence is perhaps best expressed in the debate the Reformers raised about the real presence of Jesus in the Eucharist. Catholics, Lutherans, Calvinists, and post-Reformers such as Zwingli elaborated their different positions, opposing the consubstantiation or a simple symbolization to the Catholic transubstantiation such as the real presence of Jesus Christ in the bread and wine. Luther believed in consubstantiation as the literal presence of Jesus's body and blood "alongside" the bread and wine. Huldrych Zwingli had a more a symbolic view that claimed the presence of Jesus is only a symbol. More complicated was the approach of John Calvin, which I cannot exhaustively present in this book. Calvin rejected any notion at all of a local presence and physicality of Christ in the Eucharist and believed that what was called real presence was instead only the spirit of Christ. Seminal books have been written on this very topic. Among them, see Alister McGrath, *Reformation Thought: An Introduction* (Hoboken, NJ: Wiley-Blackwell, 2012); Christopher Elwood, *The Body Broken: The Calvinist Doctrine of the Eucharist and the Symbolization of Power in Sixteenth-Century France* (New York, NY: Oxford University Press, 1999); Thomas Davis, *This Is My Body: The Presence of Christ in Reformation Thought* (Grand Rapids, MI: Baker Academic, 2008); Gary Macy, *The Theologies of the Eucharist in the Early Scholastic Period: A Study of the Salvific Function of the Sacrament according to the Theologians c.1080-c.1220* (Oxford, UK: Oxford University Press, 1984); Lee Palmer Wandel, *The Eucharist in the Reformation* (Cambridge, UK: Cambridge University Press, 2005).

18. On the relationship between art and real presence, see the magisterial work of Hans Belting, *Likeness and Presence: A History of the Image before the Era of Art* (Chicago, IL: Chicago University Press, 1994).

19. Matthew Engelke, *A Problem of Presence: Beyond Scripture in an African Church* (Los Angeles: University of California Press, 2007).

20. Robert Orsi, *Between Heaven and Earth: The Religious Worlds People Make and the Scholars Who Study Them* (Princeton, NJ: Princeton University Press, 2006), 74.

21. By *aesthetics* here I do not refer narrowly to the sense of beauty and art but to *aesthesis*, such as the Aristotelian science of feeling, perceiving, exploring, and knowing the world through the senses.

22. On the media turn in the study of religion, see Matthew Engelke, "Religion and the Media Turn: A Review Essay," *American Ethnologist* 37, no. 2 (May 1, 2010). This development has sought to question the dominant understanding of religion as an intellectual and mental relationship with the divine and the supernatural that sharply opposes religious meanings to the material world of things. On the materiality, sensuality, and aesthetics of religion see Birgit Meyer and Dick Houtman, eds., *Things: Religion and the Question of Materiality* (New York, NY: Fordham University Press, 2012); Birgit Meyer, ed., *Aesthetic Formations: Media, Religion, and the Senses* (New York, NY: Palgrave Macmillan, 2009); Birgit Meyer, "Aesthetics of Persuasion: Global Christianity and Pentecostalism's Sensational Forms," *South Atlantic Quarterly* 109, no. 4 (2010): 741–63; Brent Plate and Walter Benjamin, *Religion and Aesthetics: Rethinking Religion through Art* (London, UK: Routledge, 2005); David Morgan, *Religion and Material Culture: The Matter of Belief* (London, UK: Routledge, 2010); Daniel Miller, ed., *Materiality* (Durham, NC: Duke University Press, 2005); Diana Espirito Santo and Nico Tassi, eds., *Making Spirits: Materiality and Transcendence in Contemporary Religions* (London, UK: I.B. Tauris, 2013); Sally Promey, ed., *Sensational Religion: Sensory Cultures in Material Practice* (New Haven, CT: Yale University Press, 2014); Paula Findlen, ed., *Early Modern Things: Objects and Their Histories, 1500–1800* (London: Routledge, 2013).

23. Manuel Vazquez, *More Than Belief: A Materialist Theory of Religion* (Oxford, UK: Oxford University Press, 2010).

24. Harvey Cox, *Fire From Heaven: The Rise of Pentecostal Spirituality and the Reshaping of Religion in the 21st Century* (Boston, MA: Da Capo, 2001), 184.

25. See Bernice Martin, "The Pentecostal Gender Paradox: A Cautionary Tale for the Sociology of Religion," in *The Blackwell Companion to Sociology of Religion*, ed. Richard Fenn (Hoboken, NJ: Wiley-Blackwell, 2003), 52–66; André Droogers, "Essentialist and Normative Approaches," in *Studying Global Pentecostalism: Theories and Methods*, ed. Allen Anderson et al. (Los Angeles: University of California Press, 2010), 30–50.

26. Matthews Ojo, *The End-Time Army: Charismatic Movements in Modern Nigeria* (Trenton, NJ: Africa Research & Publications, 2007).

27. Annalisa Butticci, "Crazy World, Crazy Faith! Prayer, Power and Transformation in a Nigerian Prayer City," in *Prayer in Religion and Spirituality*, ed. Giuseppe Giordan, and Linda Woodhead (Leiden, Netherlands: Brill, 2013), 243–62.

28. Allan Anderson, *An Introduction to Pentecostalism* (Cambridge, UK: Cambridge University Press, 2004), 112.

29. On Christianity and paganism, see Christopher Jones, *Between Pagan and Christian* (Cambridge, UK: Harvard University Press, 2014); Arnoldo Momigliano, *The Conflict between Paganism and Christianity in the Fourth Century*

(Oxford, UK: Oxford University Press, 1963); Éric Rebillard, *Christians and Their Many Identities in Late Antiquity, North Africa, 200–450 CE* (Ithaca, NY: Cornell University Press, 2012); Alan Cameron, *The Last Pagans of Rome* (New York, NY: Oxford University Press, 2011); Anna Fedele, *Looking for Mary Magdalene: Alternative Pilgrimage and Ritual Creativity at Catholic Shrines in France* (New York, NY: Oxford University Press, 2013).

30. Several scholars, including Thomas Csordas, Meredith McGuire, Mary Joe Neitz, and recently Emanuela Contiero and Marco Marzano in Italy have devoted themselves to the study of Catholic charismatics. Compare Thomas Csordas, *Language, Charisma, and Creativity: The Ritual Life of a Religious Movement* (Los Angeles: University of California Press, 1997); Mary Jo Neitz, *Charisma and Community: A Study of Religious Commitment within the Charismatic Renewal* (Piscataway, NJ: Transaction, 1987); Meredith McGuire, *Lived Religion: Faith and Practice in Everyday Life* (New York: Oxford University Press, 2008); Marco Marzano, *Cattolicesimo magico: Un'indagine etnografica* (Milan, Italy: Bompiani, 2009); Emanuela Contiero, "Pluralism and Rituals in Italian Catholicism: The Spiritual Approach of Renewal in the Spirit," in *Testing Pluralism: Globalizing Belief, Localizing Gods*, ed. Giuseppe Giordan and William Swatos (Leiden, Netherlands: Brill, 2013), 39–55; Emanuela Contiero, "Italian Catholicism and the Differentiation of Rituals: A Comparison of the Neocatechumenal Way and Renewal in the Spirit," in *Mapping Religion and Spirituality in a Postsecular World*, ed. Giuseppe Giordan and Enzo Pace (Leiden, Netherlands: Brill, 2012), 9–26.

31. Antonio Gramsci, *Prison Notebooks*, trans. Joseph Buttingieg (New York, NY: Columbia University Press, 2011). Recently, expressions such as *popular* or *folk* religions have been criticized. Scholars saw in the use of these terms the reification of an evolutionary and hierarchical approach to religions whereby popular religions, along with popular piety, magic, and superstitions, are at the lowest level. Gramsci did not have this hierarchy in mind when he used these terms and did not use the words *folk* or *popular* as derogatory or to refer to inferior forms of religion. He argued that folk religions and common sense are the philosophy of life of people. In this work, I use the words *folk religions* or *popular Catholicism* as Gramsci used and conceived them, namely, as part of the culture, emotions, passions, and philosophy of the people.

32. On popular Catholicism and devotional practices, see (among others) Michael Carroll, *Madonnas that Maim: Popular Catholicism in Italy since the Fifteenth Century* (Baltimore, MD: Johns Hopkins University Press, 1992); Michael Carroll, *Veiled Threats: The Logic of Popular Catholicism in Italy* (Baltimore, MD: Johns Hopkins University Press, 1996); Luigi Berzano, Alessandro Castegnaro, Enzo Pace, eds., *La religiosita' popolare nella societa' post-secolare* (Padua, Italy: Edizioni Messaggero, 2015).

33. My approach to contact zones is inspired by the work of postcolonialist theoretician Mary Louise Pratt, who coined the term *contact zone* to describe a social space of negotiation where cultures meet, clash, and grapple with each

other, often in contexts of highly asymmetrical relations of power. In this book, the contact zone is not the result of colonial expansionism or Western Eurocentrism. It is not an exotic or colonial frontier, or a border zone far from Europe or the West. The study I present here flips the Eurocentric mapping and makes Europe, and in this specific case Italy, the very contact zone in the heart of Europe.

34. Birgit Meyer, ed., *Aesthetic Formations: Media, Religion, and the Senses* (New York, NY: Palgrave Macmillan, 2009); Birgit Meyer, "Aesthetics of Persuasion: Global Christianity and Pentecostalism's Sensational Forms," *South Atlantic Quarterly* 109, no. 4 (2010): 741–63.

35. Nikolas Kompridis, *The Aesthetic Turn in Political Thought* (London, UK: Bloomsbury Academic, 2014), xx.

36. Key authors that looked at the relationship between aesthetics and politcs are Terry Engleton, Ernst Bloch, Georg Lukács, Bertolt Brecht, Walter Benjamin, and Theodor Adorno. Their works focus on the question of how the political is represented in the aesthetic domain, and conversely on how aesthetics itself is an expression of political power within the socioeconomic and political domain. See Theodor Adorno et al., *Aesthetics and Politics* (New York, NY: Verso, 2007). Moving beyond the work of these scholars, other scholars such as Jacques Rancière, Davide Panagia, Arnold Berleant, and Crispin Sartwell developed a new type of inquiry about the relationship between politics and aesthetics. Their approach expands the concept of aesthetics beyond the art field and looks at senses and sensations as well as environmental and social aesthetics as intrinsic to negotiation of power and politics. See Jacques Rancière, *The Politics of Aesthetics*, trans. Gabriel Rockhill (London, UK: Bloomsbury Academic, 2006); Davide Panagia, *The Political Life of Sensation* (Durham, NC: Duke University Press, 2009); Arnold Berleant, *Aesthetics beyond the Arts: New and Recent Essays* (Farnham, UK: Ashgate, 2012); Crispin Sartwell, *Political Aesthetics* (Ithaca, NY: Cornell University Press, 2010).

37. Rancière, *The Politics of Aesthetics*, 10.

38. Elisabeth Arweck and William Keenan, eds., *Materializing Religion: Expression, Performance and Ritual* (Farnham, UK: Ashgate, 2006), 12.

39. Ferruccio Gambino, *Migranti nella tempesta: Avvistamenti per l'inzio del nuovo millennio* (Verona, Italy: Ombre Corte, 2003); Ferruccio Pastore, "Europe, Migration and Development: Critical Remarks on an Emerging Policy Field," *Development* 50, no. 4 (2007): 56–62.

40. Valentin Mudimbe, *The Invention of Africa: Gnosis, Philosophy, and the Order of Knowledge* (Bloomington: University of Indiana Press, 1988); Edward Said, *Orientalism* (London, UK: Routledge, 1978). On Italy and postcolonial critiques, see (among others) Jacqueline Andall and Derek Duncan, eds., *Italian Colonialism: Legacy and Memory* (Bern, Switzerland: Peter Lang, 2005); Graziella Parati, *Migration Italy: The Art of Talking Back in a Destination Culture* (Toronto, Canada: University of Toronto Press, 2005); Cristina Lombardi-Diop and Caterina

Romeo, eds., *Postcolonial Italy: Challenging National Homogeneity* (New York, NY: Palgrave Macmillan, 2012).

1. African Pentecostalism in the Storm

1. The religious field is one of the theoretical concepts that Bourdieu articulated in his sociology of religion. To Bourdieu, the social world is divided up into a variety of distinct arenas, or fields of practice, such as education, religion, art, law, and so on. These arenas have their unique set of knowledge, rules, and forms of capital, and their own set of positions and struggles for position as people mobilize their capital to make their claims within a particular social field. Each is relatively autonomous from the others, although they can overlap. Bourdieu considers the religious field, like other fields, to be an arena of competition and relations between religious agents. What is at stake in the relations and transactions are specific forms of religious capital and the administration of the sacred. Compare Pierre Bourdieu, "Genesis and Structure of the Religious Field," trans. Jenny Burnside, Craig Calhoun, and Leah Florence, *Comparative Social Research* 13, no. 1 (1991): 1–44.
2. Istat 2014 (Italian National Institute of Statistics).
3. Ferruccio Gambino, *Migranti Nella Tempesta: Avvistamenti per L'inzio Del Nuovo Millennio* (Verona, Italy: Ombre Corte, 2003).
4. Sandro Mezzadra, "The New European Migratory Regime and the Shifting Patterns of Contemporary Racism," in *Postcolonial Italy: Challenging National Hegemony,* ed. Christine Lombardi Diop and Caterina Romeo (New York, NY: Palgrave Macmillan, 2012), 47. At its beginnings, the Northern League was a federalist populist party born out of the protest against a centralized state and the assistance programs toward what this party considered the unproductive South of Italy at the expense of what it considered the productive North. Within years, the Northern League Party started to bear all the hallmarks of a classic and modern party of the extreme right. It was anti-European, xenophobic, Islamophobic, homophobic, and on many occasions, explicitly racist. Their lurid provocations ranged from bringing pigs to pastures close to mosques to publicly comparing the former African Congolese Italian minister to an orangutan.
5. In this regard, see Jacqueline Andall, *Gender, Migration and Domestic Service: The Politics of Black Women in Italy* (Farnham, UK: Ashgate, 2000); Floya Anthias and Mojca Pajnik, *Contesting Integration, Engendering Migration: Theory and Practice* (New York, NY: Palgrave Macmillan, 2014); Luisa Passerini Lyon and Enrica Capussotti, eds., *Women Migrants from East to West: Gender, Mobility and Belonging in Contemporary Europe* (Oxford, NY: Berghahn, 2009).
6. Migrants represent 36 percent of the prison population in Italy. Of the migrant population, black Africans make up 6 percent; the most represented nationality is Nigerian (4.5 percent), followed by Senegalese (1.7 percent).

See "Detenuti presenti stranieri per area geografica—Anni 2007–2014," *Ministero della Giustizia*, December 31, 2014, http://www.giustizia.it/giustizia/it/mg_1_14_1.wp?facetNode_1=2_0&previsiousPage=mg_1_14&contentId=SST679902. On the criminalization of migrants, see Salvatore Palidda, ed., *Racial Criminalization of Migrants in the 21st Century* (Farnham, UK: Ashgate, 2013); Alvise Sbraccia, *Migranti tra mobilità e carcere: Storie di vita e processi di criminalizzazione* (Milan, Italy: FrancoAngeli, 2010); Alvise Sbraccia, *More or Less Eligibility? Theoretical Perspectives on the Imprisonment Process of Irregular Migrants in Italy* (Messina, Italy: C.I.R.S.D.I.G., 2008); Dario Melossi, "'In a Peaceful Life': Migration and the Crime of Modernity in Europe/Italy," *Punishment & Society* 5, no. 4 (2003): 371–97; Asale Angel-Ajani, "Italy's Racial Cauldron: Immigration, Criminalization and the Cultural Politics of Race," *Cultural Dynamics* 12, no. 3 (2000): 331–52; Asale Angel-Ajani, "A Question of Dangerous Races?," *Punishment & Society* 5, no. 4 (2003): 433–48; Emilio Reyneri, *Migrant Insertion in the Formal Economy, Deviant Behaviour, and the Impact on Receiving Societies: Some Hypotheses for a Cross-National Research*, TSER Report (European Commission, 1996).

7. In this regard, see Heather Merrill, "Migration and Surplus Populations: Race and Deindustrialization in Northern Italy," *Antipode* 43, no. 5 (2011): 1556–57; Angel-Ajani, "A Question of Dangerous Races?," 439.

8. On the Western imaginary and the construction of Africa, see the magisterial work of Valentin Mudimbe, *The Invention of Africa: Gnosis, Philosophy, and the Order of Knowledge* (Bloomington: University of Indiana Press, 1988); Achille Mbembe, *On the Postcolony* (Los Angeles: University of California Press, 2001); Edward Said, *Orientalism* (London, UK: Routledge, 1978), among others.

9. Nimi Wariboko, *Nigerian Pentecostalism* (Rochester, NY: University of Rochester Press, 2014), 225.

10. Angel-Ajani, "A Question of Dangerous Races?," 439.

11. See Nwando Achebe, "The Road to Italy: Nigerian Sex Workers at Home and Abroad," *Journal of Women's History* 15, no. 4 (2004): 178–85; Esohe Aghatise, "Trafficking for Prostitution in Italy: Possible Effects of Government Proposals for Legalization of Brothels," *Violence Against Women* 10, no. 10 (2004): 1126–55; Jørgen Carling, *Migration, Human Smuggling and Trafficking from Nigeria to Europe*, PRIO Report (International Organization for Migration, 2006). Several investigations led to officials at the Italian Embassy in Nigeria being sentenced in court for selling visas for considerable sums of money ranging from $1,000 to $3,000 in a country where a monthly salary of $30 is considered decorous. The racket apparently involved several local lordlings in Nigeria and women (*mamans*) who were trafficking prostitutes in Italy; they would lend the money to girls and then oblige them to pay it back, together with their airfare, from their earnings as prostitutes. The number of Nigerian girls arriving in Italy in recent years has been estimated at around 30,000, although the figures vary and will probably never succeed in providing a real idea of the enormity of this phenomenon. There are approximately

10,000 such Nigerian *mamans*, who are generally themselves former prostitutes; they know the market and the risks involved. Together with the traffickers, they keep the girls moving from one town to another as they strive to keep a step ahead of the police. The girls involved are practically all under twenty-five years old and have no documents.

12. Maurizio Ambrosini, *Un'altra globalizzazione: La sfida delle migrazioni transnazionali* (Bologna, Italy: Il Mulino, 2008).

13. Stefano Pasta, "Jerry Essan Masslo, 25 anni dal suo assassinio nella terra dei Casalesi," *La Repubblica,* August 24, 2014, http://www.repubblica.it/solidarieta/diritti-umani/2014/08/16/news/anniversario_masslo-93894017/.

14. For further analysis on the question of the cost of labor in the Italian orange orchards and the tensions between local farmers and multinationals (such as Fanta and Coca-Cola), see "Immigration in Italy: Southern Misery," *The Economist,* January 14, 2010, http://www.economist.com/node/15271071. The investigations clearly identified the underhanded policies of the multinationals setting their (very low) price on agricultural products. One farmer who was interviewed said that his laborers receive the minimum legal wage, i.e., €25, but the market price for his produce had dropped below the production cost. In addition to earning a pittance, the farm workers live in conditions no better than a prisoner-of-war camp. In Rosarno, a small town that has become well known for its oranges harvested by sub-Saharan migrants, the NGO Emergency sets up a twice-weekly mobile doctor's surgery in a van with space for medical examinations and the basic instruments needed for minor surgical procedures. The volunteers said that they attend to at least forty patients per day who present with breathing problems and muscle and joint pain, and who very often needed to be seen by a specialist. Many of the migrants' health problems relate directly to their work, and especially to the improper use of pesticides and fungicides during the harvest season. They suffer from contact dermatitis on their hands and faces, and conjunctivitis because their eyes are not protected. Angelo Moccia, director of the clinic, said the conditions are worse than what he saw in Congo, and Andrea Freda, the nurse responsible for the project, added, "The situation is not very different from Afghanistan." See "Aranciata amara a Rosarno," *Internazionale,* http://www.internazionale.it/news/italieni-2/2012/03/02/aranciata-amara-a-rosarno/.

15. Hans Lucht, *Darkness before Daybreak: African Migrants Living on the Margins in Southern Italy Today* (Los Angeles: University of California Press, 2012). See also Giorgio Agamben, *State of Exception,* trans. Kevin Attell (Chicago, IL: University of Chicago Press, 2005).

16. Steven Vertovec, "Super-Diversity and Its Implications," *Ethnic and Racial Studies* 30, no. 6 (2007): 1024–54.

17. Afe Adogame, *The African Christian Diaspora: New Currents and Emerging Trends in World Christianity* (London, UK: Bloomsbury Academic, 2013); Kim Knibbe, "Geographies of Conversion: Focusing on the Spatial Practices of

Nigerian Pentecostalism," *Pentecostudies: An Interdisciplinary Journal for Research on the Pentecostal and Charismatic Movements* 9, no. 2 (2010): 175–94; Gerrie ter Haar, "African Christians in the Netherlands," in *Strangers and Sojourners: Religious Communities in the Diaspora* (Leuven, Belgium: Peeters, 1998), 153–72; Rijk van Dijk, "From Camp to Encompassment: Discourses of Transsubjectivity in the Ghanaian Pentecostal Diaspora," *Journal of Religion in Africa* 27, no. 2 (1997): 135–59; Rijk van Dijk, "The Soul Is the Stranger: Ghanaian Pentecostalism and the Diasporic Contestation of 'Flow' and 'Individuality,'" *Culture and Religion* 3, no. 1 (2002): 49–65; Hermione Harris, *Yoruba in Diaspora: An African Church in London* (New York, NY: Palgrave Macmillan, 2006); Boris Nieswand, *Theorising Transnational Migration: The Status Paradox of Migration* (London, UK: Routledge, 2012); Abel Ugba, *Shades of Belonging: African Pentecostals in Twenty-First Century Ireland* (Trenton, NJ: Africa World Press, 2009).

18. Another interesting case concerns the African Pentecostal churches in Campania, where the Africans have kept alive the churches initially set up by African American soldiers between the 1960s and 1980s. See Paolo Naso, Alessia Passarelli, and Tamara Pispisa, *Fratelli e sorelle di Jerry Masslo: L'immigrazione Evangelica in Italia* (Torino, Italy: Claudiana, 2014).

19. See Annalisa Butticci, "Le Chiese Neopentecostali e carismatiche Africane," in *Le religioni nell'Italia che cambia: Mappe e bussole*, ed. Enzo Pace (Rome, Italy: Carocci, 2013), 85–96.

20. Ingo Schröder, "Catholic Majority Societies and Religious Hegemony: Concepts and Comparisons," in *Religious Diversity in Post-Soviet Society: Ethnographies of Catholic Hegemony and the New Pluralism in Lithuania*, ed. Milda Ališauskiene and Ingo Schröder (Burlington, VT: Ashgate, 2012), 17–36.

21. On the political role of the Catholic Church in contemporary Europe, see (among others) Mark Donovan, "The Italian State: No Longer Catholic, No Longer Christian," in *Church and State in Contemporary Europe: The Chimaera of Neutrality*, ed. Zsolt Enyedi and John Madeley (London, UK: Routledge, 2004), 92–112.

22. The concordat (or Lateran Treaty) was formally approved by Benito Mussolini on February 11, 1929. The articles it contained gave the Catholic Church a number of privileges, chief among them that the Catholic faith was declared the "only state religion." In modern Europe, the states that stipulated agreements with the Roman Catholic Church include Austria and Germany in 1933, Italy in 1929, Portugal in 1940, and Spain in 1953. In 1984, the Italian concordat was revised after lengthy and difficult negotiations, but this did not change the obligation to teach Catholic religion in the country's schools. The revised article 9, section 2, stated that the Italian Republic recognized the value of its culture, and bearing in mind that the principles of Catholicism were part of the historical heritage of the Italian people, it would continue to assure that the goals of education would include teaching the Catholic religion in all state-run schools of every order and grade, apart from

the universities. The qualification to teach Catholic religion was awarded by the territorially competent bishop, based on an assessment of the interested party's "proper doctrine" and proof of his "Christian lifestyle" and "teaching ability," as laid down in canons 804 and 805 of the Codex Juris Canonici, according to which the bishop also had the right to remove, or demand the removal of, teachers of religion "for reasons of religion or behavior." Because this teaching was imparted to all state schools, the corresponding economic burden fell entirely to the state. One of the novelties of the revised concordat was that attendance of these lessons was no longer compulsory, even though they were among the school's teaching goals.

23. The revised concordat enacted in 1984, which required lengthy procedures and political maneuvering, granted specific benefits in an agreement (intesa) with the Waldensian Church. The same law later extended similar benefits to the Seventh Day Adventist Church and the Assemblies of God (1988); Jews (1989); Baptists and Lutherans (1995); Mormons, Orthodox, and Apostolics (2012); and Buddhists and Hindus (2013). For the religions legitimized by the state and their practitioners, the *intesa* allows for ministers of religion to access state hospitals, prisons, and military barracks; it links religious ceremonies to civil records of marriage; it grants state funding for religion, fosters the teaching of religion in state schools, facilitates special religious practices for funerals, regulates rental contracts, and exempts students from attending school on religious holidays. If the religious community so requests, an *intesa* can provide for state subsidies by means of tax revenue collection. The laws of the Fascist era (1929–30) on the status of religious minorities in Italy remain in force today, however. For the past fifteen years, there has been strong pressure from the Italian Protestant churches to enact a law on religious freedom in Italy, especially concerning the teaching of religion in schools. The Catholic Church has criticized this movement, claiming that all religions being equally free does not mean they should all have the same rights. Yet despite the active lobbying of these religious groups and the obvious conflict between the Fascism-based laws and the principle of religious freedom granted by the Italian Constitution, no major political party, prime minister, or House of Parliament has taken significant steps to replace the law.

24. Compare Carmine Napolitano, "The Development of Pentecostalism in Italy," in *European Pentecostalism*, ed. William Kay and Anne Dyer (Leiden, Netherlands: Brill, 2011), 189–204; Salvatore Esposito, *Un secolo di Pentecostalismo Italiano: Cenni sulle origini, le discussioni Parlamentari, L'assetto contemporaneo delle Assemblee di Dio in Italia* (Milan, Italy: The Writer, 2015). On Italian Pentecostalism, see also Salvatore Cucchiari, "Between Shame and Sanctification: Patriarchy and Its Transformation in Sicilian Pentecostalism," *American Ethnologist* 17, no. 4 (1990): 687–707.

25. In this regard, see Giorgio Spini, "La persecuzione degli Evangelici in Italia," *Il Ponte* 1 (1953): 1–14; Giorgio Spini, "Movimenti Evangelici nell'Italia contemporanea," *Rivista Storica Italiana* 80, no. 5 (1968): 463–98.

26. Religions with an *intesa* (special agreement) with the state are: the Walde-
    sian/Methodist Church; the Jewish community; the Assemblies of God; the
    Lutheran, Baptist, Apostolic Churches, and Orthodox Church; the Church of
    Jesus of the Latter-Day Saints; the Seventh Day Adventist Church; and the
    Buddhist and Hindu communities.

27. Adu Akosua, "Peaceful Demonstration by Christ, Peace and Love Church to
    Be Held in Bergamo," *International African Herald*, November 24, 2012,
    http://www.theafricaninternationalherald.com/index.php/quick-guide/
    item/241-peaceful-demonstration-by-christ-peace-and-love-church-to-be-
    held-in-bergamo.

28. Ibid.

29. Ibid.

30. Franco Garelli, *Catholicism in Italy in the Age of Pluralism* (Lanham, MD: Lex-
    ington, 2010); Franco Garelli, *Religion Italian Style: Continuities and Changes in
    a Catholic Country* (Burlington, VT: Ashgate, 2014); Giuseppe Giordan and
    Enzo Pace, eds., *Mapping Religion and Spirituality in a Postsecular World* (Leiden,
    Netherlands: Brill, 2012); Giuseppe Giordan and Enzo Pace, eds., *Religious
    Pluralism: Framing Religious Diversity in the Contemporary World* (New York, NY:
    Springer, 2014).

31. Enzo Pace and Marco Marzano, "Introduction: The Many Faces of Italian
    Catholicism in the 21st Century," *Social Compass* 60, no. 3 (2013): 299–301;
    Enzo Pace, "Achilles and the Tortoise: A Society Monopolized by Catholicism
    Faced with an Unexpected Religious Pluralism," *Social Compass* 60, no. 3
    (2013): 315–31; Marco Marzano, "The 'Sectarian' Church: Catholicism in
    Italy since John Paul II," *Social Compass* 60, no. 3 (2013): 302–14.

32. Bourdieu defines *habitus* as a structure that organizes practices and the per-
    ception of practices. Habitus is a certain perception of the world and a special
    structure of feelings internalized through social experiences in a given social
    context. It is therefore a way of life inscribed in the body rather than a con-
    scious reflection. See Pierre Bourdieu, *Distinction: A Social Critique of the Judg-
    ment of Taste*, trans. Richard Nice (Cambridge, MA: Harvard University Press,
    1984), 170.

33. See also Pace, "Achilles and the Tortoise: A Society Monopolized by Catholi-
    cism Faced with an Unexpected Religious Pluralism," *Social Compass* 60, no.
    3 (2013): 315–31.

34. Marco Marzano, *Quel che resta dei Cattolici: Inchiesta sulla crisi della Chiesa in
    Italia* (Milan, Italy: Feltrinelli Editore, 2012); Marco Marzano and Nadia Ur-
    binati, *Missione impossibile: La riconquista Cattolica della sfera pubblica* (Bologna,
    Italy: Il Mulino, 2013).

35. Grace Davie, *Religion in Modern Europe: A Memory Mutates* (Oxford, UK: Ox-
    ford University Press, 2000); Grace Davie, "Vicarious Religion: A Method-
    ological Challenge," in *Everyday Religion: Observing Modern Religious Lives*, ed.
    Nancy Ammerman (New York, NY: Oxford University Press, 2006), 21–37.

36. There is a rich and nuanced body of works on Gramsci's hegemony. Scholars who contributed to it are, among others, Jean Comaroff and John Comaroff, *Of Revelation and Revolution*. Volu. 1, *Christianity, Colonialism, and Consciousness in South Africa* (Chicago, IL: University of Chicago Press, 1991), 23; Walter Adamson, *Hegemony and Revolution: A Study of Antonio Gramsci's Political and Cultural Theory* (Los Angeles: University of California Press, 1983); Peter Thomas, *The Gramscian Moment: Philosophy, Hegemony and Marxism* (Leiden, Netherlands: Brill, 2009); Kate Crehan, *Gramsci, Culture and Anthropology* (Los Angeles: University of California Press, 2002); Chantal Mouffe, *Gramsci and Marxist Theory* (London, UK: Routledge, 2014).

37. On the funeral lamentation, see Alberto Cirese, *Cultura egemonica e culture subalterne* (Palermo, Italy: Palumbo Editore, 1971). Gramsci also gave good examples. In his letters, Gramsci often recalled episodes and characters from the religious popular world steeped in passions and creative spirit. The people who Gramsci remembered were always a little over the top, slightly mad, certainly imaginative; they challenged the conception of the world and feeling rules of the dominant hegemonic culture. Among them it is worth mentioning the folkloristic character called Donna Bisodia. Writing to his sister Teresina from prison on November 16, 1931, Gramsci recalled an episode of his youth in one of his letters from the prison.:

> Do you remember that Aunt Grazia really believed there had been a "Donna Bisodia" who was so pious that her name was always mentioned in the Pater Noster. It came from the words "dona nobis hodie" that she, like many others, took to mean "Donna Bisodia" and imagined was a dame of bygone times, when everyone went to church and there was still some religion in this world. You could write a short story about this imaginary "Donna Bisodia" who was named as an example. I wonder how many times Aunt Grazia must have said to Grazietta, Emma, and you too perhaps: "Ah, you're certainly not like Donna Bisodia!" when you didn't want to go to confession before Easter.

Donna Bisodia is a character created by popular Catholicism in Sardinia, born of a manipulation or mispronunciation of a line in the "Our Father" that was recited exclusively in Latin up until the Second Vatican Council (in the 1960s), although only very few people could understand the meaning of the Latin words. According to popular Sardinian tradition, Donna Bisodia was Saint Peter's mother. Many elderly women would recite the Pater Noster as "Panem nostrum quotidianum Donna Bisodia," instead of "Panem nostrum quotidianum dona nobis hodie." The faithful would swear that they heard the priest at the altar mention Donna Bisodia's name. She was remembered as a model of piety and devotion, but also as a jealous schemer who obliged her son, the apostle Peter, to make sure that her name was included in the prayer. So Peter came to have a shrewish mother who was jealous even of Jesus—because he

could work miracles but her son Peter could not. The Sardinian writer Giammario Demartis took up Gramsci's idea for a short story about Donna Bisodia
and wrote an "apocryphal gospel" entitled "A misciammureddu" (in Sardinian), or "The Gospel according to Donna Bisodia." It is an unusually scathing,
amusing, and ironic portrait of a type of matriarchal woman and of a poor and
humble Sardinian world that yet pulses with life. Giammario Demartis, *Il Van-
gelo di Donna Bisodia; Centotre contos a misciamurreddu* (Cagliari, Sardinia: Isola
Editrice, 2011).

38. Milingo served as a parish priest in Zambia from 1958 to 1965. In 1965, he left
to study sociology and education in Rome and Dublin. He returned to Zambia
and started what is still remembered as a quasi revolution. He joined the Catholic charismatic renewal movement and became a national figure owing to his
outspoken personality and healing ministry that attracted thousands of people. He was made a bishop by Pope John Paul II in 1969 at the age of thirty-
nine. Controversies over his "too Africanized" Catholicism and his statements
against white Christianity and non-African missionaries, who constituted the
majority of the priests in Lusaka at that time, resulted in his forced relocation
to Rome. After almost one year in Rome, Milingo met Pope John Paul II. At
that meeting, the pope acknowledged Milingo's healing ministry and, according to historical sources, told him: "Healing is your bent. Let us discuss together what you can do in Rome." At that point, the pope and his closest col-
laborators did not know Milingo's potential impact. After the meeting, the
presence of Milingo in Rome became a thorn in the side of the Vatican. Milingo
built his own ministry that attracted thousands of Italians. The crowds that
flocked to Milingo's mass healings and exorcisms were so vast that the
churches he was using could not contain the people. Followers of Milingo
perpetually stood on the stairs of his apartment in Via di Porta Angelica, facing
the walls of the Vatican, to ask for blessings and healings. Among Milingo's
followers were people from all walks of life, including Giovannino Agnelli, late
president of the automobile firm Fiat. Milingo's popularity soon became a
problem for the Vatican. He had a long list of supporters, but longer yet was
the list of his opponents. The story became more and more complicated.
Milingo's provocations and actions, including his marriage, brought about the
final break with the Catholic Church that, after vainly trying to redeem him
(by forcing him to a protected exile under the custody of the Catholic Focolar
movement), excommunicated him and warned him not to wear Catholic
vestments, conduct Mass, or baptize anybody.

See Gerrie ter Haar, *Spirit of Africa: The Healing Ministry of Archbishop
Milingo of Zambia* (Trenton, NJ: Africa World Press, 1992); Vittorio Lanter-
nari, *Medicina, magia, religione, valori* (Liguori, MO: Liguori, 1994); Thomas
Csordas, *Language, Charisma, and Creativity: The Ritual Life of a Religious Move-
ment* (Los Angeles: University of California Press, 1997); Phyllis Zagano,
Women & Catholicism: Gender, Communion, and Authority (New York, NY:

Palgrave Macmillan, 2011); Giordana Charuty, "L'africaniste en Italie : Le cas Milingo," *Archives de Sciences Sociales Des Religions* 161 (2013): 93–111.

39. Lanternari, *Medicina, magia, religione, valori*, 299.

40. In this regard, see Csordas's current research: Thomas Csordas, "Hammering the Devil with Prayer (Prayer to Relieve Affliction from Evil Spirits)," *Reverberations*, February 26, 2013, http://forums.ssrc.org/ndsp/2013/02/26/hammering-the-devil-with-prayer-prayer-to-relieve-affliction-from-evil-spirits/.

41. Antonio Gramsci, *Prison Notebooks*, ed. Derek Boothman (Minneapolis: University of Minnesota Press, 1995), 9.

42. Philip Jenkins, *The Next Christendom: The Coming of Global Christianity* (New York, NY: Oxford University Press, 2011).

2. Contact Zones and Religious Short Circuits

1. Mary Louise Pratt, *Mary Louise Pratt, Imperial Eyes: Travel Writing and Transculturation* (London: Routledge, 2007), 4–6.

2. Jacques Rancière, *The Nights of Labour*, trans. John Drury (Philadelphia, PA: Temple University Press, 1989).

3. Michel de Certeau, *The Practice of Everyday Life* (Los Angeles: University of California Press, 1984), 25.

4. de Certeau, *The Practice of Everyday Life*, 25.

5. These numbers are not precise. Being a foreign state, the Holy See is not obliged to report to the Italian authorities on its real estate. That is why nobody knows exactly how many buildings it owns and what activities go on inside them. The immense heritage of properties is almost entirely tax free, thanks to the provisions made by the various governments that have ruled Italy over time, including the last of Silvio Berlusconi's governments. See Marzio Bartolini, "Chiesa, 2mila miliardi di immobili nel mondo," *Il Sole 24 ORE*, February 15, 2013, http://www.ilsole24ore.com/art/notizie/2013-02-15/chiesa-2mila-miliardi-immobili-082813.shtml?uuid=Ab3cTeUH; Ettore Livini, "Palazzi, scuole, alberghi e ospedali tutti gli immobili di 'Vaticano Spa,'" *La Repubblica*, December 8, 2011, http://www.repubblica.it/economia/2011/12/08/news/vaticano_ici_miliardo-26266053/.

6. Paolo Ojetti, "Vaticano S.p.A," *L'Europeo*, January 7, 1977.

7. On the Pentecostal diaspora in Europe, and the practices of space, including worshiping in church buildings that belong to other denominational churches, see also Regien Smit, "The Church Building: A Sanctuary or a Consecrated Place? Conflicting Views between Angolan Pentecostals and European Presbyterians," *African Diaspora* 2, no. 2 (2009): 182–202. Smit's piece is part of a special issue of *African Diaspora* edited by Kim Knibbe and Marten van der Meulen. Compare Kim Knibbe and Marten van der Meulen, "The Role of Spatial Practices and Locality in the Constituting of the Christian," *African Diaspora* 2, no. 2 (2009): 125–30.

8. On the controversy of tithes and prosperity gospel, see also Devaka Pre-mawardhana, "Transformational Tithing: Sacrifice and Reciprocity in a Neo-Pentecostal Church," *Nova Religio: The Journal of Alternative and Emergent Religions* 15, no. 4 (May 1, 2012): 85–109, doi:10.1525/nr.2012.15.4.85. Premawardhana especially looks at this practice among underclass Cape Verdeans in a Boston branch of the Universal Church of the Kingdom of God. Premawardhana analyzes the role of tithes in this community and addresses the transformative role of giving as a strategy of empowerment born out of a spirituality centered on sacrifice and reciprocity. On Pentecostalism and prosperity gospel, see also Attanasi Kasi and Yong Amos, *Pentecostalism and Prosperity: The Socio-Economics of the Global Charismatic Movement* (New York: Palgrave Macmillan, 2012).

9. Members of Celestial Church of Christ do not wear shoes during their worship service and wear their traditional *sutana*, a long, white garment that led to them being known as the "white garment church," along with the Church of the Cherubim and Seraphim. On these churches, see Hermione Harris, *Yoruba in Diaspora: An African Church in London* (New York: Palgrave Macmillan, 2006); Afe Adogame, "Ranks and Robes: Art Symbolism and Identity in the Celestial Church of Christ in the European Diaspora," *Material Religion: The Journal of Objects, Art and Belief* 5, no. 1 (2009): 70–87; Afe Adogame, "Engaging the Rhetoric of Spiritual Warfare: The Public Face of Aladura in Diaspora," *Journal of Religion in Africa* 34, no. 4 (2004): 493–522; Elisha Renne, "Consecrated Garments and Spaces in the Cherubim and Seraphim Church Diaspora," *Material Religion: The Journal of Objects, Art and Belief* 5, no. 1 (2009): 70–87.

10. John 3: 5–8, NIV.

11. Literature on being Pentecostal and born again is vast and ranges from theology to anthropology, sociology to history. Particularly relevant for this book are the works of Ruth Marshall and Nimi Wariboko. Compare Ruth Marshall, *Political Spiritualities: The Pentecostal Revolution in Nigeria* (Chicago, IL: Chicago University Press, 2009); and Nimi Wariboko, *Nigerian Pentecostalism* (Rochester, NY: University of Rochester Press, 2014).

12. Simon Coleman, *The Globalisation of Charismatic Christianity* (New York, NY: Cambridge University Press, 2000), 198. See also Simon Coleman, "Words as Things: Language, Aesthetics and the Objectification of Protestant Evangelicalism," *Journal of Material Culture* 1, no. 1 (1996): 107–28.

13. Mattijs van de Port used this term to describe the ecstatic moments he witnesses in his fieldwork on Bahian Candomblé. See Van de Port, *Ecstatic Encounters: Bahian Candomblé and the Quest for the Unknown* (Amsterdam, Netherlands: Amsterdam University Press, 2011), 18.

14. Wariboko, *Nigerian Pentecostalism*, 134.

15. Randall Collins, *Interaction Ritual Chains* (Princeton, NJ: Princeton University Press, 2004). According to Collins, emotional energy is generated when there is a physical assembly of the group and bodies in proximity; the group

has some form of identity markers; and people share actions, awareness, symbols, and objects.

16. The field of the study of religion and emotion is certainly vast and rich. Among other things, scholars have explored the foundational role of emotions in shaping moral or religious norms, communities, rituals, material worlds, and languages. Examples of these works include Ole Riis and Linda Woodhead, *A Sociology of Religious Emotion* (Oxford, UK: Oxford University Press, 2007); John Corrigan, *The Oxford Handbook of Religion and Emotion* (Oxford, UK: Oxford University Press, 2007); John Corrigan, *Religion and Emotion: Approaches and Interpretations* (Oxford, UK: Oxford University Press, 2004); Douglas Davies, *Emotion, Identity, and Religion: Hope, Reciprocity, and Otherness* (Oxford, UK: Oxford University Press, 2011).

17. Michael Jackson, "Knowledge of the Body," *Man* 18, no. 2 (1983): 328.

18. Pierre Bourdieu, *Outline of a Theory of Practice* (Cambridge, UK: Cambridge University Press, 1977), 93–94.

19. Certainly, as I also said in the introduction, Catholicism is not a homogeneous religious and social world, and it includes differences in theological questions and even styles of prayer. The Catholic charismatic prayer style, for instance, is more similar to a vibrant Pentecostal gathering than to the Catholic Sunday prayer at the Tempio della Pace. The same can be said about the Pentecostal heterogeneous world and its diverse engagement, for instance, with dance and music. The question of the diversity of prayer, as well as its social and religious role, has been the subject of various studies developed across a variety of disciplines. In the field of social sciences, Marcel Mauss's seminal (uncompleted) work has been an important reference for several significant studies of prayer as social activities. He identified prayer as a social phenomenon, an institution, a social reality, and collective fact. See Marcel Mauss, *On Prayer*, ed. W. S. F Pickering (Oxford, NY: Berghahn, 2003). Sociological studies on prayer look at the relationship between prayer and community: Mary Jo Neitz, *Charisma and Community: A Study of Religious Commitment within the Charismatic Renewal* (Piscataway, NJ: Transaction, 1987); Nancy Ammerman, "Religious Identities and Religious Institutions," in *Handbook of Sociology of Religion*, ed. Michele Dillon (Cambridge, UK: Cambridge University Press, 2003), 207–24; Meredith McGuire, *Lived Religion: Faith and Practice in Everyday Life* (New York: Oxford University Press, 2008); as well as prayer and power: William Swatos, "The Power of Prayer: A Prolegomenon to an Ascetical Sociology," *Review of Religious Research* 24, no. 2 (1982): 153–63; and prayer and the body: Thomas Csordas, *Embodiment and Experience: The Existential Ground of Culture and Self* (Cambridge, UK: Cambridge University Press, 1994); Thomas Csordas, *Body/Meaning/Healing* (New York, NY: Palgrave Macmillan, 2002). Scholars have conceptualized the multidimensionality of prayer and the variety of practices: Friedrich Heiler, *Prayer: A Study in the History and Psychology of Religion* (Oxford, UK: Oxford University Press, 1932); as well as its influence on people's psychophysical well-being: Margaret Poloma and Brian Pendleton, "The Effects of

Prayer and Prayer Experiences on Measures of General Well-Being," *Journal of Psychology & Theology* 19 (1991): 71–83; Margaret Poloma and Gordon Gallup, *Varieties of Prayer: A Survey Report* (Harrisburg, PA: Trinity, 1991). Also, prayer has been studied as a coping and antianxiety strategy: Laurence Brown, *The Human Side of Prayer: The Psychology of Prayer* (Birmingham, AL: Religious Education, 1994); Kenneth Pargament, *The Psychology of Religion and Coping: Theory, Research, Practice* (New York, NY: Guilford Press, 1997); and as a means of compensating economic and social deprivation: Mary Patillo-McCoy, "Church Culture as a Strategy of Action in the Black Community," *American Sociological Review* 63, no. 6 (1998): 767–84; Ronald Inglehart and Pippa Norris, *Sacred and Secular: Religion and Politics Worldwide* (Cambridge, UK: Cambridge University Press, 2004); Neal Krause and Linda Chatters, "Exploring Race Differences in a Multidimensional Battery of Prayer Measures among Older Adults," *Sociology of Religion* 69, no. 2 (2005): 23–43; Joseph Baker, "An Investigation of the Sociological Patterns of Prayer Frequency and Content," *Sociology of Religion* 69, no. 2 (2008): 169–85; Rodney Stark and William Bainbridge, *A Theory of Religion* (New Brunswick, NJ: Rutgers University Press, 1987).

20. On touch in Ghanaian Pentecostalism, see Marleen de Witte, "Touch," *Material Religion: The Journal of Objects, Art and Belief* 7, no. 1 (2011): 148–55.

21. However, over the years, the approach of the Catholic Church to evil and exorcism has undergone various changes. Since recent times, the Catholic Church seems to be more and more open to publicly engaging this thorny question. Pope Benedict and the current Pope Francis often refer(red) to Satan and to his activities in the church and the world, and there are frequent authorized special training sessions, schools, and workshops on exorcism in Italy. In 2015, for instance, the European University in Rome, in collaboration with the Catholic Istituto Sacerdos, held a course on exorcism open to priests, psychologists, doctors, teachers, and social workers. The teachers included priests, philosophers, historians, and intellectuals, and topics ranged from how to recognize the devil to how to defeat him. Various national newspapers reported on the course. See, for instance, Orazio la Rocca, "Lezione di esorcismo: 'Il male si sconfigge,'" *La Repubblica,* January 4, 2015, http://roma. repubblica.it/cronaca/2015/04/01/news/lezione_di_esorcismo_ il_male_si_sconfigge_-110942419/. On the broader question of exorcism and deliverance in Catholicism, see the seminal works and recent research of Thomas Csordas on the Catholic Charismatic movement in the United States and Italy that extensively analyzes the various prayers and practices of exorcism, the complex physical and psychiatric features of spirit possession, their collective representations and cosmology, as well as the social role of exorcism as individual and communal process of reformation. See Csordas, *Body/Meaning/Healing*; Thomas Csordas, *The Sacred Self: A Cultural Phenomenology of Charismatic Healing* (Los Angeles: University of California Press, 1997). For his recent research on Catholic charismatic exorcism and healing, see Thomas Csordas, "Hammering the Devil with Prayer (Prayer to Relieve Affliction

from Evil Spirits)," *Reverberations*, February 26, 2013, http://forums.ssrc.org/ndsp/2013/02/26/hammering-the-devil-with-prayer-prayer-to-relieve-af-fliction-from-evil-spirits/.

22. Franz Fanon, *Black Skin, White Masks: The Experiences of a Black Man in a White World* (New York, NY: Grove, 1967), 92. Concerning the Italian imaginary about the presumed cannibalism in Africa, I will mention only one example that emerged during the World Cup and that involved the only black Italian soccer player, Mario Balotelli. The demise of the Italian team and what the general public regarded as Balotelli's poor performance triggered a slew of harsh critiques and vicious verbal attacks on Balotelli. In a public statement, the soccer player said that the public never would have treated him in such a rude and aggressive way in Africa. The response of a couple of popular actors was that that he should be happy to be in Italy because in Africa they would have cooked him in a pot. On this event, see Antonio Nasso, "La battuta razzista di Giovanni: 'Balotelli e gli Africani? Magari L'avrebbero messo nel pentolone,'" *La Repubblica TV*, June 26, 2014, http://video.repubblica.it/dossier/brasile-2014-mondiali-calcio/la-battuta-razzista-di-giovanni-balotelli-e-gli-africani-magari-l-avrebbero-messo-nel-pentolone/170595/169084.

23. Images of Bishop Diana shot that same day can be found in Annalisa Butticci, ed., *Na God: Aesthetics of African Charismatic Power* (Padua, Italy: Grafiche Turato Edizioni, 2013); and on my research website, available at http://www.pentecostalaesthetics.net.

24. On this matter, see Brigid Sackey, "Charismatism, Women, and Testimonies: Religion and Popular Culture in Ghana," *Ghana Studies* 8 (2005): 169–96; Maria Frahm-Arp, *Professional Women in South African Pentecostal Charismatic Churches* (Leiden, Netherlands: Brill, 2010); Jane Soothill, *Gender, Social Change and Spiritual Power: Charismatic Christianity in Ghana* (Leiden, Netherlands: Brill, 2007); Afe Adogame, "'I Am Married to Jesus!,'" *Archives de Sciences Sociales des Religions* 143 (2008): 129–49; H. Jurgens Hendriks et al., eds., *Men in the Pulpit, Women in the Pew? Addressing Gender Inequality in Africa* (Stellenbosch, South Africa: African Sun Media, 2012); Rosalind Hackett, "Sacred Paradoxes: Women and Religious Plurality in Nigeria," in *Women, Religion and Social Change*, ed. Y. Haddad and E. Findly (Albany, NY: SUNY Press,1985), 247–70; Rosalind Hackett, "Women as Leaders and Participants in Spiritual Churches," in *New Religious Movements in Nigeria*, ed. Rosalind Hackett (Lewiston, NY: Edwin Mellen, 1987).

25. Bruno Reinhardt, "Soaking in Tapes: The Haptic Voice of Global Pentecostal Pedagogy in Ghana," *Journal of the Royal Anthropological Institute* 20, no. 2 (2014): 315–36.

26. John Kwabena Asamoah-Gyadu, "Anointing through the Screen: Neo-Pentecostalism and Televised Christianity in Ghana," *Studies in World Christianity* 11, no. 1 (2005): 9–28.

27. Ayo Oritsejafor is the president of the Christian Association in Nigeria. His leadership sparked much criticism for his controversial comments on the

violence in Northern Nigeria. He was further criticized when he bought a private jet to celebrate his forty years of ministry.

28. Ayo Oritsejafor, speech, Padua, Italy, September 2012.

29. In her work, Jean Comaroff examines the embodied forms of resistance, or the "beguiling cultural patchwork" of the Tsidi people of South Africa against the oppressive capitalist system introduced by the apartheid regime. Jean Comaroff, *Body of Power, Spirit of Resistance: The Culture and History of a South African People* (Chicago, IL: University of Chicago Press, 1985).

30. Alain Badiou, *Being and Event*, trans. Oliver Feltham (New York, NY: Bloomsbury Academic, 2013). On the concept of political event, see also Nick Hewlett, *Badiou, Balibar, Rancière: Re-Thinking Emancipation* (London, UK: A&C Black, 2010).

31. Compare Matthew Engelke, *A Problem of Presence: Beyond Scripture in an African Church* (Los Angeles: University of California Press, 2007); Birgit Meyer and Dick Houtman, "Material Religion—How Things Matter," in *Things: Religion and the Question of Materiality*, ed. Birgit Meyer and Dick Houtman (New York, NY: Fordham University Press, 2012), 1–23; Reinhardt, "Soaking in Tapes: The Haptic Voice of Global Pentecostal Pedagogy in Ghana"; Simon Coleman, "Materializing the Self: Words and Gifts in the Construction of Charismatic Protestant Identity," in *The Anthropology of Christianity*, ed. Fenella Cannell (Durham, NC: Duke University Press, 2006), 163–84; Coleman, "Words as Things: Language, Aesthetics and the Objectification of Protestant Evangelicalism."

3. Holy Bones

1. Examples of the various powers and identities of relics in various religious traditions are beautifully presented in a collection of essays edited by Alexandra Walsham. See Alexandra Walsham, ed., *Relics and Remains* (Oxford, UK: Oxford University Press, 2010).

2. For some key contributions on the study of relics in various religious traditions, see Sergius Bulgakov, *Relics and Miracles* (Grand Rapids, MI: Wm. B. Eerdmans, 2011); Patrick Geary, *Phantoms of Remembrance: Memory and Oblivion at the End of the First Millennium* (Princeton, NJ: Princeton University Press, 1994); Peter Brown, *The Cult of the Saints: Its Rise and Function in Latin Christianity* (Chicago, IL: University of Chicago Press, 1982); Caroline Bynum, *Fragmentation and Redemption: Essays on Gender and the Human Body in Medieval Religion* (New York, NY: Urzone, 1991); Caroline Bynum, *The Resurrection of the Body in Western Christianity, 200–1336* (New York, NY: Columbia University Press, 1995); Caroline Bynum and Paula Gerson, "Body-Part Reliquaries and Body Parts in the Middle Ages," *Gesta* 36, no. 1 (1997): 3–7; Caroline Bynum, *Metamorphosis and Identity* (New York, NY: Zone, 2001); Caroline Bynum, *Wonderful Blood: Theology and Practice in Late Medieval Northern Germany and Beyond* (Philadelphia: University of Pennsylvania Press,

2007); Caroline Bynum, *Christian Materiality: An Essay on Religion in Late Medieval Europe* (New York: Zone, 2011); Sally Cornelison and Scott Montgomery, eds., *Images, Relics, and Devotional Practices in Medieval And Renaissance Italy* (Tempe: Arizona Center for Medieval and Renaissance Studies, 2006); Benedicta Ward, "Relics and the Medieval Mind," *International Journal for the Study of the Christian Church* 10, no. 4 (2010): 274–86; Charles Freeman, *Holy Bones, Holy Dust: How Relics Shaped the History of Medieval Europe* (New Haven, CT: Yale University Press, 2012).

3. The anxiety about the integrity of the body was a reflection of the anxiety about integrity of personhood and the community of the Christians. According to Bynum, the doctrine of resurrection that undergirds the veneration of relics was a reassuring vision meant to consolidate the vulnerable sense of personhood and community. See Caroline Bynum, *Christian Materiality: An Essay on Religion in Late Medieval Europe.*

4. Ibid., 257.

5. Bynum, *The Resurrection of the Body in Western Christianity, 200–1336*, ii.

6. Several scholars who have devoted their study to the reliquaries illuminate the intrinsic role of these often magnificent objects for the cult of relics. In Europe, ever since the Middle Ages, relics have been placed in precious reliquaries and frequently displayed in crypts and, on special occasions, celebrated and venerated in processions and other liturgical ceremonies. Compare Hans Belting, *Likeness and Presence: A History of the Image before the Era of Art* (Chicago, IL: University of Chicago Press, 1994); Erik Thunø, *Image and Relic: Mediating the Sacred in Early Medieval Rome* (Rome, Italy: L'Erma di Bretschneider, 2002); Bynum and Gerson, "Body-Part Reliquaries and Body Parts in the Middle Ages"; Bynum, *Christian Materiality: An Essay on Religion in Late Medieval Europe.* These scholars have noted that these sophisticated gold reliquaries studded with precious stones have played an important part in pointing the gaze of the devout heavenward, not keeping it on the material substance of those embellishments. In this sense, reliquaries glorify and sublimate the matter of decay and putrefaction.

7. Charles Stinger, *The Renaissance in Rome* (Bloomington: Indiana University Press, 1998), 95.

8. In this regard, see Patrick Geary, *Furta Sacra: Thefts of Relics in the Central Middle Ages* (Princeton, NJ: Princeton University Press, 2011); S. A. Smith, "Bones of Contention: Bolsheviks and the Struggle against Relics 1918–1930," *Past & Present* 204, no. 1 (2009): 155–94; Julia Smith, "Rulers and Relics c.750–c.950: Treasure on Earth, Treasure in Heaven," *Past & Present* 206, no. 5 (2010): 73–96; Guy Lazure, "Possessing the Sacred: Monarchy and Identity in Philip II's Relic Collection at the Escorial," *Renaissance Quarterly* 60, no. 1 (2007): 58–93.

9. Daniel Olukoya, *Prayer Rain* (Mountain of Fire and Miracles Ministries, 2013), 380–82.

10. On Veronica's veil, see the work of Ewa Kuryluk, *Veronica and Her Cloth: History, Symbolism, and Structure of a "True" Image* (Hoboken, NJ: Blackwell, 1991).

11. Walsham, "Introduction," in *Relics and Remains*, 23.

12. On the social and political power of the relics, see Brown, *The Cult of the Saints: Its Rise and Function in Latin Christianity*; Geary, *Phantoms of Remembrance: Memory and Oblivion at the End of the First Millennium*; Christine Quigley, *Skulls and Skeletons: Human Bone Collections and Accumulation* (Jefferson, NC: McFarland, 2001); Guy Lazure, "Possessing the Sacred: Monarchy and Identity in Philip II's Relic Collection at the Escorial."

13. "La santa reliquia del cuore di San Camillo vola con Alitalia verso il Brasile," *Alitalia Social,* June 27, 2012, http://corporate.alitalia.it/static/upload/14c/14 c153aefb7594c354c6f93e16ec77e3.pdf

14. The procession with Saint Anthony's relics is an important spiritual experience for those taking part, an exercise of faith and devotion. It is also an important ritual of confessionalization. During the period of the confessionalization of European cities in the sixteenth to eighteenth centuries, the processions had a strong impact on the cities' urban layout and civic communities. See in this regard Heinz Schilling, "Calvinist and Catholic Cities: Urban Architecture and Ritual in Confessional Europe," *European Review* 12, no. 3 (2004): 293–312.

15. For examples, see "Vent'anni fa il furto delle reliquie del santo: Il racconto con i titoli del *Mattino*," *Il Mattino di Padova*, September 26, 2011, http://mattinopadova.gelocal.it/padova/foto-e-video/2011/09/26/fotogalleria/vent-anni-fa-il-furto-delle-reliquie-del-santo-il-racconto-con-i-titoli-del-em-mattino-em-1.1138647#1; Antonello Francica, "Felice maniero ordino' il furto di Sant'Antonio," *La Repubblica*, February 11, 1995, http://ricerca.repubblica.it/repubblica/archivio/repubblica/1995/02/11/felice-maniero-ordino-il-furto-di-sant.html.

16. Nicoletta Masetto, "Felice Maniero: 'Un boss non è un eroe,'" *Il Messaggero di Sant'Antonio,* October 11, 2011, Special Issue edition, 44.

17. Masetto, "Felice Maniero: 'Un boss non è un eroe,'" 45–46.

18. Oddly enough, another of Saint Anthony's relics was stolen in 2011, but this time from a church in Long Beach, California. The relic had been donated by the Vatican in 1903 when the parish in Long Beach was dedicated to Saint Anthony. A few days after the theft, the relic was recovered from the home of a devout woman who had it on display in her sitting room. See "Usa: Rubate le reliquie di Sant'Antonio di Padova a Long Beach," *Il Giornale*, June 15, 2011, http://www.ilgiornale.it/news/usa-rubate-reliquie-santantonio-padova-long-beach.html.

19. Unfortunately, the literature on Nana Ntona is very scanty. Historians who have mentioned the story of Nana Ntona are Hans Debrunner, *A History of Christianity in Ghana* (Accra, Ghana: Waterville, 1967), 220; de Graft in Harris Mobley, *The Ghanaian's Image of the Missionary: An Analysis of the Published Critiques of Christian Missionaries by Ghanaians 1897–1965* (Leiden, Netherlands: Brill, 1970), 17–18; Ralph Wiltgen, *Gold Coast Mission History, 1471–1880* (Techny, IL: Divine Word, 1956), 145, 164; Nolwenn l'Haridon and

Jean Polet, "Les statuettes funéraires en terre cuite de La Côte de l'Or té-moignent-elles d'une première Christianisation?," *Journal Des Africanistes* 75, no. 2 (2005): 65–86; Pashington Obeng, *Asante Catholicism: Religious and Cultural Reproduction among the Akan of Ghana* (Leiden, Netherlands: Brill, 1996), 105; Helena Pfann in John Kofi Agbeti, *West African Church History* (Leiden, Netherlands: Brill, 1986), 104.

20. The Dutch attacked Elmina in 1637. As Debrunner wrote, their fury against the Portuguese and the local people did not spare the Catholic churches and local shrines. The locals also tried to save part of the Catholic paraphernalia including a statue of Saint Anthony of Padua, a statue of Mary, and a statue of Saint Francis. The statue of the Virgin Mary later became the object of worship by a group of devotees called Santa Mariafo, which means "the Santa Maria people," while the statue of Saint Anthony found refuge in a local shrine.

21. Larry Yarak, "'Creative [and] Expedient Misunderstandings': Elmina-Dutch Relations on the Gold Coast in the Nineteenth Century," unpublished paper, 2014.

22. See http://w2.vatican.va/content/john-paul-ii/en/apost_exhortations/documents/hf_jp-ii_exh_14091995_ecclesia-in-africa.html. However, concerning the veneration of ancestors it is important to note that until the Second Vatican Council even the Catholic Church, along with the Protestants and Pentecostals, looked with suspicion on what appeared to be a local idolatrous cult.

23. Alisa La Gamma, *Eternal Ancestors: The Art of the Central African Reliquary* (New Heaven, CT: Yale University Press, 2007).

24. Compare Ogbu Kalu, "Ancestral Spirituality and Society in Africa," in *African Spirituality: Forms, Meanings, and Expressions*, ed. Jacob K. Olupona (New York: Crossroad, 2000), 54–84; Michael Jindra and Joel Noret, eds., *Funerals in Africa: Exploration of a Social Phenomenon* (Berghahn, 2013); Olatunde Lawuyi, "Obituary and Ancestral Worship: Analysis of a Contemporary Cultural Form in Nigeria," *Sociological Analysis* 48, no. 4 (1988): 373–79; Meyer Fortes, "Some Reflections on Ancestor Worship in Africa," in *African Systems of Thought*, ed. Meyer Fortes and Germaine Dieterlen (Oxford, UK: Oxford University Press, 1964), 122–42.

25. Art. 946, *The Catechism of the Catholic Church (English Translation for the Catholic Church in the United States of America* (Vatican City: Libreria Editrice Vaticana, 1994), 247.

26. "Relics of St. Therese to be in South Africa during World Cup," *Catholic News Agency*, May 6, 2010, http://www.catholicnewsagency.com/news/relics_of_st._therese_to_be_in_south_africa_during_world_cup/.

27. Daniel Wesangula, "A Saint's Hand Is Coming to Nairobi," *Nation*, September 3, 2011, http://www.nation.co.ke/news/A-saints-hand-is-coming-to-Nairobi-/-/1056/1229936/-/tuilvbz/-/index.html.

28. Nimi Wariboko, *Nigerian Pentecostalism* (Rochester, NY: University of Rochester Press, 2014), 104–5.

29. Several scholars studied the intensification of "witchcraft" discourses and practices in many postcolonial states in Africa. Among them are: Birgit Meyer, "Translating the Devil: An African Appropriation of Pietist Protestantism: The Case of the Peki Ewe, 1847–1992" (PhD dissertation, University of Amsterdam, 1995); Birgit Meyer, "'Make a Complete Break with the Past': Memory and Post-Colonial Modernity in Ghanaian Pentecostalist Discourse," *Journal of Religion in Africa* 28, no. 3 (1998): 316–49; Adam Ashfort, *Witchcraft, Violence, and Democracy in South Africa* (Chicago, IL: University of Chicago Press, 2005); Apter Andrew, "Atinga Revisited: Yoruba Witchcraft and the Cocoa Economy, 1950–1951," in *Modernity and Its Malcontent: Ritual and Power in Postcolonial Africa*, ed. Jean Comaroff and John Comaroff (Chicago, IL: University of Chicago Press 1993), 111–28; Jean Comaroff, John Comaroff, and Sally Falk Moore, "Occult Economies and the Violence of Abstraction: Notes from the South African Postcolony," *American Ethnologist* 26, no. 2 (1999): 279–303; James Ferguson, *Global Shadows: Africa in the Neoliberal World* (Durham, NC: Duke University Press, 2006); Rijk van Dijk, "Witchcraft and Skepticism by Proxy: Pentecostalism and Laughter in Urban Malawi," in *Magical Interpretations, Material Realities: Modernity, Witchcraft, and the Occult in Postcolonial Africa*, ed. Henrietta Moore and Todd Sanders (London, UK: Routledge, 2001), 97–117; James Howard Smith, *Bewitching Development: Witchcraft and the Reinvention of Development in Neoliberal Kenya* (Chicago, IL: Chicago University Press, 2008); Peter Geschiere, *The Modernity of Witchcraft: Politics and the Occult in Postcolonial Africa*, trans. Janet Roitman and Peter Geschiere (Charlottesville, VA: University of Virginia Press, 1997); Henrietta Moore and Todd Sanders, eds., *Magical Interpretations, Material Realities: Modernity, Witchcraft, and the Occult in Postcolonial Africa* (London, UK: Routledge, 2001); Gerrie ter Haar, *Imagining Evil: Witchcraft Beliefs and Accusations in Contemporary Africa* (Trenton, NJ: Africa World Press, 2007).

30. Prayers against witchcraft, overheard at Mountain of Fire and Miracles Ministries.

31. This enigmatic embodied response has attracted the curiosity of several scholars from a variety of disciplines. The literature on disgust is vast, but some of the most popular works include William Miller, *The Anatomy of Disgust* (Cambridge, MA: Harvard University Press, 1998); Aurel Kolnai, *On Disgust*, ed. Carolyn Korsmeyer and Barry Smith (Chicago, IL: Chicago University Press, 2004); Winfried Menninghaus, *Disgust: Theory and History of a Strong Sensation*, trans. Howard Eiland and Joey Golb (Albany, NY: SUNY Press, 2003); Daniel Kelly, *Yuck! The Nature and Moral Significance of Disgust* (Cambridge, MA: MIT Press, 2013); Martha Nussbaum, *Hiding from Humanity: Disgust, Shame, and the Law* (Princeton, NJ: Princeton University Press, 2006); Susan Miller, *Disgust: The Gatekeeper Emotion* (Hilldale, NJ: Analytic Press, 2004); Colin McGinn, *The Meaning of Disgust* (New York, NY: Oxford University Press, 2011); Mojca Kuplen, "Disgust and Ugliness: A Kantian Perspective," *Contemporary Aesthetics* 9 (2011).

32. Miller, *The Anatomy of Disgust*, 9.

33. Ibid.

34. Ibid., 206.

35. Wariboko, *Nigerian Pentecostalism*, 104.

36. On disgust as in-between space, see McGinn, *The Meaning of Disgust*; and Kolnai, *On Disgust*.

37. Jacques Rancière, *Dissensus: On Politics and Aesthetics*, trans. Steven Corcoran (London, UK: Continuum, 2010).

38. Jacques Rancière, *Disagreement: Politics and Philosophy*, trans. Julie Rose (Minneapolis: University of Minnesota Press, 1998), x.

39. Gernot Böhme, "Atmosphere as the Fundamental Concept of a New Aesthetics," *Thesis Eleven* 36, no. 1 (1993): 114.

40. Book of Revelation 4:1–6, KJV.

41. I am particularly grateful to my colleague Ato Quayson for the engaging conversation we had at the African Studies Association 2013 meeting on the aesthetics of disgust, and especially on the concept of terrible beauty.

42. Carolyn Korsmeyer, *Savoring Disgust: The Foul and the Fair in Aesthetics* (New York, NY: Oxford University Press, 2011), 171.

43. For a deeper discussion of terrible beauty, see Carolyn Korsmeyer, "Terrible Beauties," in *Contemporary Debates in Aesthetics and the Philosophy of Art*, ed. Matthew Kieran (London, UK: Wiley-Blackwell, 2005), 51–63; Emily Brady, "The Sublime, Terrible Beauty, and Ugliness," in *The Sublime in Modern Philosophy: Aesthetics, Ethics, and Nature* (Cambridge, UK: Cambridge University Press, 2013), 166–82.

44. Brian Larkin coined the term to describe the way in which urban residents of the city of Kano in northern Nigeria attune their hearing in order to capture only the sounds coming from the speakers of their own religious affiliations. Be they Christians or Muslims, they navigate in an urban environment saturated with prayers, sermons spoken by pastors and imam, and Christian and Muslim music. See Brian Larkin, "Techniques of Inattention: The Mediality of Loudspeakers in Nigeria," *Anthropological Quarterly* 87, no. 4 (2014): 989–1015.

4. Afro-Pentecostal Renaissance

1. The film was produced as part of the West African Pentecostalism in Southern Europe: The Spiritual Power, Engendered Spaces, and Aesthetic Practices project that was supported by the Progetto di Eccellenza of the Cariparo Foundation (2009–12) and by a Marie Curie Fellowship (2012–15). It can be found at http://www.pentecostalaesthetics.net/documentary/.

2. Giorgio Vasari, *Lives of the Most Eminent Painters, Sculptors, and Architects*, trans. Mrs. Jonathan Foster (London: H. G. Bohn, 1851), 51.

3. Christian K. Kleinbub, *Vision and the Visionary in Raphael* (Philadelphia: Pennsylvania State University Press, 2011).

4. Mark 9:2–9, NIV.

5. Mark 9:14–29, NIV.

6. Literature on Raphael is rich and vast. Examples of works that explore Raphael's genius and his artistic, religious, and political relevance are Sydney Freedberg, *Painting in the High Renaissance in Rome and Florence* (Cambridge, MA: Harvard University Press, 1961); Hans Belting, *The Invisible Masterpiece*, trans. Helen Atkins (Chicago, IL: University of Chicago Press, 2001); Roger Jones and Nicholas Penny, *Raphael* (New Haven, CT: Yale University Press, 1983), 235–39; Christa Gardner von Teufel, "Sebastiano Del Piombo, Raphael, and Narbonne: New Evidence," *Burlington Magazine* 126 (1984): 765–66; Fabrizio Mancinelli, *Primo piano di un capolavoro: La* Trasfigurazione *di Raffaello* (Vatican City: Libreria Editrice Vaticana, 1979); Jodi Cranston, "Tropes of Revelation in Raphael's *Transfiguration*," *Renaissance Quarterly* 56, no. 1 (2003): 1–25; Maurizio Calvesi, "Raffaello; La *Trasfigurazione*," in *Oltre Raffaello, aspetti della cultura figurativa del cinquecento Romano*, ed. Luciano Cassanelli and Sergio Rossi (Rome, Italy: Multigrafica, 1984), 1–41; David Alan Brown, "Leonardo and Raphael's *Transfiguration*," in *Raffaello a Roma: Il convegno del 1983*, ed. Christoph Luitpold Frommel and Matthias Winner (Rome, Italy: Edizioni l'Elefante, 1986), 237–43; Patricia Rubin, "Il contributo di Raffaello allo sviluppo della pala d'altare Rinascimentale," *Arte Cristiana* 78 (1990): 169–82.

7. On Pope Clement and his special appreciation of altarpieces, see also Opher Mansour, "Censure and Censorship, ca. 1600: The Visitation of Clement VIII and the Visual Arts," in *The Sensuous in the Counter-Reformation Church*, ed. Marcia Hall and Tracy Cooper (New York, NY: Cambridge University Press, 2013), 136–48.

8. Compare Marcia Hall and Tracy Cooper, eds., *The Sensuous in the Counter-Reformation Church* (New York, NY: Cambridge University Press, 2013); Alexander Nagel, *The Controversy of Renaissance Art* (Chicago, IL: Chicago University Press, 2011).

9. On the "imperfect" iconoclastic attitude of reformers, see, for instance, Willem van Asselt et al., eds., *Iconoclasm and Iconoclash: Struggle for Religious Identity* (Leiden, Netherlands: Brill, 2007).

10. Bette Talvacchia, "The Word Made Flesh: Spiritual Subjects and Carnal Depictions in Renaissance Art," in Hall and Cooper, *The Sensuous in the Counter-Reformation Church*, 49–73; Marcia Hall, "Introduction," in Hall and Cooper, *The Sensuous in the Counter-Reformation Church*, 1–20.

11. Hans Belting, *Likeness and Presence: A History of the Image before the Era of Art* (Chicago, IL: Chicago University Press, 1994).

12. The literature on Renaissance theory of visuality is vast, and it is beyond the scope of this book to acknowledge and engage the richness of the work developed by the various scholars who intensely studied this exhilarating moment in the history of art. Among the work that particularly resonates with the aim of this chapter, see Hans Belting, *Florence and Baghdad: Renaissance Art*

and Arab Science, trans. Deborah Lucas Schneider (Cambridge, MA: Belknap, 2011); on Renaissance art and theories of vision and perception, compare Robert Nelson, Jeffrey Hamburger, and Anne-Marie Bouché, eds., *Visuality Before and Beyond the Renaissance: Seeing as Others Saw* (New York, NY: Cambridge University Press, 2000); Jeffrey Hamburger and Anne-Marie Bouché, eds., *The Mind's Eye: Art and Theological Argument in the Middle Ages* (Princeton, NJ: Princeton University Press, 2005); John Hendrix and Charles Carman, eds., *Renaissance Theories of Visions* (Farnham, UK: Ashgate, 2010); David Summers, *Vision, Reflection, and Desire in Western Painting* (Chapel Hill: University of North Carolina Press, 2007); Christopher Braider, *Refiguring the Real: Picture and Modernity in Word and Image, 1400–1700* (Princeton, NJ: Princeton University Press, 1993); Michael Ann Holly, *Past Looking: Historical Imagination and the Rhetoric of the Image* (Ithaca, NY: Cornell University Press, 1996); James Elkins and Robert Williams, eds., *Renaissance Theory* (New York, NY: Routledge, 2008); Nicholas Temple, *Disclosing Horizons: Architecture, Perspective and Redemptive Space* (New York, NY: Routledge, 2007); Dalibor Vesely, *Architecture in the Age of Divided Representation: The Question of Creativity in the Shadow of Production* (Cambridge, MA: MIT Press, 2004).

13. Brigitte Bedos-Rezak, *When Ego Was Imago: Signs of Identity in the Middle Ages* (Leiden, Netherlands: Brill, 2010), 177.

14. Kleinbub, *Vision and the Visionary in Raphael*, 23.

15. Martin Rosenberg, "Raphael's *Transfiguration* and Napoleon's Cultural Politics," *Eighteenth-Century Studies* 19, no. 2 (1985): 180–205; Martin Rosenberg, *Raphael and France: The Artist as Paradigm and Symbol* (Philadelphia: Pennsylvania State University Press, 1995).

16. Rosenberg, "Raphael's *Transfiguration* and Napoleon's Cultural Politics," 195. The wedding of Napoleon was painted by Benjamin Zix, who portrayed the wedding procession at the foot of the *Transfiguration* and other paintings by Raphael.

17. J. Rickard, "Peace of Tolentino, 19 February 1797," *History of War*, February 3, 2009, http://www.historyofwar.org/articles/peace_tolentino.html.

18. Christopher Johns, *Antonio Canova and the Politics of Patronage in Revolutionary and Napoleonic Europe* (Los Angeles: University of California Press, 1998), 8. See also Belting, *The Invisible Masterpiece*.

19. As I also discussed in the introduction, a growing body of work now emphasizes the importance of concepts of mediation in the study of religion. Among scholars who look at religion as practice of mediation, see the pioneering work of Birgit Meyer, and in particular her chapter "Religious Sensations: Why Media, Aesthetics, and Power Matter in the Study of Contemporary Religion," in *Religion: Beyond a Concept*, ed. Hent de Vries (New York, NY: Fordham University Press, 2008), 704–23; Birgit Meyer, "Introduction: Special Issue Media and the Senses in the Making of Religious Experience," *Material Religion: The Journal of Objects, Art and Belief* 4, no. 2 (2008): 124–35; Birgit Meyer, "Mediating Absence—Effecting Spiritual Presence: Pictures

and the Christian Imagination," *Social Research: An International Quarterly* 78, no. 4 (2011): 1029–56. See also Patrick Eisenlohr, "The Anthropology of Media and the Question of Ethnic and Religious Pluralism," *Social Anthropology* 19, no. 1 (2011): 40–55; Charles Hirschkind, "Media, Mediation, Religion," *Social Anthropology* 19, no. 1 (2011): 90–97; Peter Pels, "The Modern Fear of Matter: Reflections on the Protestantism of Victorian Science," *Material Religion: The Journal of Objects, Art and Belief* 4, no. 3 (2008): 264–83; Matthew Engelke, *A Problem of Presence: Beyond Scripture in an African Church* (Los Angeles: University of California Press, 2007); Matthew Engelke, "Religion and the Media Turn: A Review Essay," *American Ethnologist* 37, no. 2 (2010): 371–77; Matthew Engelke, "Number and the Imagination of Global Christianity: Or, Mediation and Immediacy in the Work of Alain Badiou," *South Atlantic Quarterly* 109, no. 4 (2010): 811–29; Matthew Engelke, "Material Religion," in *The Cambridge Companion to Religious Studies*, ed. Robert Orsi (Cambridge, UK: Cambridge University Press, 2012). These scholars have discussed, among others, the role of mediation in religion, working in various ways with the ideas of Hent de Vries. See Hent de Vries and Samuel Weber, eds., *Religion and Media* (Redwood City, CA: Stanford University Press, 2010). Some of these scholars built on McLuhan's theory of media and developed what Matthew Engelke has nicely defined as the *media turn* in the study of religion. Compare Marshal McLuhan's work in Marshall McLuhan and Quentin Fiore, *The Medium Is the Message: An Inventory of Effects* (New York, NY: Random House, 1967). The statement "the media is the message" emblematically describes the conflation of the signifier and the signified that happens in religious mediations. Several scholars have argued that McLuhan's approach to media theory recalls the fundamental sacramental logic intrinsic to the incarnational thinking of the Catholic Church. McLuhan being a fervent Catholic, critics did not spare their comments on this unequivocal link like the ironic critiques of Theodore Roszak in "The Summa Popologica of Marshall McLuhan," *New Politics* 5, no. 2 (1966): 22–29. On this, see also de Vries and Weber, *Religion and Media*; S. Brent Plate, "Introduction: The Mediation of Meaning, or Re-Mediating McLuhan," *CrossCurrents* 62, no. 2 (2012): 156–61; Patrick Eisenlohr, *What Is a Medium? Theologies, Technologies and Aspirations* (Oxford, UK: Blackwell, 2011).

20. On remediation, see David Bolter and Richard Grusin, *Remediation: Understanding New Media* (Cambridge, MA: MIT Press, 2000). On remediations in African cultures, see Birgit Meyer, "Religious Remediation: Pentecostal Views in Ghanaians Video-Movies," *Postscript* 1.2/1.3 (2005): 155–81; and Matthias Krings, *African Appropriations Cultural Difference, Mimesis, and Media* (Bloomington: Indiana University Press, 2015).

21. Bolter and Grusin, *Remediation: Understanding New Media*, 60.

22. Interestingly, in discussing mediation, remediation, and immediacy of modern virtual realities, Bolter and Grusin track the genealogy of immediacy to Renaissance art including altarpieces, paintings, and cabinets. Of course, as

the two scholars note, these concepts are not "universal aesthetic truths" but cultural practices and assumptions that change in specific times.

23. Annalisa Butticci, ed., *Na God: Aesthetics of African Charismatic Power* (Rubano, Italy: Grafiche Turato Edizioni, 2013), 62.

24. Michael Taussig, *Mimesis and Alterity: A Particular History of the Senses* (New York, NY: Routledge, 1993). In his work, the Australian anthropologist looked at the encounter of the Cuna Indians from San Blas, Panama, with their colonizers. In this encounter, Taussig observed the Cuna's practices of reproduction of their colonizers' visual and material world including, for example, the Cuna's healing figurines that depict their white colonizers. Through an extensive analysis of the healing rituals involving these figurines, as well as other mimetic objects, Taussig showed that those copies were not mere representations but "presentifications" of the "re-presented" that collapse the boundaries of self and other (in Taussig's case, the boundaries between the colonized and colonizers) and turn the otherness of the colonizer into sameness. In this sense, mimesis is a creative process through which imitations and copies act as if they were real, with density and substance. Mimesis has been the object of research in different colonial contexts, including Fritz Kramer's classic comparative study on foreign representations in African statuary and performances and Paul Stoller's analysis of the mimetic performances of the Hauka cults of Niger. See Fritz Kramer, *The Red Fez: Art and Spirit Possession in Africa*, trans. Malcolm Green (London, UK: Verso, 1987); Paul Stoller, *Embodying Colonial Memories: Spirit Possession, Power, and the Hauka in West Africa* (New York, NY: Routledge, 1995).

25. Taussig, *Mimesis and Alterity: A Particular History of the Senses*, 129.

26. Ibid.

27. Stoller, *Embodying Colonial Memories: Spirit Possession, Power, and the Hauka in West Africa*, 75–76. On Paul Stoller's approach on sensuous mimesis, see also Paul Stoller, *Sensuous Scholarship* (Philadelphia: University of Pennsylvania Press, 1997).

28. Kleinbub, *Vision and the Visionary in Raphael*, 130.

29. In his work, Kleinbub discusses the various interpretations emphasizing either disjunction or cohesiveness that critics gave to the unusual compilation of the two scenes. Kleinbub seems to privilege—as do I—the cohesive interpretation of Wolfgang von Goethe. As reported by Kleinbub, Goethe writes: "What is the point then of separating the upper section from the lower? Both are one. Below are those who are suffering and need help: above is the active power that gives succour: both are inseparably related in their interactions." Kleinbub, *Vision and the Visionary in Raphael*, 433.

30. Birgit Meyer, "'There Is a Spirit in That Image': Mass-Produced Jesus Pictures and Protestant-Pentecostal Animation in Ghana," *Comparative Studies in Society & History* 52, no. 1 (2010): 101.

31. See Hans Belting, "Image, Medium, Body: A New Approach to Iconology," *Critical Inquiry* 31, no. 2 (2005): 302–19. The aesthetic engagement of images

and material forms is not limited to sight. Beyond sight (that has shaped the ocularcentric Western approach) touch, smell, hearing, and taste also form religious aesthetics and are important media by which to experience the divine. Several authors have called attention to a broad range of sensuous engagement that give birth to what Birgit Meyer called *religious sensations*. On the place and role of the various senses in the study of religion, see Birgit Meyer, ed., *Aesthetic Formations: Media, Religion, and the Senses* (New York, NY: Palgrave Macmillan, 2009); David Freedberg, *The Power of Images: Studies in the History and Theory of Response* (Chicago, IL: Chicago University Press, 1989); Webb Keane, "The Evidence of the Senses and the Materiality of Religion," *Journal of the Royal Anthropological Institute* 14, no. 1 (2008): 110–27; Martijn Oosterbaan, "Sonic Supremacy Sound, Space and Charisma in a Favela in Rio de Janeiro," *Critique of Anthropology*, no. 29, 1, (2009): 81–104. Marleen de Witte, "Accra's Sounds and Sacred Spaces," *International Journal of Urban and Regional Research* 32, no. 2 (2008): 690–709; Marleen de Witte, "Touch," *Material Religion: The Journal of Objects, Art and Belief* 7, no. 1 (2011): 148–55; David Chidester, *Word and Light: Seeing, Hearing, and Religious Discourse* (Urbana: University of Illinois Press, 1992). For a broader view on the "sensory turn" in anthropology, see the seminal work of David Howes, *Varieties of Sensory Experience: A Sourcebook in the Anthropology of the Senses* (Toronto, Canada: Toronto University Press, 1991); Constance Classen, *Worlds of Sense: Exploring the Senses in History and Across Cultures* (New York, NY: Routledge, 1993); Louise Vinge, *The Five Senses: Studies in a Literary Tradition* (Lund, Sweden: LiberLäromedel, 1975); Jojada Verrips, "'Haptic Screens' and Our 'Corporeal Eye,'" *Etnofoor* 15, no. 1/2 (2002): 21–46; Jojada Verrips, "Aisthesis and An-Easthesia," *Ethnologia Europea* 35, no. 1/2 (2006): 27–33.

32. On the power relations between people and objects, see Bruno Latour, *Reassembling the Social: An Introduction to Actor-Network-Theory* (Oxford, UK: Oxford University Press, 2005); Bruno Latour, *On the Modern Cult of the Factish Gods* (Durham, NC: Duke University Press, 2010). For empirical research in West Africa on this approach, see Karin Barber, "How Man Makes God in West Africa: Yoruba Attitudes towards the Òrìsà," *Africa: Journal of the International African Institute* 51, no. 3 (1981): 724–45; Judy Rosenthal, *Possession, Ecstasy and Law in Ewe Voodoo* (Charlottesville: University of Virginia Press, 1998); Peter Probst, "Contested Presence: Memory and Media in a Yoruba Kingdom," in *Sites of Memory in Africa: Thinking through Time and Place*, ed. Suzanne Blier and Prita Meier (Cambridge, MA: Harvard University Press, forthcoming).

33. On the troubled relationship between Pentecostalism and African traditional religion, see Jacob Olupona, *The City of 201 Gods* (Los Angeles: University of California Press, 2011); Richard Burgess, *Nigeria's Christian Revolution: The Civil War Revival and Its Pentecostal Progeny (1967–2006)* (Oxford, UK: OCMS, 2008); Peter Probst, *Osogbo and the Art of Heritage: Monuments, Deities, and Money* (Bloomington: University of Indiana Press, 2011); Ogbu Kalu, *African Pentecostalism: An Introduction* (New York, NY: Oxford University Press, 2008); John

Kwabena Asamoah-Gyadu, *African Charismatics: Current Developments within Independent Indigenous Pentecostalism in Ghana* (Leiden, Netherlands: Brill, 2005); John Kwabena Asamoah-Gyadu, *Contemporary Pentecostal Christianity: Interpretations from an African Context* (Eugene, OR: Wipf & Stock, 2013).

34. Marco Agostini, "Il quadro più bello del mondo," *L'Osservatore Romano*, n.d., http://www.vatican.va/news_services/or/or_quo/cultura/2010/179q04a1.html.

35. David Morgan, *The Sacred Gaze: Religious Visual Culture in Theory and Practice* (Los Angeles: University of California Press, 2005); David Morgan, *The Lure of Images: A History of Religion and Visual Media in America* (New York, NY: Routledge, 2007). Another interesting image often shared by African Pentecostals and Catholics is the image of the sacred heart of Jesus. Compare Rhoda Woets, "The Moving Lives of Jesus Pictures in Ghana: Art, Authenticity and Animation," in *Creativity in Transition*, ed. Birgit Meyer and Maruška Svašek (Oxford, UK: Berghahn, forthcoming); Meyer, "'There Is a Spirit in That Image': Mass-Produced Jesus Pictures and Protestant-Pentecostal Animation in Ghana"; David Morgan, "Rhetoric of the Heart: Figuring the Body in Devotion to the Sacred Heart of Jesus," in *Things: Religion and the Question of Materiality*, ed. Birgit Meyer and Dick Houtman (New York, NY: Fordham University Press, 2012), 90–111.

36. Agostini, "Il quadro più bello del mondo."

37. Jacques Derrida and Henri Ronse, *Positions* (Chicago, IL: University of Chicago Press, 1982), 41.

38. Mark Lewis Taylor, *The Theological and the Political: On the Weight of the World* (Minneapolis, MN: Fortress, 2011), 15.

39. Ibid., 179.

40. Kleinbub, *Vision and the Visionary in Raphael*, 143.

41. On the concept of transimmanence, see also Jean Luc Nancy, *The Muses*, trans. Peggy Kamuf (Redwood City, CA: Stanford University Press, 1997); Ben Hutchens, *Jean-Luc Nancy and the Future of Philosophy* (Kingston, Canada: McGill-Queens University Press, 2005); Ernesto Laclau, *On Populist Reason* (New York, NY: Verso, 2005).

42. Taylor, *The Theological and the Political: On the Weight of the World*, 9.

43. Jean Comaroff, *Body of Power, Spirit of Resistance: The Culture and History of a South African People* (Chicago, IL: University of Chicago Press, 1985), 262.

44. Michel de Certeau, *The Practice of Everyday Life* (Los Angeles: University of California Press, 1984), xiii.

45. Ibid., xix.

Conclusion

1. *Oyibo* is a West African pidgin English word that means "white people" or "European."

2. Francisco Cartaxo Rolim, *Pentecostalismo* (Petropolis, Italy: Vozes, 1995).

3. Harvey Cox, *Fire from Heaven: The Rise of Pentecostal Spirituality and the Reshaping of Religion in the 21st Century* (Cambridge, MA: Da Capo, 2013), 178.

4. Compare Matthews A. Ojo, *The End-Time Army: Charismatic Movements in Modern Nigeria* (Trenton, NJ: Africa Research & Publications, 2007); Richard Burgess, *Nigeria's Christian Revolution: The Civil War Revival and Its Pentecostal Progeny 1967–2006* (Oxford, UK: Regnum, 2008); Paul Gifford, *African Christianity: Its Public Role* (Bloomington: Indiana University Press, 1998); J. Kwabena Asamoah-Gyadu, *Contemporary Pentecostal Christianity: Interpretations from an African Context* (Eugene, OR: Wipf & Stock, 2013); Ogbu Kalu, *African Pentecostalism: An Introduction* (Oxford, UK: Oxford University Press, 2008); Ruth Marshall, *Political Spiritualities: The Pentecostal Revolution in Nigeria* (Chicago, IL: University of Chicago Press, 2009); Nimi Wariboko, *Nigerian Pentecostalism* (Rochester, NY: University of Rochester Press, 2014).

5. Robert Orsi, *Between Heaven and Earth, The Religious Worlds People Make and the Scholars Who Study Them* (Princeton, NJ: Princeton University Press, 2006), 73.

6. In this regard, see the work of Xavier Bray et al., *The Sacred Made Real: Spanish Painting and Sculpture, 1600–1700* (London, UK: National Gallery, distributed by Yale University Press, 2009).

7. Michael Taussig, *Mimesis and Alterity: A Particular History of the Senses* (New York, NY: Routledge, 1993).

8. Slavoj Žižek, *On Belief* (New York, NY: Routledge, 2003), 131.

9. Slavoj Žižek, *The Puppet and the Dwarf: The Perverse Core of Christianity* (Cambridge, MA: MIT Press, 2003).

10. On the sacred as a space of infinite possibility, see Richard Fenn, "Sociology and Religion: Searching for the Sacred," in *The Oxford Handbook of Religion and Science*, ed. Philip Clayton and Zachary Simpson, 253–70 (Oxford, UK: Oxford University Press, 2006).

11. Harvey Cox, *Fire from Heaven: The Rise of Pentecostal Spirituality and the Reshaping of Religion in the 21st Century*, 178.

12. On the debate about Cox's approach on primal spirituality, see Nimi Wariboko, *The Charismatic City and the Public Resurgence of Religion* (New York, NY: Palgrave Macmillan, 2014), 84.

13. On Žižek and incarnation, see Frederiek Depoortere, "The End of God's Transcendence? On Incarnation in the Work of Slavoj Žižek," *Modern Theology* 23, no. 4 (2007): 497–523.

14. Holder, quoted in *Ethics and Time: Ethos of Temporal Orientation in Politics and Religion of the Niger Delta* (Trenton, NJ: Africa World Press, 2008), 48.

15. Nimi Wariboko, *Ethics and Time: Ethos of Temporal Orientation in Politics and Religion of the Niger Delta* (Playmouth, UK: Lexington Books, 2010), 48.

16. On Weber and Catholicism, see Werner Stark, "The Place of Catholicism in Max Weber's Sociology of Religion," *Sociological Analysis* 29, no. 4 (1969): 202–10, 204.

17. Jean-Luc Nancy, *Noli Me Tangere: On the Raising of the Body*, trans. Sarah Clift, Pascale-Anne Brault, and Michael Naas, 1st ed. (New York, NY: Fordham University Press, 2008).

18. In Greek, the words of Jesus are translated as "Cease holding on to me" or "Stop clinging to me."

19. John 20:17, KJV.

20. Jean-Luc Nancy, *Noli Me Tangere: On the Raising of the Body*, 42.

21. See Chantal Mouffe, *The Democratic Paradox* (Brooklyn, NY: Verso, 2000); and *On the Political* (London, UK: Routledge, 2011).

22. Jacques Rancière, *On the Shores of Politics* (Brooklyn, NY: Verso, 1995), 32–33.

23. See in this regard Jean-Pierre Reed, "Theorist of Subaltern Subjectivity: Antonio Gramsci, Popular Beliefs, Political Passion, and Reciprocal Learning." *Critical Sociology* 39, no 4 2012.: 561; Michalinos Zembylas, "Revisiting the Gramscian Legacy on Counter-Hegemony, the Subaltern and Affectivity: Toward an 'Emotional Pedagogy' of Activism in Higher Education." *Cristal: Critical Studies in Teaching and Learning* 1, no 1 (2013): 1–21;, Gustavo Fischman and Peter McLaren, "Rethinking Critical Pedagogy and the Gramscian and Freirean Legacies: From Organic to Committed Intellectuals or Critical Pedagogy, Commitment, and Praxis." *Cultural Studies <=> Critical Methodologies* 5 (4) (2005): 425–46.

24. In the 1970s and 1980s, Padua was one of the pulsating centers of the student movement. The political science faculty was defined as the faculty of the "bad teachers" because of the political activism of some of its teachers.

25. Among them, David Smilde looked at the agency and intentionality that Pentecostal churches provide lower-class males in Caracas; Ruth Marshall analyzed the Pentecostals' techniques and government of the self as a response to Nigerian postcolonial stasis; and Kevin O'Neal, baffled between expectations and disappointment, studied Pentecostals' practices of citizenship in Guatemala. Compare Ruth Marshall, Political Spiritualities: *The Pentecostal Revolution in Nigeria* (Chicago, IL: University of Chicago Press, 2008); David Smilde, *Reason to Believe: Cultural Agency in Latin American Evangelicalism*, 1st ed. (Berkeley: University of California Press, 2007); Kevin Lewis O'Neill, *City of God: Christian Citizenship in Postwar Guatemala* (Los Angeles: University of California Press, 2010).

26. Jean Comaroff, *Body of Power, Spirit of Resistance: The Culture and History of a South African People* (Chicago, IL: University of Chicago Press, 1985), 196.

27. Ruth Marshall, *Political Spiritualities*, 34.

28. Johannes Fabian, *Moments of Freedom: Anthropology and Popular Culture* (Charlottesville: University Press of Virginia, 1998), 91.

29. On the limits of meaning, see Matthew Engelke and Matt Tomlinson, eds., *The Limits of Meaning: Case Studies in the Anthropology of Christianity* (Oxford, UK: Berghahn, 2006); and Hans Gumbrecht, *The Production of Presence: What Meaning Cannot Convey* (Redwood City, CA: Stanford University Press, 2003).

Acknowledgments

I HAD IMAGINED that writing the acknowledgments after I had finished this research project and book would be an immense joy and certainly a relief. After three and a half years of fieldwork and one year of intense thinking, writing, and revising, I was looking forward to this moment like a runner anticipating the finish line. While I was doing the challenging work of writing, I was imagining the excitement of reaching the end. But instead of joy, I am overwhelmed by nostalgia. These acknowledgments are a thank you and also a goodbye to my companions on this journey.

It is to the Nigerian and Ghanaian Pentecostals in Italy that I offer my first words of gratitude. Without their support and trust, my fieldwork would have been as impossible as climbing a mountain of sheer ice. They allowed me to see and find more than I ever expected. In the book, I deliberately do not give their full names, and in some cases I use pseudonyms to protect their privacy and safeguard the members of their congregations whose lives are already constantly exposed to others' invasive gaze and to institutional control. Here I only want to let them know that I am humbled by the precious gift they gave both to me and to the readers of this book.

I also would like to thank the priest of the Tempio della Pace parish and the other priests I interviewed for their generosity of time, interactions, and also their reaction to my work. Their interest in my study and their support was an enormous contribution. My deep gratitude also goes to the rector, the friars, and the security staff of the Basilica of Saint Anthony of Padua. They sincerely welcomed my ethnography at the Basilica and allowed me to observe and capture some of the most crucial moments of this research.

The initial phase of interviews with Nigerian and Ghanaian Pastors in Italy was facilitated by the generous support of Théophile Nsabimana, Charles Isoken Obayagbona, and John Baptist Onama, while the kind assistance and guidance of professor Matthews Ojo and Oyeronke Olademo made possible my preliminary fieldwork in Nigeria. The Mountain of Fire and Miracle Ministries hosted me in Lagos. I am deeply grateful to Daniel Kolawole Olukoya and his team of pastors for their kindness, patience in responding to my never-ending questions, and the tragic humor with which they challenged my Catholic upbringing. For my time in Nigeria, I thank also my friend T. Y. Bello and her family for the enthusiasm with which they followed my work, and for their love and affection; Azu Nwagbogu and the African Artists' Foundation for the logistic support they provided to me at the very beginning of my fieldwork in Lagos, and Martin Ameh of the Nigerian Consulate in Rome for his assistance in my various travels. In Ghana, professor Elom Dovlo welcomed me and introduced to me one of his most brilliant students, Edem Damanka, who helped me to explore the Ghanaian Pentecostal scene and its protagonists.

I would like to extend a special thanks to Andrew Esiebo, the photographer and filmmaker with whom I produced and directed the film *Enlarging the Kingdom: African Pentecostals in Italy* that preceded this book. This book is a continuation of the work we started together. I hope that these pages will be able to match the stunning beauty of the images and soundscapes that he was able to capture during our joint fieldwork in Nigeria and Italy.

The research and writing of this book have benefited from the support of a number of institutions, including a University of Padua postdoctoral research grant; the Cariparo Project of Excellence grant; the New York University postdoctoral grant at the Department of Social and Cultural Analysis; the Global Prayer grant, which funded part of my research in Lagos; and the Marie Curie Outgoing fellowship (WASE 302240) that enabled me to spend two years at Harvard University and one year at Utrecht University. I would particularly like to thank professor Jacob Kehinde Olupona for making my stay at Harvard possible. He generously shared his immense knowledge of Nigeria with me and his students, and gifted us with more beautiful oral histories of Nigeria than I have ever read in any book.

The administrative staff of the various departments that hosted me at the University of Padua, New York University, and Harvard and Utrecht Universities generously gave me access to their resources. I deeply thank all of you for your work and patience.

In Italy, I had the opportunity to discuss my work at the various meetings of the Italian Sociological Association and at the summer schools of religion of San Giminiano. I am particularly grateful to Enzo Pace for supporting the first stage of my research. I will always be indebted to Ferruccio Gambino for the seeds of critical thinking that he sowed in my mind; to Chantal Saint Blancat for spurring me to action when I was slowing down; to Giuseppe Giordan for his feedback on my first stage of my work; to Khalid Razzhali for our comradeship; and to Valter Zanin for seasoning our long hours of conversation with his unique genius.

Over the last four years, I have had the benefit of the comments of participants of seminars, workshops, and conferences at the University of Ibadan and the University of Ilorin in Nigeria; at the University of Legon, Accra, in Ghana; New York University; Rutgers University; the Center for the Study of World Religions and the African Studies Center of Harvard University; the Gordon Conwell Theological School; the Department of Religion at the University of Toronto, the University of California, Los Angeles, Department of History–Atlantic History Cluster; the École Normale Supérieure in Paris; the Religion and Society Research Center at the University of Western Sydney, Australia; the Transatlantic Roundtable on Religion and Race; the research colloquiums of the CIRE-LANMED; the Meertens Institute in Amsterdam; the Department of Philosohy and Religious Studies at the University of Utrecht; and at the various annual meetings of the American Academy of Religion, the Society for the Scientific Study of Religion, the International Society for the Sociology of Religion, the African Association for the Study of Religion, and the African Studies Association.

On these and other occasions, I met colleagues and friends whose critical responses to my work were a great source of inspiration. These colleagues are dispersed across the academy in Europe, Africa, and the United States. I am very glad that their engagement with the arguments I developed in this book pushed me to explore new directions. These colleagues are: Hans Belting, Jean and John Comaroff, Susan Cook, Andrew Apter, Simon Coleman, Ruth Marshal, Ato Quayson, Manuel Vazquez, Frank Clooney, Todd Johnson, Devaka Premavardhana, the late Juan Flores, Miriam Jimenez, the late Otto Maduro, Paul Freston, James Spickard, Hauwa Ibrahim, Martha Frederiks, Markus Balkenhol, Daan Beekers, Adrian Hermann, Bruno Reinhardt, Irene Stengs, Jojada Verripis, Sandra Milena Rios Oyola, Mattjis van de Port, Marleen de Witte, Peter-Ben Smith, Christoph Baumgartner, Afe Adogame, Laura Grillo, Jeremy Battle, Rosalind Hackett, Katrien Pype, Damola Osinulo, Peggy Levitt, Nidhani de Andrado, Sebastian Fath, William Ackah, and R. Drew Smith.

I am particularly grateful to the students in the course on Pentecostalism as Global Religion that I cotaught with professor Harvey Cox at Harvard University; the students in the course African Diasporas in the Mediterranean Lands that I taught at New York University; and the undergraduate and graduate students I met along my journey in Italy, Nigeria, Ghana, the United States, and the Netherlands. Their response to my work has always been a challenging testing ground for the clarity of the arguments I made in this book.

I am also thankful to the anonymous reviewers of the manuscript for their enthusiasm for this work.

This book has benefitted from the work of a wonderful team of proofreaders and translators. Part of this manuscript was initially written in Italian. Frances Coburn beautifully translated it into English. Suzanne van Geuns ably edited notes and bibliography. Darlene Marie Slagle edited part of the first draft with her unique gift of working with non-native English writers and Ulrike Guthrie worked on the whole manuscript, gifting every single page of this manuscript with her superb and elegant editing.

I am deeply grateful to my editor Sharmila Sen at Harvard University Press. Our collaboration is the fruit of her adventurous openness of mind and remarkable intuition.

More than I can adequately express, I am grateful to the four people whose works and unfaltering support have had a tremendous impact on the writing of this book and on my academic journey. These are Harvey Cox, Nimi Wariboko, Jean Comaroff, and Birgit Meyer. At Harvard University, I was immensely fortunate to benefit from the guidance of Harvey Cox. He sustained my process of discovery and encouraged me to engage with audacity several thorny questions concerning the relationship between Pentecostalism and Roman Catholicism. Also at Harvard, I had the fortune to meet Jean Comaroff and share with her the complicated moment of the first stage of the writing of this book when I was overwhelmed by three years of ethnographic notes and haunted by analytical theories. Through her unparalleled erudition and her passion as a mentor, she taught me how to dwell in the complexity, cultivate critical thinking, and challenge adversities. While I was in Boston, I had several opportunities to discuss my work with Nimi Wariboko. He challenged my work as no one else has done, which made our conversations a terrific challenge and a tremendous bliss.

Finally, I will never be able to repay the debt that I owe to Birgit Meyer. By agreeing to supervise my last three years of research as a Marie Curie Fellow, she supported me beyond my expectations. She accompanied the flourishing of my thoughts, discussed my sprouting ideas, read every single page of this book and made generous comments, offered challenging questions and constructive critiques. She has been an incredible source of inspiration; those who are familiar with her work will recognize this in the arguments I make in this book. But above all, she gifted me by her work ethic and integrity, as well as by her devotion and talent for mentoring young scholars.

My last thoughts are for my friends and family, who installed all sorts of software and programs to follow me virtually on my various research trips and visiting scholarship programs across the Atlantic. Their real and virtual presence was the joy of my heart. I would like to thank all of them, including those that I sadly lost along the way. My thanks go to Dr. Emanuela Trainito (she knows why), Isabella Robbiani, Marcella Scala, Angelo Aprile, Barbara Saguatti, Paolo Bettella, Francesca Turcato, Ana Helman, Adriano Marmora, Lisa Lee, Shuling Wu, Nidhani De Andrado, to my best friend Marina and to my young cousin Emiliana who both died too soon, and with so much left to do together. I deeply thank my extended family, including those who are not with me anymore, for supporting me along the journey in whatever way they could. To my sister, Caty, and my brother, Giovanni, go my unconditional love and gratitude for embracing all the metamorphosis of my being as well as the joys and pains of my life choices. To my father, I owe my deep tie to Africa and to my beloved mother and grandmother, I owe both my strength and vulnerability. I am sure they are lovingly watching me, living through the blues and bliss of their memory, adding a little bit of sugar to the more bitter moments. I dedicate this journey to them.

Index

CPSIA information can be obtained
at www.ICGtesting.com
Printed in the USA
LVHW090228141121
703271LV00004B/36/J